The

Garden

○ OF ○

INVENTION

THE PENGUIN PRESS

New York

2009

The

Garden

∘ OF ∘

INVENTION

LUTHER BURBANK AND THE
BUSINESS OF BREEDING PLANTS

Jane S. Smith

THE PENGUIN PRESS
Published by the Penguin Group
Penguin Group (USA) Inc., 375 Hudson Street, New York, New York 10014, U.S.A. · Penguin Group
(Canada), 90 Eglinton Avenue East, Suite 700, Toronto, Ontario, Canada M4P 2Y3 (a division of Pearson
Penguin Canada Inc.) · Penguin Books Ltd, 80 Strand, London WC2R 0RL, England · Penguin Ireland,
25 St. Stephen's Green, Dublin 2, Ireland (a division of Penguin Books Ltd) · Penguin Books Australia
Ltd, 250 Camberwell Road, Camberwell, Victoria 3124, Australia (a division of Pearson Australia Group
Pty Ltd) · Penguin Books India Pvt Ltd, 11 Community Centre, Panchsheel Park, New Delhi – 110 017,
India · Penguin Group (NZ), 67 Apollo Drive, Rosedale, North Shore 0632, New Zealand (a division
of Pearson New Zealand Ltd) · Penguin Books (South Africa) (Pty) Ltd,
24 Sturdee Avenue, Rosebank, Johannesburg 2196, South Africa

Penguin Books Ltd, Registered Offices:
80 Strand, London WC2R 0RL, England

First published in 2009 by The Penguin Press,
a member of Penguin Group (USA) Inc.

Library of Congress Cataloging-in-Publication Data

Smith, Jane S.
The garden of invention : Luther Burbank and the business of breeding plants / Jane S. Smith.
p.   cm.
Includes bibliographical references and index.
ISBN 978-1-59420-209-4
1. Burbank, Luther, 1849–1926.   2. Plant breeders—United States—Biography.
3. Plant breeding—United States—History.   I. Title.
SB63.B9S635   2009
630.92—dc22
[B]   2009001822

Printed in the United States of America
1   3   5   7   9   10   8   6   4   2

Designed by Meighan Cavanaugh

Once Again
To Carl

OVER FIFTY YEARS OF
PLANT INVENTION

Luther Burbank developed more than eight hundred new varieties of fruits and vegetables, flowers, nuts, and grains between 1873 and 1925. These are some of his most famous introductions.*

1873 ° Burbank potato
1885 ° Himalaya blackberry
1886 ° Satsuma plum
1893 ° Paradox walnut
1893 ° Royal walnut
1893 ° Van Deman quince
1893 ° Lemon Giant calla lily
1894 ° Iceberg white blackberry
1894 ° Wickson plum
1895 ° Tarrytown canna lily
1899 ° Burbank rose

*Adapted from *Fifty Famous Favorites*, 1989.
Courtesy Luthur Burbank Home & Gardens, Santa Rosa, California.

1899	◦	New Gladiolus hybrids
1899	◦	White agapanthus
1900	◦	Crimson Winter rhubarb
1901	◦	Miracle (stoneless) plum
1901	◦	Shasta daisy
1903	◦	Burbank cherry
1903	◦	Santa Rosa dahlia
1904	◦	Burbank Crimson California poppy
1904	◦	Santa Rosa Shirley poppies
1905	◦	Rutland plumcot
1906	◦	Burbank's Giant Hybrid amaryllis
1906	◦	Santa Rosa plum
1907	◦	Spineless cacti
1908	◦	Burbank Admiral pea
1910	◦	America Evening primrose
1911	◦	Black Giant cherry
1911	◦	Rainbow corn
1911	◦	Santa Rosa artichoke
1914	◦	Hybrid sunflowers
1915	◦	New Burbank Early tomato
1917	◦	Surprise day lily
1919	◦	Elephant garlic
1920	◦	Robusta strawberry
1920	◦	Sebastopol thornless blackberry
1922	◦	Molten Fire amaranthus
1923	◦	Tower of Gold knophoria (poker plant)
1925	◦	Burbank Giant Dahlia zinnia
1927	◦	Gold nectarine (introduced after Burbank's death)
1932	◦	July Elberta peach (introduced after Burbank's death)

CONTENTS

PART III
POSSESSING THE GARDEN

Not one man in a thousand has accuracy of eye and judgment sufficient to become an eminent breeder. If gifted with these qualities, and he studies his subject for years, and devotes his lifetime to it with indomitable perseverance, he will succeed, and may make great improvements; if he wants any of these qualities, he will assuredly fail.

—CHARLES DARWIN, *On the Origin of Species by Means of Natural Selection*, 1859

"A good tree takes no more room than a poor one. Have the good one."

Luther Burbank's Santa Rosa Nurseries catalog, 1880s.

PROLOGUE

On September 14, 1905, over two hundred of California's leading businessmen, bankers, politicians, and professors gathered at San Francisco's luxurious Palace Hotel for a "Complimentary Banquet in Honor of Luther Burbank," hosted in grand style by the State Board of Trade.

The guest of honor was a handsome, well-dressed transplant from New England with shrewd blue eyes and a closely trimmed mane of wavy gray hair. At fifty-six, Burbank was the most famous gardener on the planet. For almost thirty years, his name and his portrait had appeared around the world in newspaper stories about the latest botanical inventions of the man called the Edison of the Garden and the Wizard of Santa Rosa. From his home in Santa Rosa, California, in the green heart of Sonoma County north of San Francisco, and from his experimental farm amid the orchards of nearby Sebastopol, he sent out a flood of catalogs advertising a cornucopia of new and improved plants for both home gardens and commercial farms and orchards. He developed novelties like the white blackberry and staples like the blight-resistant potato that was exported to Ireland to revive that country's leading crop. He was at the height of a career he had invented: that of a discoverer, improver, and, to use his own term, evoluter of new plants.

Luther Burbank didn't touch alcohol, detested tobacco, and frequently declared that he would rather make a flower than a speech. As the other banquet guests ate and drank and very likely smoked cigars on that September evening, the speakers hailed Burbank as "a man whose life from boyhood has been spent in community with nature." And then they talked about how he had made California rich and famous as a new center for the international market in fruits, vegetables, flowers, and nuts.

The tributes that night were long and florid, but they are worth revisiting if we want to understand the brave new world of abundance and prosperity that made our grandparents, and their parents before them, so very enthusiastic about the prospect of new and better plants.

The first topic was the economic benefits of innovation. The value of California fruit exports had risen over a hundredfold from 1880 to 1904 and had long since surpassed the economic importance of wheat, once the state's principal agricultural product, according to N. P. Chipman, the president of the Board of Trade. Oranges and lemons brought wealth to southern California, and the raisin grape was making Fresno rich. But it was California's sun-dried tree fruits (and particularly prunes) that had changed Europe from an exporter to an importer of fruit over the previous fifteen years. And Luther Burbank had done more than anyone to perfect and introduce the new varieties of plums on which that industry was built.

More than that, Chipman said, Burbank was helping his adopted state achieve its divine destiny as the modern Eden, the garden center of the world. Whenever newspapers in other places carried stories about the "Wizard of California Horticulture," which was often, readers were reminded of the Golden State's wonderful climate and its unparalleled prospects for farmers and home seekers. Best of all, the speaker continued, Burbank did it without self-interest, scorning profit and maintaining "the simple dignity and modesty of his daily life."

The governor of California, George C. Pardee, went further. He described Burbank as an explorer who had led the way to new lands of opulent riches. "[When] we want a better plum, a larger berry, a brighter, more fragrant flower, we turn to Burbank, and he gives it to us," Pardee said. "Like Columbus, Burbank has shown us the way to new continents, new forms of life, new sources of wealth, and we, following in his footsteps, will profit by and from his genius."

Next came Senator George C. Perkins, returning from Washington to assure his constituents that the federal government was also doing its part to promote agriculture. Perkins had grown up in Maine, stubbing his bare toes against the stones of the fields while he planted corn and beans, and he had a special interest in all aspects of cultivation. The Department of Agriculture was created in 1862, he reminded his audience, taking over the national programs of agricultural advancement that had originally been performed by the Patent Office. Its annual budget was almost seven million dollars. Using that money, it sent out over twelve million useful publications to the farmers and gardeners of the United States, sponsored forty-two State Agricultural Experiment Stations, and provided forty million packets of free vegetable and flower seeds distributed annually by Congress.

And then Senator Perkins paused. As impressive as the activities of the Department of Agriculture were, he said, the government had much to learn from Luther Burbank. "He is doing more to instruct, interest, and make popular the work in the garden than any man of his generation."

David Starr Jordan, president of Stanford University and a highly respected biologist, rose to tell of Burbank's mastery of science and his priceless contributions to the advancement of human knowledge. More speakers followed, extolling the innovative genius of Luther Burbank. They told of the cacti he had bred to lose their spines, the plums that ripened without a stone, and the California poppies he had coaxed from their usual orange to crimson red. They lauded the great simplicity of his generous soul.

The last toast of the evening came from Albert G. Burnett, a judge of the Superior Court for Sonoma County and a neighbor of Burbank's in Santa Rosa. Speaking for his fellow townspeople, Judge Burnett expressed their sense of honor "that this wholesome, serious, earnest, kindly, loving, talented and enthusiastic revealer of Nature's most valuable secrets is content to live with us." Because of Luther Burbank, he said, Santa Rosa had become a shrine to which the great and wise come from the ends of the earth "to sit at the feet of this great apostle and prophet of beauty and happiness . . . and to catch some measure of his matchless inspiration." Meanwhile, Burnett insisted, Burbank himself worked only "to bring more of the sunshine of comfort and happiness into the cottages of the poor as well as the palaces of the rich."

Even by the standards of early-twentieth-century banquet oratory, where understatement had no place, these were striking claims. Taken literally, they were rather absurd. Obviously, no one individual could exert more influence than all the programs of the federal government, single-handedly unlock the mysteries of genetics, and become the transforming force of California agriculture, especially if he was also busy cultivating humility and receiving pilgrims at his gate. Outside the Palace Hotel, thousands of other people were expanding the business of farms and gardens in new directions on huge swaths of land where the crops had nothing to do with Luther Burbank's plant inventions.

In another sense, however, the speakers at the Board of Trade banquet were expressing what was, for a time, a view as common and as cherished as faith in progress itself. A vast number of people eagerly wanted to believe in Luther Burbank and in the extraordinarily diverse qualities he had come to represent. Scientist, inventor, salesman, artist, social reformer, guardian of the values of nature, embodiment of the best of traditional New England character, promoter of contemporary California—no matter what kind of hero you wanted, it seemed Luther Burbank was a leading candidate. The man behind the adulation had the usual number of foibles and failings, of course, but that was not the point. In an era in which agriculture was becoming a science and science was becoming a business, Burbank was the human face of the modern garden. The praise that was heaped upon him revealed the hopes and calculations his admirers held for the future he represented.

As speaker followed speaker at the Board of Trade banquet, a few assertions kept coming up that were too important to be obscured even by the great billowing clouds of rhetoric. One was that the future would derive huge benefits from new plants that would surpass all others in productivity, usefulness, and beauty. A second was that Burbank's deep understanding of the workings of nature would advance the progress of science and agriculture, while his spiritual wisdom extended far beyond cultivation of land and crops. And the last, which encompassed the others (including that selfless indifference to profits), was that Burbank's plants, his ideas, his spiritual aura, and even his fame were all valuable commodities that could be possessed and sold by others.

These three drives—for invention, for understanding, and for ownership—were the powerful, often conflicting human desires that shaped contemporary attitudes toward the natural world in the period of Luther Burbank's career, and they were all on display that night, swirling about amid the elaborate toasts and the heady scent of flower garlands that cascaded over the white linen tablecloths of the Palace Hotel.

THERE ARE NOT VERY MANY agricultural celebrities. Burbank did not design gardens. He did not advocate for one diet system or another. He cared a great deal about the taste, aroma, and appearance of his creations, but he was no cook and no gourmet, either. Burbank's talent was much more elemental. He expanded the range of plants that became the meal, the ornamental garden, and the bouquet. And he did this at a time when the vast majority of people agreed that improving on nature was, in fact, a very good thing to do.

It takes a long look back to understand why Luther Burbank was so very famous—or, to put it a slightly different way, to remember why our not-so-distant ancestors were so remarkably eager for plant improvements that they lionized the inventor of a bigger fruit, a better-yielding vegetable, or a longer-blooming flower. The modern supermarket carries a global array of fruits, vegetables, and flowers, obliterating all sense that there might be such things as regional or seasonal differences. Even markets that sell only what is locally grown by independent farmers, without pesticides or genetically modified seeds, have brimming bins stocked with an astonishing profusion of varieties, many of them brought back from the neglected corners of our great-grandparents' gardens after having been ignored for decades as too small, too fragile, or too expensive for commercial production.

In 1905, markets offered fewer choices. There were a number of types of apples and tomatoes, but many of them didn't taste very good or travel well. Refrigerated railcars existed, but refrigerated trucks had not yet been invented to carry produce from the rail depot to the consumer. Two years after the Wright brothers made their historic twelve-second flight, air freight, like commercial air travel, was still very far in the future.

If you wanted to eat something out of season, something you couldn't store in the root cellar or in an unheated pantry in the back of the kitchen, it would probably have to be canned or pickled or dried. Only a few kinds of produce could survive the trip from distant climates, and those were luxury items reserved for the very rich. Even exotic delicacies usually came in bottles and tins. Frozen food was another marvel that wouldn't come on the market for another twenty years. In the ornamental garden, the flowers that bloomed in the spring were gone by June, the rose was an emblem of fleeting pleasure, and hothouse flowers, like hothouse fruits, were a sign of conspicuous wealth.

Today, people debate whether it is miraculous or ominous that breeders can use genetic engineering to make better-looking, hardier, more prolific, better-selling crops, but nobody disputes the obvious fact that it can be done. When Luther Burbank was born in 1849, plant reproduction was a far greater mystery than the breeding of animals, and the idea of creating new kinds of plants was more common in the realms of fantasy and fiction than of fact.

Over the next seventy-five years—after Darwin had popularized the idea of change as a natural process in the organic world, when the new field of genetics was just being discovered, and long before contemporary advances in molecular biology began—plant breeding was a wide-open frontier. During those years, Luther Burbank was one of the people transforming the materials of the modern farm and garden.

The story could end there, and Burbank would be remembered as a colorful pioneer of the early days of modern agriculture and horticulture: talented, productive, enormously influential, often overpromoted, and now largely forgotten. What that account would miss, however, is the way this single individual's almost mythic reputation reflected—and still reflects—a host of contradictory attitudes about the place of human ingenuity in the natural world. Idealist and businessman, Burbank embodied both the passionate closeness to the living garden that many people today are trying to recover and the very beginnings of the large-scale manipulation of plants that has made commercial agriculture so remote from ordinary experience.

He also reminds us of a time when most people regarded "new and improved" as a phrase without irony. Burbank's story stretched across the continent and extended through much of our national history. His father was born when George Washington was president, and his widow lived into the administration of Jimmy Carter. Still, he was unmistakably a product of his own era, the expansive commercial years between the Civil War and the Great Depression, when a plot of ground could be both a business incubator and, quite literally, a research park.

There were many other people involved in the same enterprise, of course, though few of them ever approached Burbank's level of fame. Only a small percentage of those contemporaries could be mentioned here without turning this into an encyclopedia of agriculture, which it is not. It's not a biography, either, if that means a thorough account of all aspects of a person's life. This began as a book about the origins of modern garden varieties in the days before genetic engineering, and about a single charismatic breeder who was a very celebrated part of that new bounty. It quickly grew into a story about marketing and codifying nature, which led to the much larger consideration of how an earlier generation responded to the unprecedented idea that the vegetable kingdom could be mastered, directed, and even claimed as private property.

In another sense, though, this is a very ancient tale. In these pages, I use the word "garden" in the most inclusive way, to refer to any cultivated space. By business, I mean not just a way of earning a living, but also a vocation, an occupation, and even a preoccupation. Invention is another word of many meanings, encompassing everything from discovery to contrivance to bright idea.

None of these multiple meanings is at all new. As everyone since Adam has discovered, our relationship to growing things is never simple, and the ways in which we define that relationship always reveal hopes and assumptions that extend far beyond a mere botanical description. Every garden is a haven but also an arena, a fertile field for contesting ideas as well as for growing fruits and flowers. Its separation from unmediated nature is what makes it a garden, treasured for what it excludes as well as for what it contains, and the question of who controls the grounds is never very deeply buried. What made the garden of invention so very exciting was the possibility, for a time, that anyone could enter and see what might take root.

PART I

Inventing the Garden

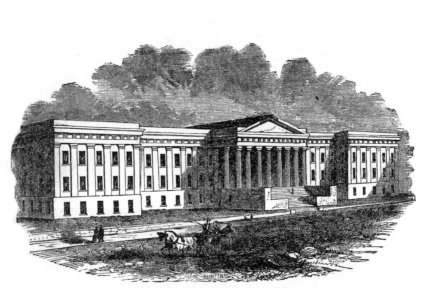

PATENT OFFICE, WASHINGTON.

From *Master Spirits of the World*, 1872

NATURE IN AN AGE
OF INVENTION

The greatest service which can be rendered to any country is to add a useful plant to its culture. —THOMAS JEFFERSON, 1800

WHEN the United States was a very young country and the introduction of new seeds and plants was a central object of national policy, agricultural development was supervised by the Department of State, which was also responsible for patents. In 1827, President John Quincy Adams formalized a long-standing policy when he instructed naval and consular officers to collect any foreign plants or seeds that might be useful and send them to Washington. A decade later, when the Patent Office, newly separated from the State Department, was preparing to move into a grandly neoclassical building rising out of the capital city's prevailing mud, Henry Leavitt Ellsworth, the first commissioner of patents, saw the expansion as an opportunity to do something with all those seeds.

Ellsworth envisioned his office as the center of a vast national program of agricultural improvement. As a graduate of Yale University, a lawyer, and a son of Oliver Ellsworth, chief justice of the United States under George Washington, he knew his Constitution. The purpose of the Patent Office was not simply to evaluate and record patent applications, but "to promote the Progress of Science and the Useful Arts." In a nation of farmers, what could be more progressive and more useful than promoting agriculture?

At a time when the entire country could still be considered an experiment, Ellsworth saw every farm and field as a potential laboratory of agricultural innovation. The Great Hall of the new Patent Office building would be used to display agricultural acquisitions. Members of Congress would distribute new plants and seeds, supplied by the Patent Office, to their constituents across the country. Reports on the successes and failures of new plantings would come back to Washington, and so would information on regional crop prices. In 1839, in the first federal appropriation ever made for agriculture, Congress granted Ellsworth a thousand dollars to distribute seeds and gather information on agricultural markets. National progress, invention, and the search for new and better plants were united as official policy.

WHEN LUTHER BURBANK WAS BORN a decade later in Lancaster, Massachusetts, mechanical inventions seemed a much more likely way to get ahead. Farming in New England was already in decline, and woods were beginning to reclaim some of the land earlier settlers had so laboriously cleared. In north-central Massachusetts, where Lancaster had been settled in 1653, sawmills, gristmills, and factories for nails, paper, and cotton now dotted the banks of the Nashua River as it twisted and forked through a rolling landscape of fields, marshes, ponds, and woods. Wealthy merchants, many of them arriving from Boston to settle closer to their factories, lined Lancaster's main street with stately new homes where marble statues sat on mahogany pedestals and the perils of the wilderness seemed very far away. The textile mills of Lowell and the machine shops of Worcester were close by, helping make Massachusetts the most industrialized state in the nation.

The first of the Burbanks had arrived from England in the 1630s, and the family had tended to teaching, preaching, and manufacturing for as long as anybody could remember. Luther's grandfather, Nathaniel Burbank, had owned a paper mill in Harvard, Massachusetts, that he sold in 1797, moving his family six miles away to a large farmhouse with one hundred acres of land on the north side of Lancaster. The new farm had a kitchen garden and an orchard, but more important were its rich deposits of clay, good for forming bricks, and abundant timber that would fire the kilns to bake them. Just five years earlier John Chapman had left the Lancaster neighborhood and set out for Ohio, becoming the itinerant orchardist who would eventually earn the popular name of Johnny Appleseed, but Luther Burbank's family had no such ambitions.

Of the various Burbank occupations, brickmaking was by far the most profitable. The little schoolhouse where Luther first studied was made of Burbank bricks, as were the Lancaster Gingham Mills and the Crocker-Burbank Paper Mills in Fitchburg, a few miles away. Lancaster's Fifth Meeting House, built on the village green between 1815 and 1817, still stands as a proud monument to Burbank bricks; it is one of the masterpieces of Charles Bulfinch, who had also designed the Boston State House and would go on from Lancaster to contribute his architectural talents to the design of the United States Capitol in the newly created District of Columbia.

Luther's mother was Olive Burpee Ross. The Rosses had arrived from Scotland in the seventeenth century and the Burpees some time later from France. Olive always took credit for Luther's love of flowers and liked to point out his relationship to her distant cousin, famed seed seller W. Atlee Burpee, but her background was no more agricultural than her husband's. She was born in 1813 in Sterling, Massachusetts, where her father was a cabinetmaker. Apart from the temperance pledge Olive took at age thirteen, the chief event of her childhood seems to have been the famous day her younger class-mate, Mary Sawyer, was followed to school by her little lamb, as was soon memorialized in the popular nursery rhyme.

The self-sufficient farm, to the extent that such an Arcadian enterprise had ever existed in New England, had faded into nostalgic myth by the middle of the nineteenth century. Those who attempted to live off the land without consideration of the marketplace were more likely to be philosophical dreamers than practical men of the soil. In the summer of 1843, while Luther's father, Samuel Burbank, was making bricks in Lancaster, Bronson Alcott moved his wife and four daughters, including future author Louisa May, to a farm seven miles away. Fruitlands, Alcott's uto-pian community, lasted a single winter before the threat of starva-tion drove the family off the land. Brook Farm, the transcendentalist experiment in communal agriculture satirized in Nathaniel Haw-thorne's *The Blithedale Romance*, fared little better, limping along from 1841 to 1847.

Bricks provided a more solid foundation for a cultured life. According to the rosy recollections of his devoted younger sister Emma, Luther's childhood was spent reading Emerson, Thoreau, and Longfellow, studying nature, inventing simple machines, and listening to discussions of politics, religion, and whatever other topics were introduced by the visiting ministers and lecturers his father liked to host.

Emma's account is an idyll of useful arts and letters, a nostalgic vision of refined conversation and enlightened curiosity. Other records tell the hard facts of mortality in nineteenth-century New England. Samuel Burbank's first wife, Hannah, left five living children when she died in 1840; three other offspring had predeceased her. Four years later, the second Mrs. Burbank and her two infant children were also dead. Within another year, on June 19, 1845, when he was almost fifty, Samuel married thirty-two-year-old Olive Ross, bringing her into a house of fractious teenagers who resented their new stepmother and her strict rules. Olive's first child, a girl, died at birth, and her son Henry died before he was nine months old. Luther, Samuel Burbank's thirteenth child and the first of Olive's three surviving children, was born on March 7, 1849, six months after baby Henry was buried and eight months after the death of seventeen-year-old Lucy Burbank, Samuel's daughter by his first wife. Another son, Alfred, was born two years later, and then Emma in 1854.

Little Lute, as the family called him, was painfully shy. It was even a torture for him to attend classes in the small brick schoolhouse half a mile away through the family woods. When his half brother Herbert was the schoolmaster, being pulled to class on a sled was the only part of the academic experience Luther enjoyed. When he grew older and his half sister Jenny became the teacher, he bargained to do extra lessons to avoid having to recite in class. If he saw an extra plate at the table, suggesting guests, he would skip dinner rather than endure a stranger. In a letter written when his little brother was seven, Herbert noted, "Luther has his days of moroseness."

Moroseness. This is not a word you usually find attached to a child. Luther outgrew his shyness, but his oddities persisted. As a teenager, he put himself on a strict diet, weighing his portions before he ate. He insisted on bathing only in ice water. In his early teens he had a conversion experience after which he "accepted so literally the [Baptist church's] severe doctrines, and they so impressed his young mind as to make him almost morbid," according to his mother. Morbid is another word not often used to describe children. The boy was bright, but he was a worry.

The Civil War passed over the Burbank family with little direct impact. Luther's half brothers George and David had moved to California in the 1850s, in the wake of the gold rush, and the other older children were settled in homes and careers. Like many of his neighbors, Samuel Burbank was an early advocate of abolition and a later critic of Lincoln's generals, and Olive would read the war news aloud each night from the newspaper fetched from the railway station at Still River, but nobody in the immediate family went to battle.

What would turn out to be more significant were three pieces of legislation passed by Congress when Luther was thirteen and the Civil War was in its second deadly year. By 1862, the Patent Office building had become a military hospital where Walt Whitman and Clara Barton (formerly a Patent Office copyist) tended Union casualties. Even in the midst of war, however, the cultivation of new plants was too important to neglect. On May 15, 1862, President Abraham Lincoln signed the Organic Act, which removed the Division of Agriculture from the Patent Office and created a separate Department of Agriculture to expand the vital work of spreading new seeds and plants as well as information on how to grow them. Then, on May 20, Lincoln signed the Homestead Act, offering 160 acres of public land to settlers who would fence, improve, and inhabit their holding for at least five years.

And finally, on July 2, he signed the Morrill Act, better known as the Land-Grant College Act, providing funds for every state to establish "at least one college where the leading object shall be . . . to teach such branches of learning as are related to agriculture and the mechanic arts."

Much later, after Luther Burbank was famous as the Wizard of Santa Rosa, accounts of his childhood highlighted his early signs of horticultural genius. From infancy, his mother reported, she could quiet him by giving him a flower to hold. He planted a patch of ground near the house with the local daisy that his father considered a weed, and bore in silence his punishment for this transgression. He discovered flowers blooming in the snow, warmed by a thermal spring, and took it as a lesson in how to speed plants to maturity. When he was fifteen, he asked his half brother George to send him seeds from California.

These are slender threads from which to weave a tale of destiny. Had Burbank become a famous lawyer, no doubt other anecdotes would have been remembered: early signs of a passion for justice, perhaps, or an argumentative streak. The simple truth is that there was approximately nothing in Burbank's background that would have predicted a desire to become an inventor of new plants.

There was, however, a great deal to suggest he might become an inventor of something, because that was what bright young men of his time and place were encouraged to do. The Burbanks shared the widespread national opinion that new inventions could and would increase comfort and prosperity in every sphere of the human endeavor, and they were proud of their son's mechanical ingenuity. Years later, family members boasted that young Luther had built a steam whistle from an old teakettle to call the workers in from the brickyard; he persuaded his father to dam a stream that ran through the property, claiming it would improve the cranberry bog but secretly wanting to create a pond for skating; he discovered a better way of loading bricks on the wagons he had been driving into town ever since he was big enough to hold the reins. Growing up, he saw ample evidence that inventors were heroes who improved life for everybody, and that scientific knowledge could lead to immediate practical applications.

Wealth was also a natural part of the inventor's life, or so it must have seemed. In 1865, when he was sixteen, Burbank used the money he earned gathering fruit to buy a book whose ponderous title speaks equally to the young man's dreams and to the commercial preoccupations of the age in which he lived: *Instructions on How to Obtain Letters Patent for New Inventions: Including a Variety of Useful Information Concerning the Rules and Practice of the Patent Office; How to Sell Patents; How to Secure Foreign Patents; Forms for Assignments and Licenses, Together with Engravings and Descriptions of the Condensing Steam-Engine, and the Principal Mechanical Movements, Valuable Tables, Calculations, Problems, Etc. Etc.*

Over fifty years later, Luther's half sister Jenny still felt he had missed the great rewards that came to the inventors of machines and industrial processes. "He was very ingenious," she recalled, "and would have won honor, renown and riches, if his intense love for flowers had not drawn all his inventive powers toward them."

The telegraph and the cotton gin may have seemed more glamorous and rewarding inventions than flowers, but the idea of getting rich by marketing a new breed of plant or animal was grounded in familiar experiences, or at least familiar hopes. Frenzies of agricultural speculation swept through the United States with some frequency in the nineteenth century, and better plants and animals, like better plows and reapers, commanded high prices when they were first introduced.

Farmers early in the century had rushed to take advantage of rising prices for wool, creating a demand for merino sheep imported (or, more accurately, smuggled) from Spain. Between 1807 and 1810 the price of rare and precious merino lambs rose from a hundred dollars each to over a thousand dollars before collapsing a few years later to less than twenty dollars. During the 1830s, the prospect of government subsidies to promote a domestic silk industry led enthusiastic speculators to plant great tracts of Chinese mulberry trees, the preferred food of the precious silkworm. Unfortunately, few investors shared the same enthusiasm for the difficult, boring job of actually raising silkworms, unraveling their cocoons, and spinning the silk into thread. The mulberry boom, like the merino sheep bubble, collapsed under the deflating forces of oversupply and lack of demand.

Other agricultural fads and bubbles quickly followed. Everywhere east of the Mississippi, farmers were breeding Berkshire hogs and madly planting broom corn, Rohan potatoes, and an array of new kinds of wheat that may have all actually been the same variety sold under different exotic names: Italian, Siberian, California, Egyptian, Santa Fe, Osage. Periodicals like the *Farmer's Cabinet*, the *American Farmer*, and the *Cultivator* promoted new plant cultivars and animal breeds that they assured their readers would make them wealthy. Advertisements urged growers to buy an extremely expensive cottonseed that didn't even need a name, but was described only as "a new species."

Novelty paid. In November 1849, just a few months after Luther Burbank's birth, Boston had hosted the first American exhibition of fancy poultry, setting off a dizzying upward spiral of prices for

PORTRAIT OF THE " COCHIN-CHINA " FOWL !

FROM *The History of the Hen Fever,* 1855

exotic chickens and their eggs that lasted several years. The story of the poultry bubble is recorded in George P. Burnham's very amusing and still instructive 1855 volume, *The History of the Hen Fever,* which he dedicates "to the Amateurs, Fanciers, and Breeders of Poultry, the Successful and Unfortunate Dealers throughout the United States; and the Victims of Misplaced Confidence in the Hen Trade Generally." As Burnham reports and other accounts confirm, the speculative passion for new chicken varieties like the Cochin-China, Shanghai, Chittagong, and Dorking was as irrationally exuberant as any other investment mania, be it for tulips, real estate, or Internet stocks. And so, while New England's bachelors were rushing off to California to pan for gold, the more settled members of the middle class were ready to pay fifty dollars or more for rare barnyard specimens that would never be part of anybody's Sunday dinner. This was the common news and conversation in the Burbank house when Luther was a child, along with the latest literary efforts of Mr. Emerson and Mr. Thoreau, the exciting new craze for séances, and the price of bricks.

Still, it is clear that Burbank's parents envisioned an indoor career for their son. At seventeen, Luther was walking three miles to the center of town to the Lancaster Academy, where he studied Shakespeare and French grammar, memorized the principal rivers of the world, and worked arithmetic problems involving the price of firewood and the yards of wallpaper needed to cover a room.

He was five feet eight inches tall, hovered between 120 and 130 pounds, and was already prone to mysterious bouts of fatigue that would plague him for the rest of his life. During the summer, instead of the heavy labor of making bricks or farming, Burbank was sent to work designing manufacturing patterns at the Ames plow factory in Worcester, Massachusetts. Olive's brother was a manager there, and it seemed like a good way to develop the boy's mechanical skills. When he was at home, he amused himself making small clay disks, inscribing them with his name and the date, and burying them around the farm. It would be like a pirate treasure, he thought. The only one that has been recovered is inscribed "Luther Burbank" and dated 1867. He was eighteen, which might seem old for pirate games, but Luther was not like those precocious young businessmen who were starting to appear in the popular novels of Horatio Alger. Drawn to literature and philosophy, in love with the natural world, and good at tinkering, the adolescent Burbank had no idea what he was going to do in life.

SAMUEL BURBANK DIED in December 1868, abruptly ending any plans for his son's further education. Luther returned to the plow factory in Worcester, earning money and taking what advantage he could of the larger options the city offered to a young man of limited funds, high aspirations, and no particular direction. Fond of drawing, he was one of over two hundred Worcester artisans and teachers who signed up for public drawing classes with the legendary professor George Gladwin, a highly eccentric but inspiring art teacher at Worcester Polytechnic Institute. He joined the Mechanics Institute and attended a series of lectures by Professor W. D. Gunning, who spoke on Darwin, evolution, and the importance of science. As a child, Burbank had learned botany and geology from his older cousin Levi Sumner Burbank, who had in turn studied natural history with Louis Agassiz, the spellbinding lecturer and founder of the Museum of Comparative Zoology in Boston. Now Burbank roamed the hills and woods around Worcester, which were full of interesting rocks and flowers to study, once stopping to write his mother a letter describing the view of "grand Waschusett," the highest mountain in the area, and "smaller hills, their sides just beginning to be clothed in the robe of summer."

Thoreau, one of Burbank's literary heroes, had described that very view in one of his essays, but there was another, more popular naturalist whose name and influence were much in the air in that summer of 1869. In September, newspapers around the state carried reports of the centennial celebration of the birth of the famed

German geographer Alexander von Humboldt, who had died only ten years before. The daylong event, held on the Boston Common, featured a stirring two-hour address by Louis Agassiz and shorter appearances by Ralph Waldo Emerson, Julia Ward Howe, Oliver Wendell Holmes, and the mayor of Boston, among others.

Humboldt had become an unlikely object of mass adulation in the United States when he visited Washington in 1804 after completing one of the first scientific surveys of the Amazon, and his fame had endured, bolstered by the publication of his book *Cosmos* in several English translations in the years before the Civil War. Humboldt's depiction of the natural world as an interconnected whole had a profound influence on writers like Emerson, Thoreau, Whitman, and Poe, as well as on scientists like Agassiz. Many years later, Burbank would list Humboldt, along with Emerson and Thoreau, as his three favorite authors, and would call himself "a Cosmist."

Unfortunately, a passion for the unity of creation does not provide an obvious way of earning a living. Emerson instructed, "Follow your genius." Burbank's family told him to find a trade. There had been talk that Luther might become a doctor, but there is no record of any actual study to that end. He was far too shy to be a teacher, and the drawings he saved, while competent, cannot have encouraged him to think of a career in art. For a time he sold hand-cranked sewing machines door-to-door in the area around Fitchburg, but Burbank was not of a temperament to see that as a career. He had suggested some mechanical improvements at the Ames plow factory that led to the offer of a more important position and a much higher salary, but he claimed that the indoor life of the factory made him ill. In the summer of 1870, when he was twenty-one, Burbank tried his luck as a merchant sailor. His boat, the *Mary Stede*, was bound for the mackeral fisheries in the Gulf of Newfoundland but sank in a storm before it ever got there, scuttling his seafaring career with it. Meanwhile, his younger brother, Alfred, had joined all the other young men going west to grow up with the country. Emma, the baby of the Burbank clan, was working as a schoolteacher. Family members began to fear that Lute would never settle down.

BURBANK DISCOVERED HIS VOCATION at the public library. While botany walks, geology lectures, and the excitement of the Humboldt centennial may all have sustained Burbank's interest in natural science, a young man needed access to a large collection of books to keep up with the voluminous literature of this enormously popular field. Luckily, the town of Lancaster was ready to meet Burbank's needs. The community had prospered during the Civil War, and when an earlier library was destroyed by fire in 1867, the town leaders embraced the loss as an opportunity for civic improvement on a noble scale. Twenty-five thousand dollars was raised to erect a building on the town green, between the Bulfinch church and the Lancaster Academy, that would be both a library and a tribute to the local men who had died preserving the Union.

Work on the Soldier's Memorial Hall and Library was completed in June 1868, and it had opened to much fanfare while Burbank was still making the long daily walk between the Lancaster Academy and the family farm. The center of the new library was a two-story-high octagonal room with a "peace window" mounted in the ceiling where the midday sunlight could strike the image of a dove bearing an olive branch through breaking clouds of war. Spiral staircases joined the two levels of bookcases that lined the perimeters, with shelf space for twenty-five thousand books, ten times the prior holdings. One of the new library's first purchases was the latest book by the controversial British naturalist Charles Darwin.

Darwin's *The Variation of Animals and Plants Under Domestication*, published in the United States in two fat volumes in 1869, was a detail-crammed response to those who had criticized *On the Origin of Species by Means of Natural Selection* as a hypothesis unsupported by sufficient proof. More a compendium than a treatise, *Variation* seemed to include every piece of evidence for biological evolution that Darwin had gathered during his entire career as a student of natural history. Although geneticists still consider it a fundamental source of data and observation, it was never the popular success of the 1859 *Origin of Species* or the 1871 *Descent of Man*. In England it sold fewer than five thousand copies, and it is likely no one has ever put it on a desert island reading list.

Burbank hadn't read *On the Origin of Species*, published when he was only ten years old, though he had certainly heard of the controversial volume. It took him a year or two to notice *Variation of Animals and Plants Under Domestication*. When he did, however, it was a momentous encounter. "It opened a new world to me," he later said. "It told me, in plain simple sentences, as matter-of-fact as though its marvelous and startling truths were commonplace, that variations seemed to be susceptible, through selection, of permanent fixture in the individual. . . . I doubt if it is possible to make any one realize what this book meant to me."

Indeed, it is an unlikely source of inspiration. The early chapters of *Variation* are devoted to exhaustive lists of the ways that domestic animals differ, from the shapes of cats' skulls to the colors of cows' hides to the myriad varieties of pigeons, a bird of which Darwin was extremely fond. Only in chapter nine, 368 pages into volume 1, did Darwin get to plants, the half of the animate creation to which Burbank would devote his career. From gooseberries to gladioli, Darwin compiled his evidence: plants changed in response to outside stimulus (like the cabbages Darwin described that changed their shape or color when planted in different countries), and these changes could happen within a short time span (like the hyacinths he said growers had managed to improve from the offerings of only a few generations earlier). The causes of the changes were still largely unknown, but their occurrence was a fact beyond dispute. This was evolution measured in human time.

In spite of its clutter of miscellaneous and sometimes inaccurate information, *Variation of Animals and Plants Under Domestication* gave Luther Burbank several big ideas. The first was that it was possible to force the emergence of latent differences in fruits and flowers, even to the point of generating what seemed to be entirely new varieties. Still more exciting was Darwin's tentative suggestion that selecting, grafting, hybridizing, or simply moving a plant to a new environment might spur changes that would persist over succeeding generations. According to Darwin, these alterations were often inadvertent, but as Burbank immediately realized, such happy accidents could also be deliberately pursued. The creation of new plant varieties, something far beyond the familiar efforts to breed the best of an existing stock, did not need to wait for the slow accumulation of natural advantages Darwin had described in his *Origin of Species*. Evolutionary change could be accelerated by human intervention.

With this new idea came another important revelation: if nature could be shocked into unanticipated changes, there was nothing wrong with trying to provide that shock. "It is an error to speak of man 'tampering with nature' and causing variability," Darwin wrote. "If organic beings had not possessed an inherent tendency to vary, man could have done nothing." For Burbank, after reading those words in the Lancaster public library, the fear of hell that had haunted his early youth was quietly replaced by a much more optimistic creed: instead of submitting to the mysteries of divine creation, one could rightly and properly help those mysteries unfold.

The last chapter of volume 1 of *Variation of Animals and Plants Under Domestication* is a grab bag of puzzling observations with the cumbersome title "Anomalous Modes of Reproduction and Variation." In it Darwin listed examples of hybrid plants seemingly formed from grafts, of plants created by cross-pollination that were literally divided in their resemblance to their different ancestors (like an apple that was red on one side and yellow on the other), and of hybrids that maintained their mixed characteristics in succeeding generations. In his concluding sentence, the famous naturalist admitted he did not understand what was behind the changes he described: "When we ask ourselves what is the cause of any particular bud-variation," Darwin confessed, using the plural pronoun to cast himself and his readers in the same fellowship of confusion, "we are lost in doubt, being driven in some cases to look to the direct action of the external conditions of life as sufficient, and in other cases to feel a profound conviction that these have played a quite subordinate part, of no more importance than the nature of the spark which ignites a mass of combustible matter."

And there at the end of volume 1, where Darwin had left him suspended between doubt and combustion, Burbank cannot have missed seeing a spark of another kind. Occupying the entire facing page, in type much larger and bolder than Darwin's text, was an advertisement for another book, the best-selling *Gardening for Profit* by Peter Henderson, in which "every thing is made perfectly plain, and the subject treated in all its details, from the selection of the soil to preparing the products for market." On facing pages, the two key ideas of Burbank's career came together. It wasn't necessary to give up his interest in the natural world or choose between the outdoor life and the inventor's bench. Plant life could be a subject for experimentation and improvement, and a commercial garden could provide a good living for an imaginative and enterprising man.

On his twenty-second birthday, March 7, 1871, in a ruled notebook where he kept his personal accounts, Luther Burbank listed his possessions, along with their value. It's a long list, ranging from two hundred dollars in the bank to a pair of skates he valued at fifty cents. Among the entries are several books, including *Education and Self-Improvement* ($1.50), *Physical Perfection* ($1.00), and *French Grammar and Dictionary* ($1.00), each an indication that Burbank still saw himself as something of a work in progress.

By the following November, the French grammar book had vanished from the inventory, replaced by useful agricultural items. A corn sheller appeared, along with two dollars' worth of cranberries and fifty cents in "vegetables." Cash on hand had grown from $4.50 to $49.25, but the $200 listed in March as a "deposit in Lancaster bank" has become "second deposit to Major Jones." On September 10, 1871, Burbank had bought seventeen acres of Jones's farmland in the nearby town of Lunenburg, where he

GARDENING FOR PROFIT,

In the Market and Family Garden.

By Peter Henderson.

FINELY ILLUSTRATED.

This is the first work on Market Gardening ever published in this country. Its author is well known as a market gardener of eighteen years' successful experience. In this work he has recorded this experience, and given, without reservation, the methods necessary to the profitable culture of the commercial or

MARKET GARDEN.

It is a work for which there has long been a demand, and one which will commend itself, not only to those who grow vegetables for sale, but to the cultivator of the

FAMILY GARDEN,

to whom it presents methods quite different from the old ones generally practiced. It is an ORIGINAL AND PURELY AMERICAN work, and not made up, as books on gardening too often are, by quotations from foreign authors.

Every thing is made perfectly plain, and the subject treated in all its details, from the selection of the soil to preparing the products for market.

Sent post-paid, price $1.50.

ORANGE JUDD & CO., 245 BROADWAY, NEW-YORK

planned to raise vegetables for market. Olive Burbank, who had already sold her share of the Lancaster farm and had been living with Emma in neighboring Groton Junction, bought a white frame house across the street from the Lunenburg town hall, where they all could live while Luther cultivated his garden. The business of inventing plants was about to begin.

American Agriculturist.

ₒ 2 ₒ

THE LUCKY SPUD

And he gave it for his opinion, that whoever could make two ears of corn, or two blades of grass, to grow upon a spot of ground where only one grew before, would deserve better of mankind, and do more essential service to his country, than the whole race of politicians put together. —JONATHAN SWIFT, *Gulliver's Travels*, 1726

Burbank's first discovery as a market gardener was that he wasn't alone in the business. The stalls in Fitchburg were crowded with competitors, many of them with larger farms, more varied produce, and well-established relations with their customers. Searching for a way to attract buyers, the novice grower began by trying to be the first to offer each new crop in season. At a time when buying local was the only option, the first fresh greens of spring commanded a good price in cold climates, and a week or two head start in getting to market could make the difference between profit and loss. Burbank planted seeds indoors before the ground had thawed and then transferred the seedlings to cold frames, glass-topped enclosures that would enable his young plants to survive the uncertainties of New England spring weather. He started his sweet corn indoors, too, sprouting the kernels in a mixture of leaf mold and manure so he could be the first to have a stock of that late-summer treat. And then, less than a year after he began farming in Lunenburg, he found his lucky spud, the plant that brought him his initial fame.

Today, the Burbank potato, better known through its variant, the Russet Burbank, is one of the most widely grown potatoes in the world. In Idaho, where the Russet Burbank dominates state agriculture, a picture of the potato and the slogan "Famous Potatoes" often appear on the state license plates. When the United Nations declared 2008 the "International Year of the Potato," it featured the Russet Burbank as "the classic American potato."

Large and oval, with white flesh and conveniently shallow eyes, the Burbank is an excellent potato. Its high starch and low moisture content produce fluffy baked and mashed potatoes. The low moisture also means it can be fried without becoming limp or soggy, while its low sugar content prevents excess browning. These virtues, along with its large size, regular shape, and distinctive nutty flavor, make the Russet Burbank the preferred variety for many potato processors. McDonald's, the largest purchaser of potatoes in the United States and a significant force in global potato markets, specifies Russet Burbanks. The Russet Burbank is also the guinea pig of the vegetable world, a favorite for laboratory experiments, perhaps because it is so widely available. When the Monsanto Corporation was looking for a plant with which to demonstrate the power of an inserted bug-repelling gene, Bt, it chose as its carrier the Russet Burbank potato.

All of this was far in the future, of course, when Burbank was tending his field in Lunenburg in 1872. Still, a potato was a good foundation on which to build his reputation. Humble and nourishing, potatoes were grown and cherished around the world.

It wasn't always that way, however. Like the tomato, its botanical cousin, the potato was greeted with fear and skepticism when it was first brought to Europe from the Americas near the end of the sixteenth century. Most people wanted nothing to do with it. The green leaves and stems of the potato plant smelled nasty, and nasty in much the same way as several well-known poisons. This is because the potato is a member of the Solanaceae family, which includes not only tomatoes, bell peppers, eggplants, and ornamental petunias, but also potentially dangerous species like deadly nightshade, jimsonweed, henbane, mandrake, and tobacco. Potatoes grow underground, a region always associated with dubious transactions, and farmers feared the plant would poison their soil. Leprosy, scrofula, and syphilis were only some of the diseases wrongly attributed to potato eating.

Even in the face of these suspicions, the potato had some very real virtues. It was easy to grow, stored well over extended periods, and produced a large yield on a small piece of land. It would take another three hundred years to learn that potatoes were high in vitamins, minerals, and protein and low in fat and cholesterol (at least before being fried or garnished with butter or sour cream), but it was clear from the earliest years that people could survive on a diet in which potatoes were the central or even the only source of nutrition.

European rulers, persuaded that the new plant from America could serve as a cheap and plentiful source of food, worked hard to impose potatoes on their subjects. Still, it took more than a century of top-down coercion to get people to eat the things, and longer than that for potatoes to lose their stigma entirely. Well into the eighteenth century, the French were still resisting potatoes. Antoine Parmentier, the chemist and public health official who served under both King Louis XVI and Emperor Napoleon Bonaparte, campaigned ceaselessly for potato cultivation, urging

Queen Marie Antoinette to wear potato blossoms to make the vegetable fashionable, hosting elaborate dinners where potatoes were featured in every course, and persuading the Paris Faculty of Medicine to make a formal announcement declaring the tuber edible. In Prussia, Frederick the Great sent potatoes to famine victims, accompanied by soldiers to make sure they ate the gift. Eventually, hunger won out over suspicion, and the potato became a staple food in much of Europe and the United States.

Potatoes are not usually grown from seed, but by a process known as vegetal reproduction. Leave a potato alone and it will begin to sprout new shoots from its buds, or "eyes." Toss it in the ground, and some of those shoots will rise up to become the leaves and vine, while others will branch off underground to produce new potatoes that can be dug up and savored in the spring or left underground until needed. Barring the odd spontaneous mutation, each potato grown this way is an exact duplicate of the parent. Doubling the yield can be as simple as dividing the original tuber (confusingly known as a seed potato) before planting. Sandy, well-drained soil is preferred, which is why the eastern end of Long Island, New York, held flourishing potato fields before the Hamptons became a prime location for millionaires' mansions. All sorts of other unpromising conditions will do, however, including piles of seaweed or fallen leaves. Commercial potato cultivation requires a great deal of care, but even a clumsy, casual, interrupted effort will usually produce enough potatoes to feed a family.

Unfortunately, vegetal reproduction is also a perfect way to transmit disease from generation to generation. The blight that destroyed the Irish potato crops—starving one and a half million people and forcing another million to emigrate, mainly to the United States—was caused by a then-mysterious disease that in a matter of days, if not hours, could transform a thriving field into a slimy, foul-smelling patch of rotting vegetation. Long before anyone knew it was a form of fungus, the disease was called late blight, a mild description of the horrible ruin it would bring to a potato field ready for harvest. Late blight was particularly devastating in Ireland because the potato was almost the only source of food for the peasant population, and also because there was only one variety of potato grown. It was a problem in other countries as well, however, including the United States.

Even without blight, beetles, or other pests, the relative ease of potato growing did not necessarily translate into an excellent crop. Early potato varieties were often small and misshaped in ways that made them difficult to cook, and many rotted during storage. The first record of successful potato cultivation in North America was in New Hampshire in 1719. The urge to improve the plant quickly followed. By 1848, the year before Burbank was born, the Massachusetts Horticultural Society listed almost one hundred varieties of potato on exhibit at its annual fair, all part of a continuing search for a better potato.

"Search" was the operative word, because the Patent Office was not alone in thinking the easiest way to find a new plant variety was to appropriate it from somewhere else. In 1850, the Reverend Chauncey Goodrich obtained several seed potatoes from somewhere in South America (accounts of the source vary), which he planted in upstate New York. In 1853 he introduced what he called the Garnet Chili potato, a round, red-skinned, white-fleshed potato that seemed to resist late blight. Albert Breese discovered a variant of the Garnet Chili he called the Early Rose and introduced in 1861. In the following decade there was still plenty of room, and demand, for improvement.

How to Make a Plant: Selection

Selection is the oldest form of plant breeding. Long before anybody was keeping records, people were choosing which particular plants to cultivate based on higher yield, better taste, superior pest or drought resistance, easier cultivation, extraordinary beauty, or other desirable traits—desirable to humans, that is, because this is artificial selection we are talking about. Natural selection, the engine of evolution identified independently by both Charles Darwin and Alfred Russel Wallace, is about surviving long enough to reproduce. It thus often rewards plants that have annoyingly selfish qualities like being extremely inconspicuous, tasting terrible, or going to seed in a fast and fabulously prolific way, leaving nothing behind to harvest. Humans, however, have other priorities.

In writing *On the Origin of Species*, Darwin began his explanation of what he called "natural selection" by comparing it to the much more familiar process of artificial selection known to every pigeon fancier, horse racer, sheep shearer, and saver of seeds. Humans have guided animals in their reproductive options for many centuries, selecting chickens to find the best egg layers and the fiercest fighters, dividing dogs into hunters and herders, and taking great pains to maintain the differences between a draft horse and a derby contender. Plants, too, were familiar objects of selection, though in the nineteenth century the process of breeding plants to maintain or improve varieties was not nearly so well understood.

The Burbank potato was not Luther Burbank's most intricate exercise in plant breeding. Certainly it was not the invention that brought him the most money. Still, it would always be his best-known claim to fame. He wasn't obsessed with finding a better potato. A breakthrough in beets would have suited him just as well. His cabbage seeds, his sorghum, and his honey had all brought cash prizes at the local agricultural fair. He was already experimenting with beans, which offer themselves up for cross-pollination in ways that are much more obvious than those of potatoes. But when the opportunity to experiment and perhaps discover a new variety of potato presented itself, Burbank was ready.

The story would be repeated for decades, an enduring part of the plant inventor's legend. Burbank was growing Early Rose potatoes on his farm in Lunenburg when he noticed a rarity: a seed ball forming on one of the plants. It was an inconspicuous little seed-carrying globe, like a tiny tomato dangling from the vine, and he claimed it was the only Early Rose seed ball he ever saw. Most farmers would have ignored the thing, since potatoes are not planted from seeds; one of the explanations offered for the scarcity of seed balls was that they had faded away after generations of selection for other qualities. Burbank remembered his reading of Darwin, however, and the master's insistence that a single plant could contain multiple variations. Vegetal reproduction hid those differences, but an enterprising experimenter could perhaps uncover them. It would be his first exercise in assisting evolution.

Burbank marked the potato with a strip of fabric torn from the hem of his shirt (a lifelong habit, to the despair of his female relatives), and waited for the seed ball to ripen. When he came one day to check on his plant and discovered that his precious seed ball had fallen from the stem, he spent three days searching on hands and knees to find the tiny thing in the potato patch. He somehow recovered it, carefully saved the twenty-three seeds inside, and waited until spring to plant them.

The results were as varied as Darwin had predicted. The twenty-three seeds produced plants with potatoes of different sizes, colors, and shapes. Some had many tiny tubers and some had almost none. Most of them would be of no interest at all to any but the most desperate farmer. Two, however, produced impressively large white tubers with smooth skins and relatively few shallow eyes. This whole experiment was already shaping up to be a case of extraordinary good fortune, but Burbank's luck went further. His new potatoes also tasted very good, and they stood up well over the winter's storage. The next summer, Burbank planted them both again. One variety produced many more potatoes than the other. It would take longer to discover that it also had superior resistance to the late blight that had devastated Ireland.

By the fall of 1874, Burbank was starting to show his new potatoes around. In September, he exhibited five of his best specimens at the Lunenburg town fair. A reporter from the Fitchburg *Sentinel* singled out for special notice the potato then known as No. 15, the seedling from the Early Rose. What caught the reporter's attention was that the plant had produced tubers weighing over three pounds, an enormous yield compared to other varieties.

Like any other inventor, whether of better potatoes or better plows, Burbank now had to decide how to maximize profit from his discovery. He could have acquired a great deal more land and become a potato farmer, but he had neither the money nor the inclination to go into the business of wholesale potato production. Besides, that would not have solved two problems that were unique to inventors of organic things: the lack of any kind of legal protection for their creations and the absence of any control over the product itself.

Burbank Scrapbook 1906.
COURTESY LUTHER BURBANK COLLECTION,
LIBRARY OF CONGRESS

According to a long-standing legal principle called the "Product of Nature" doctrine, objects found in the natural world (animal, vegetable, or mineral) could not be patented. A gold *mine* was real property, and could be fenced so that only the owner of the property could extract the gold and dispose of it in the marketplace. A new design for a *machine* to extract gold was intellectual property, controlled by its owner. The new machine could be used in secret in the gold mine or its details could be protected through a patent and revealed to the world. But gold itself located on other land was available to any lucky finder. So were potatoes.

The second difficulty for Burbank, one that applied only to inventors working in the realm of animals or vegetables, was that living things reproduce themselves. Unlike a mechanical invention, a plant is it own organic factory; any buyer could go into the potato-making business for himself, using the original purchase to grow a potentially limitless number of future products. Even a large, well-established plant merchant could count on exclusivity for only a season or two, after which other sellers would simply raise the new variety in their own fields, and Burbank's farm was neither large nor well established. The thing to do was sell the rights to his potato to someone who had the means to propagate it on a scale large enough to make a profit before the plant's exclusivity had faded and its value had decreased.

When Burbank was starting his career, seed sellers were the venture capitalists of the vegetable world, buying promising new prototypes, getting them into production, and grooming them for the market. Anyone trying to make a living by developing new plants hoped to be bought out by a large dealer in plants and seeds, which was exactly what Burbank wanted. While he was exhibiting at the Lunenburg Farmers Fair, he began writing to major seed sellers in the area, describing the wonderful virtues of his new potato.

If Burbank had been hoping for an immediate sale, he was disappointed. On October 5, 1874, he received a reply from James J. H. Gregory, a seed merchant in the Atlantic seaport of Marblehead, Massachusetts, eighteen miles north of Boston. "D[ear] S[ir]," Gregory scribbled, "I have a great number of seedlings sent me for trial and with these I shall be happy to compare yours another season. Should it prove to be a real acquisition I should so learn and would so inform you; the ownership of the potato would, of course remain in your hands to be disposed of as you might think best."

Gregory's proposal was a model of judicious evaluation, but hardly what the hopeful young plant inventor wanted to hear. Next, Burbank wrote to Washburn & Company, a large seed company in Boston. Their reply, dated December 4, was even less encouraging:

> *Dear Sir, In reply to your letter regarding the new potatoes, we can only inform you of the usual method taken by potatoe [sic] raisers—after they have a pretty fair stock they send samples to eminent agricultural gentlemen . . . to grow in their respective localities—Their report at the end of the season is the verdict by which the new potatoe [sic] will sink or swim. You will see the utility of such a method in advantage of any puffing by interested parties— We scarcely think your stock large enough to let it out this season— even for testing. Any further advice will be gladly given by us—*
>
> *yours, &c—*
> *Washburn*

At this point Burbank went back to Gregory, who had at least offered to try out what Burbank was now calling the "best white potato."

JAMES J. H. GREGORY, the eventual buyer of Burbank's potato, was not an obscure local retailer who struck it rich through another man's discovery. He was a leader in the growing ranks of seed sellers who were transforming the business of agriculture in the decades after the Civil War, and a man of considerable civic achievement. Twenty years older than Luther Burbank and a graduate of Amherst College, Gregory had been a teacher and school principal before taking over the family seed business, and he was a prolific writer and lecturer on horticultural topics. Gregory was also a poet, a collector of Native American relics, a generous donor to the town of Marblehead (his gifts included a clock, a bell for the town's new tower, and land for an oceanfront park), a selectman, a library trustee, a state senator, a benefactor of struggling families and adoptive father to a number of orphans, and an ardent believer in educational opportunity who would later give over thirty thousand books to African American colleges.

Most important, he was a man with the resources and the reputation needed to enter a new variety of potato into a crowded and competitive market. Introducing new and improved seeds to the general market was a Gregory family specialty. In the early 1840s, when James J. H. Gregory was still a schoolmaster and Luther Burbank had not yet been born, James's father had popularized the Hubbard squash, a large, lumpy variety with a sea-green rind whose appearance does not inspire immediate affection. He named it after Elizabeth Hubbard, "a very worthy lady" who had directed his attention to this previously unrecognized variety of winter squash after she had tasted one grown by another Marblehead resident, Captain Knott Martin. Martin in turn had gotten his seeds from a different Marblehead woman, doubtless also worthy but unnamed. In this slow and very local way, the squash had made the rounds of neighborhood gardens for a good twenty years before the senior Mr. Gregory took note of it, named it after the estimable Mrs. Hubbard, and put it on the market, where it remains popular today, prized for its rich, moist flavor and its ability to be stored for months without rotting. There is no record of Mrs. Hubbard receiving a finder's fee.

When James J. H. Gregory returned to Marblehead and the selling of seeds in the 1850s, he continued his father's interest in plant introductions. He devoted most of his four hundred acres to growing the plants that provided the seeds he sold through catalogs, which by midcentury was a thriving business. A certain amount of land was always set aside, though, to develop his own new selections as well as to test the submissions from other growers. After planting Burbank's sample in the summer of 1875, Gregory agreed it was a very fine potato. He also noted, however, that the market at the moment was glutted with new potatoes. He offered Burbank $150 for exclusive rights to propagate and sell the variety, which he generously decided to call the Burbank Seedling. He would list it in his catalog. It might catch on.

What was an ordinary transaction for James J. H. Gregory was a life-changing opportunity for Luther Burbank. His early success with his potato discovery convinced him that he could make a career of his passion for garden experiments. At the same time, three years of battling the rocky soil and unforgiving winters of Massachusetts had persuaded him to join the exodus to the Pacific Coast. Burbank's older half brothers George and David had been writing home about the splendors of northern California for twenty years. By 1875, his younger brother, Alfred, was also living in the area north of San Francisco. Lured by their letters and by widely circulated (if somewhat exaggerated) reports of cheap and fertile land in a perpetually balmy climate, Luther decided to go to northern California, too.

Burbank had asked five hundred dollars for rights to his discovery (the beginning of a lifetime of overoptimistic pricing), but he accepted Gregory's lower offer, which included the right to take ten seed potatoes with him to the western market. Selling his land in Lunenburg for barely enough to repay his mortgage, he packed his trunk, bade goodbye to his mother and sister, and grabbed the hamper of sandwiches and cake they had prepared for the nine-day cross-country train ride. He was transplanting his business to the other side of the continent.

"Res. of E. L. Davis, Santa Rosa, Sonoma Co., Cal."
Illustrated Atlas of Sonoma County, 1877.

THE SECOND GOLD RUSH

Within the limits of our State, every fruit of the temperate zone, and
some of the tropics, will ripen in perfection. We have soil of every
character, climate of every possibility, resources undeveloped everywhere, industries yet to be fostered, hopes to be realized, a future
which we, who live in its midst, can hardly as yet comprehend.

—Charles H. Shinn, *Pacific Rural Handbook*, 1879

Before the discovery of gold in 1848 and the rush of prospectors that began in 1849, the great bounty of California agriculture lay almost entirely in the future. Native American tribes
were hunters and fishermen, not planters. Spanish missionaries
and generals had come north from Mexico to gain converts and
consolidate their political control, not to cultivate the land, and
they had never gone very far beyond mission gardens and grazing
herds of cattle and sheep. Russians had sailed from Siberia to fish
and trap for furs, and tales of fertile valleys full of wild oats had
lured a few early pioneer farmers from the United States, but neither they nor the Spanish ranchers were ready to meet the demands of the hoards of hungry gold seekers who arrived at
midcentury to make their fortunes and stayed to transform the
entire Pacific Coast.

Food for the first prospectors arrived by boat, shipped around
Cape Horn from ports on the eastern seaboard or from Europe. A

closer source was Hawaii, a mere 2,400 miles away. Potatoes, easy
to plant and ready to eat in a single season, were the first significant food crop cultivated in gold country after 1849. The river
town of Petaluma, just north of San Francisco in Sonoma County,
grew up as a depot for a local variety, the small Bodega Red potato.
Cattle, timber, and wheat ranching followed, each requiring large
plots of land but relatively few workers, and all suited for easy
export. Twenty-five years after the gold rush, California was on
the cusp of a second boom, this one based on agricultural rather
than mineral wealth.

In 1875, the year twenty-six-year-old Luther Burbank moved
to California, the transition to garden and orchard crops was just
beginning. The luscious fruits, flowers, vegetables, and nuts for
which the state is now so famous had not yet become big business,
and in many instances they had not even been introduced to the
region. The small, sustainable network of farms and orchards that
preservationists are now struggling to maintain did not exist; Burbank was one of the people who would help to create it. For the rest
of his life, Burbank would contribute in multiple ways to the rise
of California agriculture, both by introducing new plants and,
equally important, by popularizing the idea that nature could
and should be managed to provide an almost limitless variety of
products. He was the perfect collaborator with the second generation of California boosters, eager to promote the state as a natural
cornucopia where anyone could grow anything in the willing soil.

When Burbank arrived in San Francisco on October 29, a year
after he had first tried to sell his new potato, he saw California as a
land of almost limitless possibility. He wrote back to his mother
and sister in Massachusetts, as he had every day of his trip, and
assured them that "a young man who will not drink here and is

good-natured and makes folks like him, and *who minds his own business*, has *ten thousand* chances of success where the same qualities would have *one* chance in the states." Burbank seems to have forgotten that California had been a state since 1850, but he was certain that he had arrived in a new country where great opportunities offered themselves, ready for planting if not quite ripe for the picking.

His plan was to join his brother Alfred in Santa Rosa, sixty miles north of San Francisco on the other side of the Golden Gate. The booming new city was typical of the transformation of California over the previous twenty-five years. In 1849, Rancho Cabeza de Santa Rosa had belonged to Doña Maria Carrillo, a gift from her son-in-law General Vallejo, the Mexican military governor. Two decades later, after deaths, divisions, scandal, bribes, and legal wrangles, the cattle ranch had been sold and divided many times. By 1875, when Burbank arrived, almost all of Santa Rosa was owned by more recent arrivals from the eastern United States. The town already had a college, a public school that enrolled 275 students, two private schools, two banks, a municipal water company, a brewery, a flour mill, a granite works, a Masonic Hall, at least seven churches, and twice as many saloons. Sidewalks hadn't appeared yet, but a newly completed railroad, a branch of the Southern Pacific, connected the growing town to Petaluma, and from there one could go by ferry down the Petaluma River and across the San Pablo Bay to San Francisco. The rail link to Petaluma connected Santa Rosa to the rest of the nation.

In another long letter, written on October 31, Burbank's first day in Santa Rosa, he described his surroundings in ecstatic terms. The air was delicious, the mountains lovely enough to move him to tears, the valley "covered with majestic oaks placed as no human

hand could arrange them for beauty," and the gardens full of plants
that in Massachusetts were humble flowers but in California grew
to resemble trees. "Do you suppose I am not pleased to see fuchsias
in the front yards, twelve feet high, and loaded with various colors
of blossoms?" he asked, with the boastful teasing familiar to anyone who has received a postcard photo of palm trees while shiver-
ing through a winter storm at home. *"Fruit cans are not for sale
here,"* he added, summing up the astounding abundance of fresh
local produce.

Already Burbank was scouting the area for unknown plants,
confident that novel varieties of every sort of growing thing, all
with high commercial potential, were just waiting to be discovered.
"I took a long walk to-day and found enough curious plants in a
wild spot of about an acre to set a botanist wild," he wrote to his
mother and sister in that same first letter. "I found the wild Yam
which I hunted for so much in Massachusetts, also the yerba buena
vine, which has a pleasant taste like peppermint (I send you a few
leaves). I also found a nut that no one has seen before (have planted
it), and several (to me) curious plants. I mean to get a piece of land
(hire or buy) and plant it, then I can do more work just the same."
To confirm how delighted he was by his decision to move to California, Burbank added an endorsement so avid that it has been
featured on the official letterhead of the city of Santa Rosa and in
the brochures of just about every real estate office in Sonoma
County: "I firmly believe from what I have seen that it is *the chosen
spot of all this earth* as far as *Nature* is concerned."

Chosen spot or not, life wasn't as easy as the would-be plant
inventor had expected. He was sharing an eight-by-ten-foot shack
with his brother Alfred and another man, close quarters that
weren't improved by the fact that neither of his new roommates

was a great housekeeper. Just a month before, the Bank of California had failed, leaving fourteen million dollars in debt and causing a credit crisis that stalled the construction jobs that Alfred had touted as a sure way to earn money fast. And, while Burbank had left a region of declining agricultural land values, Santa Rosa's real estate prices were rising as values were inflated by speculation. The cheap farmland he had been expecting turned out not to exist. An acre in Santa Rosa would cost at least three hundred dollars, four times the price Burbank had paid in Lunenburg. He had come west with a little over six hundred dollars, all the money he had in the world, and he was wary of losing it on a bad purchase and not having enough to support himself until he was established.

Still, the twenty-six-year-old newcomer was undaunted, at least at first. Unable to find work, he left Santa Rosa to visit his much older half brothers George and David in Tomales, some twenty miles west on the Pacific Coast. George Burbank, a solid citizen who had just been elected to the state legislature, was skeptical that anyone could make a career as a plant inventor, but he agreed to give Luther garden space to cultivate the ten seed potatoes Burbank had bargained with James J. H. Gregory to retain. It was the first step in propagating enough stock to market his own creation in the West, where there were few other growers and an expanding population. Eventually, the Burbank potato would be grown up and down the Pacific Coast, remaining a major California export into the 1940s, but "eventually" is a very long time frame for a young man with few other assets.

After George left for his new duties in Sacramento, Burbank lingered in Tomales with David Burbank and his wife, Lina, for another two weeks, explored the oceanfront sights of Tomales and

Point Reyes, and "had an outrageous good time" with his jovial rediscovered relations. David and Luther priced farmland in San Rafael, a relative bargain at only a hundred dollars an acre, but Burbank was unconvinced the foggy climate would suit his needs. Before leaving Massachusetts, he had read as much about California growing conditions as he could find, and he had set his sights on a location that would be more reliably sunny.

When Burbank returned to Santa Rosa, the construction market was still depressed. He had dreamed of getting some land on which to start his plant experiments but found himself making do with small carpentry jobs and a few commissions collecting California native plants and seeds for botanical gardens in the East. Plant collecting was a good way to get to know the local species but provided a very precarious living. When the rainy season began in November, construction jobs stopped entirely and the unpaved roads turned into deep troughs of mud. In December, even the shack had to be abandoned. Alfred took off to work in the local quarry, and Luther walked nineteen soggy miles to Petaluma, where he managed to find a job at a nursery. He lived there until a fever the following spring forced him to leave the damp greenhouse. Making his way back to Santa Rosa, he barely survived on the milk a sympathetic neighbor gave him free of charge.

Once again, Burbank's mother, Olive, and his sister Emma stepped in, joining him in California. Twenty-two-year-old Emma arrived in Santa Rosa first, in the summer of 1877, and quickly found work as an elementary school teacher. A few weeks later, Olive sold the house in Lunenburg, packed her household goods and Luther's childhood relics in barrels to be shipped by boat on the long ocean route around South America to San Francisco, and boarded the train for California. However dubious the rest of the family may have been about Luther's potential, his mother and sister regarded him as a genius whose work needed to be encouraged, supported, and vigorously promoted. The Burbank potato was beginning to receive favorable comments from eastern growers and Emma had been diligent in gathering any news reports that mentioned her brother's name. If Luther's reputation hadn't yet reached the western markets, Emma and Olive were sure that simply meant the creator needed time, space, opportunity, and support to make his career grow.

Perhaps he also needed a bit of prodding. The population of northern California in the 1870s held a great many people who had emigrated in the expectation of easy wealth, and such a rootless society was bound to experience a high degree of disappointment, particularly as newcomers compared their own circumstances with the get-rich-quick tales of gold miners and the effusive brochures put out by shipping lines and railroads to entice immigrants. Burbank's letters home included several unconvincing assurances that he was immune to the attacks of "the blues" that afflicted so many new arrivals. After Emma and Olive arrived in Santa Rosa, Luther's life became less difficult, as the sensitive young man who rhapsodized about the landscape and loved to wander the hills collecting nuts and flowers gave sudden signs of increased attention to business.

What a pair those Burbank women must have been. Olive was tiny, tireless, fretful, and proud. She insisted on her due in every transaction, including charging her son rent on the two acres behind the house she bought on Tupper Street, on the southern edge of what was then downtown Santa Rosa. Emma had grown to be a large, square-faced young woman, tight-corseted and determined ("she will never have any of her rights real or imaginary

infringed on in the least," her half brother Herbert had predicted).
She contributed her earnings to the shared household and pasted
her sheaf of clippings into the first of many scrapbooks that would
contain every mention she could gather of her brother Luther
and his achievements.

Construction had picked up by then in Santa Rosa, and Burbank was having better luck finding day jobs as a carpenter at

various building sites around the growing town. After work, he planted his rented garden with laurels, yews, cypress, roses, and whatever other trees, shrubs, vegetables, and flowers he thought would bring the quickest profit. The propagation of familiar favorites was just a temporary expedient. Burbank's plan—it would always be his plan—was to concentrate on the more important business of selecting and breeding entirely new plants, creating varieties and even species that had never been seen before, and selling his inventions to growers across the country and around the world.

To be a plant breeder in the late 1870s required a course of self-education, because there were few other ways to learn what remained an obscure and often secret trade. Over a decade after the passage of the Morrill Act of 1862, the national network of land grant colleges was still only slowly coming into being. The University of California, recently relocated to the new town of Berkeley, on the east side of San Francisco Bay, had graduated its first class of twelve students in 1873, and it had taken another two years for the university to find a director for its College of Agriculture. E. W. Hilgard, the College of Agriculture's first dean, arrived in California in 1875, at almost the same moment as Burbank. But Hilgard was a soil scientist, much more interested in improving growing conditions than in the creation of new crops, and plant breeding had little role in the early curriculum. Beyond the universities, the national program of Agricultural Experiment Stations, federally funded centers for research and plant improvement, would not begin until 1887.

Commercial sources of information were not very helpful either. Then, as now, books for gardeners concentrated on advice for sowing and nurturing plants, paying a great deal of attention to climate and pest control and very little to plant variety. The many farm journals of the day were full of information on improved methods of agriculture and horticulture but not on how to improve the plants themselves (unless you counted the advertisements that usually covered front and back covers alike with their promises of surefire miracle crops). Seed sellers enhanced their catalogs with cultivation tips, but those were aimed at the vast market of inexperienced farmers and gardeners who had taken to the land with little actual knowledge of what they were doing. And nobody had yet written much of value about the plants of California.

In this vacuum, Burbank found inspiration once again by turning to Charles Darwin, whose interest in agriculture and horticulture was almost entirely noncommercial. Darwin's *Effects of Cross and Self Fertilisation in the Vegetable Kingdom* was published in England in 1876 and in the United States the following year. It was presented as an extension of his 1862 study *On the Various Contrivances by which British and Foreign Orchids Are Fertilised by Insects*, a subject that appealed to a passionate but somewhat limited audience. To Burbank, however, Darwin's lessons reached far beyond the realm of hothouse rarities.

Burbank acquired a copy of *Effects of Cross and Self Fertilisation in the Vegetable Kingdom* as soon as the book reached San Francisco. Once again, he was seized by a passion for experimentation. Burbank's first exposure to Darwin had inspired him to accelerate evolution by seeking out and fostering the kind of spontaneous variations that created the Burbank potato. Now he took on hybridization. "One sentence in the very introductory chapter of that volume opened the door of my mind and took possession of my fancy," he later recalled. "After discussing briefly the marvel of cross- and self-fertilization in plants Darwin said: 'As plants are adapted by such diversified and effective means for cross-fertilization, it might have been inferred from this fact alone that they derive some great advantage from the process; and it is the object of the present work to show the nature and importance of the benefits thus derived.'" As Darwin went on to suggest, cross-fertilizing plants might lead to offspring that were not only *different* from either parent, producing the novelty that was so often the goal in the flower trade, but also *better:* larger, sturdier, more prolific, or faster growing.

If this was true for flowers, it was worth trying on other plants with much larger markets. Shortly after he read *Effects of Cross and Self Fertilisation*, Burbank began crossing everything from variations on a single wildflower to multiple varieties of plums and even different species like the tomato and the potato. He treated cross-fertilization (between plants of the same variety), crossbreeding (between different varieties of a single species), and hybridization (between species) as different points along a single progression of biological possibilities. He often used the terms almost interchangeably, and he was willing to try just about any sort of cross he could imagine. He cross-pollinated nut trees, fruit trees, grapes, berries, roses, lilies, native wildflowers, and local cacti, pursuing subtle variations and also mixing entirely different species, including native plants that had never been thought to have any desirable qualities that would make them worthy of a grower's attention.

Burbank began hybridizing and crossing plants in significant numbers as soon as he had his mother's garden to work in, probably in the spring of 1878. It was a surge of intense creative activity, like the inspired production of an artist turning out dozens of canvases in a matter of weeks. Burbank's later catalogs almost always dated his experiments to exactly this period—before he had anything but curiosity, ambition, and access to the most ordinary tools and plants.

How to Make a Plant:
Crosses and Hybrids

The presence of sexual reproduction in plants was neither fully understood nor widely believed until the end of the eighteenth century. By the 1830s, however, improving plant cultivars by cross-pollinating different varieties had become an exciting prospect. In 1839, when Patent Commissioner Henry L. Ellsworth petitioned Congress for funds for agriculture, he had declared that "the sexuality of plants, and the practicability of crossing the same, are no longer matters of doubt; and great improvements may be anticipated from new experiments."

By the middle of the nineteenth century the mechanics of cross-pollination were fairly well known, although the reasons for the specific outcomes would remain a mystery for another fifty years. Most people who spent any time cultivating plants were aware that wind, birds, and insects carried pollen from one plant to another. Growers would sometimes try to isolate a particularly prized specimen from random pollinators to maintain its qualities, but if they just wanted to see what happened when two different specimens of a particular plant mixed, all they had to do was transfer the pollen from one to the other. A less common exercise was the attempt to cross different *varieties* (a Jonathan apple with a McIntosh, perhaps), much less the highly irregular and even morally suspect process of crossing different *species* (plum and apricot, to take an example Burbank later made famous) in pursuit of what were then often called mongrel plants, now better known as hybrids. Hybridization was the clearest case of tampering with nature. It was also the most difficult. It would take almost another century to discover how to prevent hybrids from reverting to one or another of their sources or from being incapable of reproduction themselves. The best-known hybrid, after all, is the mule, famously stubborn and also famously sterile.

One of the many things that would make Luther Burbank so original and successful as a plant breeder was his complete indifference to these cautions, obstacles, and distinctions. He understood the challenge of hybridizing species that seemed too different for a successful union, but he tried to stretch the boundaries and was willing to wait years and even decades for results. In time, a cross of the plum and apricot created the plumcot, and a cross of the raspberry and western dewberry (a California native considered too soft for commercial production) created the popular Primus berry. A potato crossed with a tomato created a curiosity that was a great attention getter, though of no economic value. The trick was experimenting on a scale large enough to increase the chances of interesting offspring, having the patience to wait a very long time for results, and (the hardest part) recognizing whatever good resulted and finding a way to preserve it in following generations. Burbank experimented in volume, and he watched and selected and recrossed and backcrossed and watched some more, for as many seasons as it took, until he had something he wanted.

ONE OF THE THINGS Burbank wanted was a better walnut. The black walnut tree is a native of North America. In the eastern

United States, where walnut trees often grew very tall, the straight-grained timber was considered particularly suitable for elegant parlor furniture, the interiors of banks and hotel lobbies, and for gunstocks, and it commanded a very high price. In California, however, where timber was scarce and everyone, it seems, was searching for new sources of lumber, black walnuts were much smaller, growing wild as a short tree or multistemmed shrub. Sensing a market, Burbank made the walnut one of his first targets for improvement, crossing different varieties in search of both better nutmeats and faster-growing wood.

East or west, the nuts of the black walnut tree, while very good to eat, are a challenge to harvest. In autumn, ripe nut pods fall from the trees; the soft, round pod looks and feels something like an undersized tennis ball. Cutting the pod open reveals a spongy layer that surrounds the nut and that coats everything it touches with a deep, dark purple stain that soon turns to an almost indelible brown. And that is before you even get to the shell.

Here are some modern suggestions for cracking black walnut shells to get at the nutmeat inside: Roll the nut underfoot on a hard surface, such as a driveway. Put the nut on a metal mesh and drive a car over it. Drill a slightly-too-small hole in a board and pound the nut through with a hammer. Entire academic programs devote themselves to the difficulties of removing black walnuts from their shells: the Non-Timber Forest Products Program at Virginia Tech recommends first cracking the nuts by running them between large steel wheels and then extracting the meat from the cracked shell by using another series of rollers with saw teeth. Amateurs who lack this kind of equipment sometimes invest in a walnut-cracking device that looks like an oversized stapler, with the addition of a large upper handle that folds out for extra leverage.

For reasons that are probably obvious by now, the nuts of the black walnut tree are usually sold to candy makers or other large commercial markets; the walnuts sold for home consumption are a milder variety that has paler nuts and more obliging shells. These are sometimes called Persian walnuts, reflecting a common assumption about their origins, or English walnuts, a name that recalls the days when the British Empire controlled the trade. The botanical name, *Juglans regia*, means Jove's acorn, because the Romans considered it the food of the gods. The tree is not as sturdy as the black walnut, however, and modern growers often graft the Persian walnut onto a black walnut rootstock. It you look at the trees of a walnut orchard, you may be able to see the line where the dark bark of the black walnut changes to the paler bark of the Persian walnut.

When Burbank set out to make a better walnut, he turned to hybridization to combine the best traits from different walnut varieties in a single tree. His first experiment, in the spring of 1878, was to apply pollen from the Persian walnut onto the blossoms of the northern California black walnut, probably by the simple method of shaking the pollen from the first tree onto a piece of stiff paper or a watch crystal and then using his fingers to smear it on the stigma of the other tree's blossom. When the nuts had developed, he planted them.

Like the offspring of the Early Rose potato seeds, the walnut seedling results were mixed and mostly bad. Many of the new trees were not hybrids at all but seedlings of the ordinary California black walnut. Five or six did seem to be hybrids, however, and one was particularly large and vigorous. This was the only one Burbank saved. The new tree grew at a prodigious rate, at least in comparison to the usual slow pace of hardwood trees. In ten years it was twice as tall as equivalent Persian walnuts. A decade might seem like a long time to wait for results (certainly it must have seemed so to Burbank, struggling to grow his business), but Burbank's hybrid was an early example of his remarkable ability to accelerate the usually slow and deliberate processes of nature. To emphasize the fact that his new walnut was fine hardwood timber but grew as fast as softwood, reaching maturity in fifteen years instead of the normal fifty to sixty, he named it the Paradox walnut.

In 1879, while waiting to see what happened with his first walnut hybrid, Burbank began a second experiment: applying pollen from the eastern black walnut to the California black walnut blossom and again planting the nuts. The best of this second crop of hybrids didn't grow as fast as the Paradox, but it was a prolific producer of nuts that were larger, milder, sweeter, and easier to shell than those of either parent tree. This would become the Royal walnut.

JUGLANS CALIFORNICA.   JUGLANS NIGRA.   HYBRID WALNUT.
Staminate Parent.   Pistillate Parent.   All Life Size.
                              (See also page 9.)

Hybrid Walnut.

Juglans Nigra × Juglans Californica.

Burbank's walnut experiments.

COURTESY LUTHER BURBANK COLLECTION,

LIBRARY OF CONGRESS

In conducting his experiments, Burbank used the simple methods of the day, aided by an expert eye and a confident imagination. He paid close attention to determining the ideal moment of pollination, often using a magnifying lens to examine the stigma to be sure it was free of pollen, blowing away any stray grains, smearing the stigma thickly with pollen, and then leaving it to its fate. Sometimes he would put several different kinds of pollen on a single plant. Often he would make no records, merely marking the pollinated bud with a strip of cloth or an oddly shaped tag that may have matched one he kept somewhere in his increasingly cluttered office. Nor did he see any great need to protect his crosses from the interference of birds and bees—those ancient helpers of accidental hybrids and enemies of accurate records—since he was confident the cross-pollination had already occurred.

Whatever seed resulted from these crosses he carefully saved and planted, but by that time it was impossible to tell just how the cross had been achieved. For the rest of his career, Burbank's method would be an elaborate version of imperfectly documented guess-and-check, as he sorted through hundreds or even thousands of options in a way more often associated with computers than with human intelligence—especially the intelligence of a lone creator who considered nature to be his only collaborator.

WHILE ALL THIS HYBRIDIZING was going on, Burbank's nursery plantings in Santa Rosa and the potatoes in Tomales had produced an inventory large enough to market. In the fall of 1878, he gave up carpentry and went into business full-time as a nurseryman, selling flowers, seed potatoes, and seedling bushes for local customers to plant in their own gardens. A small soft-covered ledger records "Nursery Sales, 1878–9." The figures are not impressive. In 1878, a carpenter in Santa Rosa could make two dollars a day, while a stonecutter could expect to earn three; there were many days when Burbank failed to meet either of those marks. Business was sparse, and he had plenty of time to record the names of his customers, what they bought, and even how long they pondered their choices.

Most of his sales were of very ordinary nursery stock. On December 20, he sold three mountain cypress trees for twenty-five cents each, and another five the following day. Three days later a Mr. Ragsdale bought two pepper trees, two Italian cypress of different sizes, and one Chinese arbor vitae, for a grand total of one dollar and thirty cents. On December 28, a Professor Finley bought two cherry trees and an apricot tree, paying eighty cents, while Joel Crane provided the first day of decent profit by purchasing thirty-seven arbor vitae at ten cents each and two Laurentinas at eight cents each. At the end of the month, Burbank had gross sales of $15.20. Even in the 1870s, and even for someone who later insisted he worked only for the betterment of human kind, this was a very slow way of making a living.

In the East, the fame of the Burbank Seedling potato was spreading, with letters in the agricultural papers and testimonials reprinted in advertisements that Emma diligently gathered and pasted in her scrapbook. "The Burbank Seedling Potatoes are way ahead for yielding of anything I ever knew," wrote H. O. Bailey of Hammond, Pennsylvania. "I have tested over a thousand varieties of potatoes," said Andrew Lacery of Haverhill, Maine, "but the Burbank excels them all, growing the handsomest potatoes I ever saw, while their quality is fully equal to their looks." Jonathan Talcott of Rome, New York, reported that "the Burbank Seedling was planted with all my other new sorts, and so far as a single trial is concerned has beat them all handsomely in yield, appearance, and quality."

Unfortunately, the benefits of these testimonials were going to James J. H. Gregory in the form of sales, which apparently multiplied in Burbank's imagination whenever he recalled how cheaply he had relinquished his rights to market the new variety anywhere but in the western states. His discovery of the potato seed ball had been a fluke and the superiority of one of the seedlings was pure luck, but the fact remained that Burbank had put three years of patient effort into developing this new potato, and it was his creative ingenuity that had led him to search out a new variety in the first place. Now it seemed grossly unfair to him that the innovative genius was barely eking out a living in California while the seed merchant lived a life of luxury in Massachusetts. In the last months of 1877, Burbank wrote to Gregory, asking for an additional payment for what was still his only plant invention on the market. Gregory briskly turned him down, claiming that he himself had yet to make a profit, and closed with the unsatisfying assurance that if the Burbank potato ever proved of great financial merit, "I will remember you."

On March 27, 1879, three weeks after his thirtieth birthday and some six months after starting in business, Burbank devoted a page of his sales book to a recording of his accounts for the year to date. He had sold $44.50 worth of potatoes, of which $7 went to "Mother's part of potatoes" and another $3 to buying seed potatoes of other types to supplement his stock of Burbanks. California gardeners, used to the Bodega red potato that had been cultivated on the coast for twenty years, still demanded that variety, and Burbank was in no position to ignore the wishes of his customers. The greatest expense, though—the one that consumed almost all his income from selling potatoes—was $33.50 for advertising, printing, and mailing. If Gregory wouldn't share the profits Burbank was sure his potato was earning in the East, the struggling breeder would work harder to establish his own market in the West.

In 1880, Burbank issued his first catalog, a modest pamphlet that was little more than a list of plant names and prices. The big item was another "New Potato," this one called the Burbank Sport, for which he proposed to charge over ten times the price of the Burbank Seedling: fifty cents for a single pound, two dollars for five pounds, or ten dollars for a hundred-pound sack.

In appealing to customers, Burbank recast his own business problems as a plant breeder into advantages that deserved a premium price from the buyer. The easy reproduction that prevented him from retaining control of his plant inventions was now offered as a valuable asset. For as little as fifty cents, he wrote, buyers got not only an "astonishingly productive variety which is now offered for the first time . . . the result of four years' careful selection," but also an advantageous position in the race to profit from innovation. "Those who obtain seed this season will be able to sell their stock for several years for seed at good prices," the catalog explained, "as was the case with those who purchased the Burbank Seedling when it was first introduced." And then there is a footnote, an early mention of two issues that defined the plant breeding business throughout Burbank's career: the importance of reputation and the constant threat of shoddy imitations. "Beware!" Burbank warned. "Parties have been offering potatoes which they call Burbank Sport, all such are frauds, as the entire stock is now under my control, except a few which are in the hands of well known dealers, who can show that they were purchased of me this year."

Sales at the nursery improved after Burbank published his catalog, but progress was achingly slow. For the entire year of 1878, Burbank had recorded a profit of $84.00. By 1879, he had made $353.28, a significant improvement but hardly a vast sum. In 1880, the year he started advertising the Burbank Sport potato, he made $702, which was possibly more than carpentry would have earned, though not by much. Again he wrote to James J. H. Gregory, once more seeking an additional payment for the Burbank Seedling rights. On August 19, 1880, he got his reply, with Gregory's irritation leaping off the page as his pen dug deeper into the paper. "My Dear Sir," Gregory began:

> I have given you great fame by attaching your name to the potato and spreading it through the length & breath of the land. I purchased the Early Ohio at just about the same price I gave you for your seedling, did not give the originators name to it, & have made greater sale of this than of the Burbank.
>
> As to the profit of selling potatoes in my business, with the [high] cost of advertising & handling & loss by freezing & . . . the filling out of orders comes with the opening of spring, just when we are heels over head with work in filling seed orders, causing us such a week behindhand. . . . I have half resolved more than once to [quit] the whole potato business as unprofitable and a great nuisance. . . . You mistake in inferring that all this notoriety upon Burbank means money for me. It rather means fame to you. The more generally it is advertised the more completely it is taken out of my hands.
>
> I have stated the facts in the case & now enclose $25.00; for whatever I may write I know you will feel that some recompense is due you.

Burbank swallowed his pride and took the twenty-five dollars. A decade after he had been inspired by Darwin to become a plant inventor, he was still earning his living in fifteen-cent increments and could not afford to turn down any income, no matter how galling. Besides, two years of retail selling may have persuaded him of the truth of Gregory's complaints. But if there were no additional profits to be expected from that first potato discovery, and no other experimental plants ready to be brought to market, there were other ways of improving and accelerating the course of nature. In March 1881, Burbank seized an opportunity to break out of the narrow confines of a roadside nursery. It was something entirely different from the experimenting with the seed ball of an Early Rose potato, but it demonstrated again how rapidly the business of breeding and growing plants was changing—especially in California, *the chosen spot of all this earth* as far as *Nature* is concerned."

JAPANESE PLUMS—KELSEY AND SATSUMA.

California Fruits and How to Grow Them, 1889.

Faster, Better, Sweeter

The market for dried and canned fruit is absolutely unlimited, the demand always having increased faster than the supply; and here, at the present time, fruit is the only farm product which commands exorbitant prices, not on account of its scarcity but because of its very abundance and superior quality.

—Robert A. Thompson, *Resources of the Santa Rosa Valley and the Town of Santa Rosa, Sonoma County, California*, 1884

Warren Dutton was not a man to let opportunities slip by. An ambitious child of a restless family, Dutton was born in Canada and raised in New York, New England, and the Midwest. He had left home at fourteen to seek his way in the world, finding jobs as a clerk in Ohio and Indiana. In January 1849, the twenty-four-year-old Dutton was one of the first to set out for the California gold fields; by 1852 he had moved on to potato farming and cattle ranching in Tomales, and by 1880 he had amassed a comfortable fortune as a banker, merchant, and investor in railroads and wharfs.

In the early weeks of 1881, when Dutton decided to get into the business of raising plums for prunes, he went in search of twenty thousand plum trees ready for planting in the fall on land he owned in Petaluma. Raisins and prunes were small luxuries available year-round to any household, and dried fruit, easy to ship and store, was becoming a booming business. The Santa Rosa Fruit Preserving Company had opened next to the rail depot in 1876; by 1880, drying sheds were a common feature in California and north to Oregon. Dutton had spotted an expanding market he was determined not to miss.

The difficulty was finding the plum trees. There weren't enough to be had. The California prune industry had begun only a decade before, when an immigrant from France introduced a single tree from his native Agen region whose oval, purple plum dried well into a prune that kept for long periods without rotting or fermenting. The first commercial harvest, from an orchard in the Santa Clara valley south of San Francisco, was not ready until 1875, but by then growers all over California were beginning to recognize the unique advantages of their climate for certain crops. Vintners in the Napa and Sonoma valleys were delighted to discover that their grapevines actually did better without extensive irrigation and would flourish on the steep hillsides where little else could be planted. The hot, dry climate of southern California, enhanced by some of the state's earliest irrigation systems, was excellent for citrus trees, while the cooler winters to the north were better for other orchard fruits. After decades of concentrating mainly on wheat, more and more landholders were turning to other crops.

Northern California had another advantage for the emerging fruit industry. In the long, fertile valleys that stretched between the coast and the mountains, reliably rainless days from May to October made the perfect environment for sun-dried fruit. In France and other European countries, where the majority of prunes were still produced, plums were picked by hand, spread in shallow baskets to soften, then slowly dried through a laborious process in which the fruit was placed on racks in a slightly heated oven, then removed, shaken, cooled, and heated again. In California, a much cheaper, easier method was quickly gaining favor, in which plums were left to ripen on the tree, where they reached their highest sugar content. Only after the fruit had fallen to the ground was it gathered, washed, and placed on racks to dry in the sun.

When Dutton started searching for an instant orchard, he first approached other tree suppliers. No one in the area would take his enormous order. They all insisted it would be impossible to produce plum trees that would be bearing fruit by the following spring, as Dutton wanted. All but one, that is. Luther Burbank accepted the job.

Burbank's Santa Rosa Nursery was still small and local, planted with a familiar assortment of common flowers, shrubs, and trees. His biggest inventory was olive tree seedlings, another emerging commercial crop, and there was little about his operation that might have suggested large-volume production. Unlike the other nurserymen, however, Burbank was willing to experiment with unfamiliar ways of accelerating the course of nature—and to take the big risk required to expand his operation.

Burbank himself by now had changed in some important ways from the young man who had come to California on the strength of a single early success. He was still slender and soft-spoken, still fond of solitary rambles, and still far more likely to spend his evenings at home with his mother and sister, reading Emerson or Humboldt on the sublime wonders of nature, instead of joining the boisterous throngs at the carved mahogany counters of the downtown Santa Rosa hotels and saloons. But he was ready to become a gambler. After all, he had little enough to lose.

Burbank's plan for filling Dutton's order would make a major contribution to the fruit industry in California. His first innovation was production on a large scale that might seem ordinary today but which had not been previously attempted. Twenty years before Henry Ford established his first auto factory and thirty years before the first Detroit assembly line started up, Burbank developed a system for mass-producing plum trees.

His second innovation was to start with a kind of tree that was not the one his customer wanted. The challenge that had baffled the other nurserymen of the area was how to produce seedling trees that would be ready to plant in the fall. There weren't twenty thousand plum trees available at any price, so they would have to be started from seed, but plums did not grow nearly fast enough to meet Dutton's nine-month deadline. Burbank's solution was to skip the plum seeds and start with almonds, which would sprout much more quickly.

Within a week, he rented five acres of vacant land along a creek in Santa Rosa and hired a large crew of temporary workers he quickly trained in the operation he had in mind. He bought twenty thousand almond seeds, selecting for uniform large size, and had his crew set the seeds directly on the sandy bed near the creek. They then covered the almonds with a layer of coarse burlap that was itself topped with another layer of moist sand. The burlap layer, which could be lifted, made it possible to peek below the surface and see how the seeds were doing. As the almonds sprouted (and some were ready in less than two weeks), workers removed them and planted them four inches apart in rows four feet apart, all on the same rented land. Soon they would be ready for their transformation into plum trees.

How to Make a Plant: Grafting

Almost all orchard fruit is grown from branches of one variety of tree grafted onto the trunk of another. This may be surprising to the casual eater who finishes a piece of fruit and is left clutching a pit, a stone, or a core of seeds that begs to be tossed away to grow into a new version of the parent tree. Fruits exist to spread seeds, after all. They are luscious packages designed expressly to entice birds and beasts, including humans, to devour the casing and discard the reproductive part, preferably in some fertile patch of ground where it can pursue its evolutionary destiny.

From the grower's point of view, however, raising fruit trees from seed is a risky business, because the results are very unpredictable. Even the seeds from the best apple you ever ate will likely produce a tree whose fruit is small, sour, ugly, or simply not as good as the parent. Taking the chance on planting seeds just to see what happens is exactly the sort of science project Luther Burbank performed with his Early Rose potato, but trees take a good deal longer than potatoes to show results. Most growers would much rather skip the long odds of planting seeds and waiting five or even ten years to see if anything desirable emerges. They prefer a sure thing—a fruit they and their customers know and like. And so they use grafts.

Like artificial selection, grafting is a human invention to thwart nature. The process is so crude that it is difficult to believe it actually works. And yet it does and has for many centuries, because grafting is a very ancient piece of garden magic. To grow two (or twenty, or twenty thousand) duplicates of a favored variety, all one has to do is remove a small piece of a branch with dormant buds and attach it to another tree in such a way that the two parts become a united organic enterprise. The budding branch is called the scion, and it is rarely larger than a twig and often holds no more than a single bud. The host, which is usually a variety chosen for size or sturdiness or disease resistance, not for its fruit, is called the rootstock. The great essential is that the scion and rootstock be cut to expose the vascular cambium—the thin layer of tissue just under the bark in which new cells are formed—and that they be joined so that the two vascular cambiums are touching. If all goes well, the graft will take and the scion will sprout. By trimming the branches of the rootstock and fostering those of the new scion, grafters reproduce a duplicate of the original scion tree that just happens to be growing on the foundation of another plant.

Grafting is a useful art, like tying knots, and it encourages the same kind of inventive variation. There are many types of grafts. A whip graft, one of the most common, is made by selecting a slender rootstock branch of approximately the same diameter as the scion, cutting both at a shallow angle, binding them together and sealing the joint, usually with a special wax developed for just this purpose. A whip and tongue graft is similar but uses two parallel shallow slices, interlocking scion and stock for greater contact and a sturdier joint. A cleft graft, good for joining new scions to top branches of an established tree, involves splitting a branch of rootstock and inserting two smaller scions at the edges of the cleft, which is then sealed with grafting wax. Then there are the saddle graft, the four-flap graft, the banana graft, the side-stub graft, and in fact dozens of other kinds.

Burbank's plan was to graft plum scions onto the almond seedlings, which was not as unlikely as it might sound. He knew that plums and almonds both belong to the genus *Prunus* and so were related members of the enormous botanical rose family. With careful handling, there was a good possibility that a graft would take. He also knew he would have to be doing a lot of grafting in any case, since that was the only way to be sure of getting the kind of plum his customer wanted—the French one with a high sugar content that dried so well. And as it happened, grafting was a skill he had been practicing since childhood.

Orchards were common in the eastern United States in the nineteenth century, and so was grafting, but many of the new California growers were people like Dutton, who had no background in any sort of agriculture. Fortunately, George Burbank had taught his five-year-old brother how to graft apples before he left Massachusetts in 1854, and Luther was able to supplement this knowledge by his avid reading of farm journals and agricultural treatises as well as books on botany and experimental science. The grafting technique in which Burbank trained his small army of temporary workers was something he had read about but never done: June budding. Instead of joining a small branch to an existing limb, a single bud was inserted in a slit or notch cut in the bark of the rootstock. June budding was often used in peach orchards in the American South but was virtually unknown in California at the time; its advantage was that it could be done several months earlier than other types of grafts, which usually had to wait until August or September, and so could produce a new tree in a single growing season. The trick was to get the graft to take and keep the rootstock from dying, especially since the rootstock itself was so young and fragile. But time was the issue here, and grafting plums onto fast-growing almond saplings was a way of speeding nature up.

By June 1881, when the plum trees in Sonoma County were beginning to bud, Burbank's almond seedlings had grown tall enough to accept the grafts. A single plum tree can have hundreds of buds, so Burbank had no difficulty buying twenty thousand buds of what he called the French prune, which was probably the Petit d'Agen. Then he set another crew to work inserting the buds into the young almond saplings. Ten days later, when the joint had begun to close, workers snapped the tops of the almonds above the graft, about eight inches from the ground, but did not break them off. It took extra care to do this correctly, but the reward was a plant that directed its energies to the new grafted bud while not suffering the shock of a complete removal of the old growing tip, which might easily have killed the young trees. As the plum buds sprouted, the new shoots were tied to the almond to make a firmer trunk; only after the plum shoots had grown at least a foot were the almond tops cut away.

On December 1, 1881, Burbank had 19,500 trees ready to deliver. The remaining 500 had to wait for the following season, but Dutton was delighted. In nine months, Burbank had turned a few sacks of almonds into enough plum trees for a two-hundred-acre orchard, and word of the achievement soon spread to other growers. Burbank's reputation for performing the impossible, and doing it fast, was beginning to take root.

Buoyed by the success of his wholesale plum tree factory, business at Burbank's Santa Rosa Nursery grew, soon making him one of the leading nurserymen in the area. The profits from the Dutton order were not enormous, but the job brought in other big customers and a steady increase in sales. Over the next four years,

Burbank was able to buy the land he had been renting on Tupper Street and moved to four acres on Santa Rosa Avenue, building a greenhouse and a barn near the existing two-story frame house. Fruit trees—apples, pears, plums, peaches, apricots, and quinces— were his major stock, along with olives, chestnuts, walnuts, cypresses, roses, and grapes. The Burbank potato was gaining

Advertisement, Santa Rosa Nurseries, 1884.
Courtesy Luther Burbank Home & Gardens,
Santa Rosa, California

popularity in the West and would soon be a major crop in California, but Gregory had been right to say the chief benefit was that it made him famous. There was no profit in breeding potatoes, even eponymous potatoes, and Burbank no longer offered them for sale.

During the 1880s, more and more landholders established commercial orchards in northern California, and their orders now dominated Burbank's sales books. The olive industry had arrived, and Burbank stocked thousands of olive seedlings, but fruit trees were his particular pride. In a typical order in 1884, a grower named George Dornin bought 780 apple trees and 710 pear trees. The names of the different varieties Dornin chose are a melodious evocation of the days before the triumph of single-crop farming: Hoover, Greening, Belleflower, Ben Davis, Gravenstein, Wagener, and Smith's Cider apples; Bartlett, Beurre Clairgeau, Vicar of Wakefield, Winter Nelis, Le Conte, Sheldon, Duchesse d'Angouleme, and Seckel pears.

Such a list, so common in Burbank's sales books, shows how much of his business still consisted of supplying well-known favorites, not the new inventions that would soon bring him his greatest fame. He had developed some valuable ways of speeding up production, but providing the predictability that buyers like Dutton were after—the fast reproduction of a familiar fruit—was still not Burbank's goal. He wanted bigger fruits, more fragrant flowers, taller trees, and less-fragile berries of sorts that no one had ever seen before.

By the middle of the 1880s, the Paradox and Royal walnuts were part of a much larger garden of experimental plants, none of which were ready to market. Burbank was crossing different kinds of berries—raspberry and blackberry, strawberry and raspberry, different varieties of blackberries, all of them crossbred and then subject to rigorous selection to find those that bore more and bigger fruit, stronger canes, or fewer thorns. He was also experimenting with hybrid flowers. He was breeding California poppies, the familiar orange wildflower that covers the state's hillsides, hoping that multiple generations of hybridization and selection would spread the thin line of unusual red coloration he had noticed in a wild specimen until it covered the entire bloom. He was working on lilies to change both the shape and color of their petals. He was seeking a gladiolus that would have a shorter, sturdier stem and fuller blossoms than the gangly, wind-tossed flowers that were then the norm.

What he was not doing was keeping careful records. Take Burbank's garden notebook for 1881–1882, the first years of his new success. He bought a ledger bigger than the ones he had used in the past and wrote in large letters on the cover:

LUTHER BURBANK
JULY 1881
NURSERY—PLAN

Inside, there is an attempt at order. A map of the garden notes the different beds, marked with a code for which Burbank (uncharacteristically) provides a key. A circle indicated an apple tree. A double circle meant cherry. A figure eight stood for peach, a circle with a stem was fig, a circle with a cross was plum, a circle with a double bar was pear, a circle with a curved stem was quince, and a circle with a double stem was apricot.

Then it becomes a jumble of notes and memos and cryptic assessments. On July 5, he "budded over apricots cherries & pears &

peaches & plums." On July 24 he noted a "white # Nectarine in seedlings plum grafted tree." The # indicates good news, but about which seedling? There is no clue. Then it was on to the grapevines growing on trellises in the experimental beds. There were thirteen

Burbank Nursery Plan book, 1881–82.
COURTESY LUTHER BURBANK HOME & GARDENS,
SANTA ROSA, CALIFORNIA

varieties, including something marked as important and described with maddening imprecision as "mixed (Blk July. Rose Peru. Cognition, &&&)." What the proportions of the mix might be, or the name of "&&&," we will never know. "Age 32," Burbank wrote across the upper right corner of one page, showing his lifelong obsession with charting his personal and professional progress together. "Graft apricot on Peach," he reminds himself lower down. "It is the *best* stock." Somehow he grabbed the same page four months later to record, "Nov. 12, 1881—Potted Hyac., tulips, oxalis." Scrawled across the page is a separate note about gooseberries, and then a page on petunias (double, striped, crimson) with the vague locator: "near gate." A page headed "stray buds on last year's stock" lists pear, peach, almond, plum, and apple, but no indication of which trees had these stray buds or what became of them.

There is no question that Burbank was constitutionally incapable of keeping careful notes when he was working in his gardens. He was doing many things at once—checking to see if grafts had taken, searching long rows of flowers for the single superior blossom, sampling fruits for the best taste, sniffing out the most pleasing aroma, and physically marking each seedling and blossom he wanted to keep—and each of these tasks apparently seemed much more urgent and more interesting than stopping to make a record of the process.

It's also possible that Burbank's frustratingly opaque nursery books came from his desire to protect himself from imitators. Leonardo da Vinci used code to hide his experiments (and probably also to keep himself amused). Isaac Newton created an obscure system of notations that took several centuries to decipher, revealing that a significant part of his scientific work revolved around alchemy. Burbank's codes were more innocent but equally obscure. A crosshatch, #, indicated importance, and two or three meant something was very important. Notebooks and papers were scattered with these marks, but importance is a quality with many dimensions. A plant in the field was marked with a crosshatch, but so was a completed column of figures or even a fully used-up notebook. A business card from a new acquaintance would get one, two, or even three crosshatches. Was "#=done" the same as "#=good"? Did numbers correspond to names? And what about the many other strange symbols, probably indicating different varieties but possibly something else altogether? Only Burbank could say what they meant, and he wasn't talking.

The nursery plan books, the closest thing Burbank ever kept to a laboratory notebook, continued for the next four decades, but they are all palimpsests of scribbled notations and remarks. Observations start in tidy columns but soon succumb to a jumbled overlay of ink and pencil notes, drawing, stray remarks, additions, emendations, and mysterious rows of numbers that might equally well represent his age, his income, his plants under development, the generations of a particular cross, or even his payroll costs. He would trace the cut half of a fruit on a page to record its size and shape, and make notes about flavor, fragrance, color, and quality, but the description of a new fruit was usually much more detailed and precise than the record of whatever crosses had been used to produce it or how many generations of selection had occurred.

Burbank's records were a mess, but they were a bravura mess. At a time when there was no way to patent a plant invention, he had no commercial reason to record the evolution of his failures, or even of his successes. What mattered was not the process but the result: the flower in an unprecedented color; the fruit that looked and tasted better, resisted pests or rot or other infestations, extended the season by ripening earlier or later than any other, had the high sugar content needed to sun dry without fermentation, hung on the branch longer, was easily separated from its stone (the freestone peach was another Burbank project), or was simply, and wonderfully, more beautiful than anything that had come before. While other breeders specialized in grains, or berries, or a single species like the orchid, Burbank was confident that anything that grew could be improved. His curiosity was as great as his willingness to fail, and he was ready to make hundreds of crosses and nurture thousands of seedlings to find the single one that would be worth saving. The rest were consigned to bonfires that would become a flamboyant signature of his work.

To have space to do all of this, Burbank needed more land. He needed privacy, too, a protected area where customers and visitors wouldn't be dropping in at inconvenient moments and where he could hide his failures while pursuing his successes. The town of Sebastopol, just seven miles to the west but much less developed than Santa Rosa, was still planted with acres of wheat and hops. In 1885, Burbank bought ten acres of sloping, sandy land right on the road that connected the two towns. Gold Ridge Farm had its own well, didn't need draining or the cartloads of sand and manure that Burbank had brought in to improve the thick clay soil in Santa Rosa, and came with a small cottage. There was no barn, but that didn't matter, because his was not going to be the sort of farming that required the daily use of horses. This was intensive cultivation of rows of trees, vines, and flowers, closely planted for easy observation and comparison. Gold Ridge Farm was not a scientific laboratory in the conventional sense, any more than it was a recognizable production facility. Appropriately, it was a hybrid. Burbank was interested in speed and secrecy and building up an inventory of marketable products. And he was enlarging his range of options by exploring not just the area around Santa Rosa, but the entire world.

How to Make a Plant:
The Global Encounter

Finding new and economically useful plants has always been a major goal of exploration and travel, and introducing foreign crops is as old as settlement itself. In what is now the United States, maize, beans, and squash came from Mexico, Central America, and South America before the arrival of Europeans. Two weeks after their landing at Jamestown in 1607, the settlers were sowing English wheat and planting a garden with melons, potatoes, and tropical fruits picked up in the West Indies, even as they reveled in the native nuts and berries and made immediate plans to turn the native grapes to wine. Just about every major commercial crop in North America is the result of a foreign introduction, in a process that started with the seeds that immigrants brought from other countries and accelerated rapidly in a complex interplay of government encouragement, scientific advances, economic incentives, and new technologies. When Commodore Perry signed the treaty opening the way to trade between Japan and the United States in 1854, it was the start of a transpacific exchange of agricultural products. Thirty years later, the commerce in foreign plants and seeds was well established.

While he was working with hybrids, Burbank imported many new plant varieties from distant countries. Darwin had suggested that a change in environment could be enough to unsettle a plant in a way that would lead to interesting variations, and that was a possibility Burbank was very eager to explore. Sometimes he would simply introduce a foreign specimen to the American market, like the Seut Lea, a weeping evergreen pear from China he offered in 1885. Sometimes he tried to hybridize his imports with native species, or with each other, to see what changes the dislocation would bring on. He imported cacti and eucalyptus trees from Australia and lilies and quinoa grain from Brazil. What captured everybody's attention, however, were his Japanese plums.

There are several varieties of wild plums native to North America, but the most common grow on shrubby bushes and produce fruit that is small and sour. The native plum, often called a beach plum because it prefers sandy soil and endures windy conditions, is cooked for jam and preserves, if it is eaten at all. Orchard plums, like the vast majority of North American crops, started with imported stock. In California, the Petit d'Agen was favored for prunes because it had a high sugar content that was good for drying, but there were many other imported varieties, with different shapes and skin colors but always yellow flesh.

Shortly after he arrived in California in 1875, Burbank had visited the Mercantile Library in San Francisco—a place designed precisely for the shelter and education of ambitious young men without formal education—and read a sailor's tale of his adventures in Japan. The story included an account of eating a delicious red-fleshed plum that grew only in the province of Satsuma. To Burbank it seemed a mythic fruit, so distant and so very different, and it lingered for years in his memory. Perhaps the red Satsuma plum was real. If so, it would be very interesting to see how it behaved in California.

After he opened his Santa Rosa Nursery in 1878, Burbank bought imported seeds and plants from a number of dealers in different countries. One source was Isaac Bunting, an English bulb dealer based in Yokohama, Japan. Before he even expanded his experiments by buying Gold Ridge Farm, Burbank wrote to Bunting, probably in 1883, asking if he could obtain scions of a red-fleshed plum he had heard grew in Satsuma province. Bunting could and did, but all the scions that arrived a year later had died during the trip. Finally, in 1885, twelve healthy scions from several types of plum tree arrived by boat from Japan. Burbank grafted them to trees in his new experimental nursery in Sebastopol and waited to see what would emerge.

The Japanese plums that fruited the next year were very different from both the French prune plums and the small, yellow-fleshed wild plums of the region. The blood plum of Satsuma, as Burbank named his earliest introduction, had a bright red interior, a startling difference from other plums. It also ripened weeks earlier than the more familiar varieties, a boon because any plant that extended the commercial season, early or late, was always welcome. That was hardly the end of Burbank's plans, however.

As soon as the new plums had blossomed, he started cross-pollinating the Japanese fruit with European and native varieties, grafting the new buds onto established trees to accelerate the growing process. In 1887, he harvested forty-three different hybrids, none of them intended for the casual buyer. Carefully wrapped in paper and cotton, packed two to a box, the new plums were sent to prominent fruit judges like H. E. Van Deman at the U.S. Department of Agriculture, who wrote frequently on the qualities of new orchard fruit introductions. As Burbank must have hoped, Van Deman started praising both the new plums and the extensive stock of the man he called "Mr. Luther Burbank, the well known nurseryman of Santa Rosa, California." Burbank exhibited his new plums at the fruit growers' convention that met in Santa Rosa in November 1887. He sent samples to the *Pacific Rural Press* and other California papers, and as far away as Florida, where notice of his work prompted many inquiries to the Florida *Dispatch*.

In breeding his new plums, Burbank refined the method that came to mark almost all his plant experiments. First he grafted scions to established plants, so they would blossom and bear fruit as soon as possible, thus cutting several years off the maturing process. Next he cross-pollinated. Then he planted the seeds of the resulting fruit. Then, once more, he grafted the seedlings onto mature trees so they would fruit more quickly and he could evaluate the results in just a year or two, instead of four or five.

MOST NURSERY OWNERS at this point would have hired an assistant. Burbank didn't, because he wasn't a conventional nursery owner: he was a plant inventor. Seasonal workers were hired to do the heavy spading and pruning, and in later years they were trained to graft and pollinate and toss out the obvious duds, but there was never any second-in-command in Luther Burbank's garden. A manager took over much of the routine supervision of the commercial nursery, but for the all-important process of final selection, deciding which new plants to keep and which to discard, Burbank didn't trust anyone else's judgment. And in a business in which plant selections were in effect trade secrets, it is very possible that he simply didn't trust anyone else, period. Gardeners who worked for Burbank had to empty their pockets before they left for the day to make sure none of his valuable plants or seeds were being smuggled out, and secretaries were rarely allowed any insight into what went on out in the rows of the experimental gardens. Burbank's greatest genius was his extraordinary eye for differences, and he spent a great deal of time going over his grounds, quickly but patiently searching for the one plant in a thousand that was worth cultivating further.

To simplify this somewhat laborious process, Burbank developed another method that began as a way to effect efficiencies of time and scale and ended by becoming a signature piece of botanical showmanship. He grafted as many seedlings as possible onto a single tree, making it much easier to compare the different fruits. He called the hosts "nurse trees" or "mother trees," and they sometimes had five or even six hundred different cherries, plums, or apples blossoming on a single trunk. After each generation of cross-pollination, Burbank selected the best, either for further crosses or for direct production.

These fruit trees, with all their different blossoms and multicolored fruit, became a part of an increasingly famous garden that many people wanted to see. Visitors to Santa Rosa and Sebastopol were dazzled by the exotic wonders growing in Burbank's experimental grounds and took these visible results of his work as sufficient evidence of superior methods. By the end of the decade, the man behind the novelties was starting to be hailed as a wonder worker. Tales of Burbank's supernatural talent for discernment, like stories of George Washington's prowess in throwing coins across the Potomac River, were more the stuff of hero-making than of fact. Still, there can be little question that he was blessed with an unusual gift for noticing the first suggestion of a new surprise in a leaf or bud or blossom that most people never saw. Many of his experiments led nowhere and even the best took years to develop, but with so many sprouting and blossoming at once, something amazing seemed to emerge with great regularity.

As Burbank expanded his operations in the 1880s, he continued to keep his most important records only in his memory. The challenge was keeping it all in order, remembering what he had growing and where, and finding room for works in progress while still saving space for the standard varieties that he could never quite afford to stop selling.

Breeding a huge variety of different plants was intense work, and the absence of careful records did not diminish the results. With plums, with walnuts, and in fact with everything he worked on, Burbank kept multiple goals in mind as he surveyed his fields. He selected plants for yield, for novelty, for ability to withstand the rigors of shipping, or for whatever other commercial value he thought a new variety might have. He understood that breeding for one trait often diminished another, and so he was always juggling the different priorities of his market: you can't really produce thin skin and superior shipping capability in the same fruit; breeding for size, whether extra large or extra small, is different from breeding for flavor, or sugar content, or uniform ripening. Breeding for all of them was different from what anyone else was doing, and much bigger, and Burbank's rising inventory of innovative triumphs began to attract attention.

BURBANK HAD BEEN COURTING PUBLICITY from his first days as a plant breeder. In later years, the "Wizard of Santa Rosa" would often complain of the ways he was misrepresented by the press: praised for amazing advances neither he nor anyone else could ever achieve, and just as unreasonably blamed for failing to live up to claims he had never made. Throughout the 1880s, though, he was doing the writing himself, sending articles to newspapers in California and in the East and promoting himself as a knowledgeable plant breeder and nurseryman worth remembering. In the business of selling and in the business of invention, a well-known name was an advantage worth pursuing.

Many of Burbank's early feature articles were practical discussions that established his garden expertise: the importance of drainage tiles, the best times for summer pruning, instructions on the cultivation of ferns or the rooting of grapevines. Sometimes he sent out a rhapsodic description of the wonders of California, like his account of a trip to Yosemite and a glimpse behind its surging waterfalls. He penned cautionary satires on the wiles of traveling salesmen who carried beautiful paintings of trees but couldn't even identify what they were selling—part of a very contemporary campaign to persuade customers to buy from established local vendors like himself. While never happy as a public speaker, he was always ready to talk to reporters, eager to let them know how many very large orders he had recently filled and how he still had several hundred thousand other trees in stock. Increasingly, though, the news was about the wonders growing on his grounds.

Since moving to California, Burbank had gone from small retail sales to large orders for commercial growers. Now he wanted to return to his first passion—developing novel varieties and selling the rights to his inventions to the suppliers of the nation's gardens. On April 22, 1888, the Santa Rosa *Democrat* reported that Mr. R. W. Bell, "well and favorably known in Sonoma and adjoining counties," had bought a large part of Mr. Burbank's nursery business, including land and stock of 263,000 fruit trees and 5,000 ornamental trees. Burbank would retain the name Santa Rosa Nursery and continue to sell his olive and nut trees, the newspaper reported, but he was now concentrating on his "extensive horticultural experiment grounds," in both Santa Rosa and Sebastopol.

The next invention would be a new way of selling his creations. But first he took a vacation.

Souvenir List of Members of Parties

RAYMOND'S VACATION EXCURSIONS

ALL TRAVELLING EXPENSES INCLUDED.

LEAVING BOSTON, MONDAY, OCTOBER 8, 1888.

A PERSONAL INTERLUDE

Have never enjoyed a week of my life better than the last one, and never expect to be happier again. Everything went right. Had a very pleasant social party of people and have made some valued friends, ones who will remember each other as long as life lasts. . . . Have collected oceans of plants and wild seeds.

—LUTHER BURBANK, *letter to his mother*, October 1888

In the fall of 1888, soon after he sold the bulk of his retail nursery business, Burbank took a seven-week trip to Massachusetts, New York, and Washington, D.C., that was the longest time he would ever be away from his California gardens. It was a sentimental journey, a triumphal return, and a time for well-earned relaxation. It was also a business trip with multiple objectives. There were new customers to find, new plants to bring back to California, and new publicity outlets to cultivate.

Thirteen years earlier, Burbank had gone west with a small nest egg, his clothes, a few books and seeds, ten seed potatoes, and a hamper of food. Now he armed himself with three hundred dollars in cash, five hundred dollars in bank checks, and an array of California wonders to dazzle the folks back home. He brought copper ore, abalone shells, petrified wood, and samples of redwood, olive, palm, and eucalyptus—all natural curiosities as yet unknown in Massachusetts. He packed a large box of prunes so he could offer

samples to the crowd that came to hear him speak at the Lunenburg cattle fair, an annual event that carried much honor for the
local boy made good. He enjoyed giving interviews to all the local
papers that now ran long stories on his many marvelous plant
creations. When asked for suggestions on what farmers in Massachusetts should raise, his favorite joke was to answer, "Enough
money to move to California."

But he himself was in no overwhelming hurry to return. For
two weeks he visited family and friends, complaining in a good-
humored way of the rush from house to house and the discomforts
of too much hospitality, but meanwhile loving it all. Whatever
resentment he had harbored toward his first important customer
was gone. "Mr. Gregory expects to have a monument raised on the
spot where the Burbank potato originated," he proudly wrote to
his mother. He met the girl who had discouraged his attentions
before he left Lunenburg and they laughed at their old flirtation,
if it had even deserved so grand a name. He hired a photographer
to take pictures of the old house in Lancaster and the views from
Lunenburg. But the commercial breeder in him did not rest.
Everywhere he went, Burbank took notes on the trees and wildflowers, gathered seeds and cuttings, labeled them all, and mailed
them back to California. The journey east was his own private
voyage of botanical exploration and acquisition.

Two side trips took him to cultural and political centers that
were both very remote from his life in California. The first was a
simple series of visits (pilgrimages, really) to the homes of the
writers and philosophers who had shaped the ideas of his youth.
Burbank visited the house in Cambridge, Massachusetts, where
Henry Wadsworth Longfellow had lived until his death six years
earlier. He went to nearby Concord and carefully pocketed three

nuts that had fallen from an immense horse chestnut tree in front of Ralph Waldo Emerson's home. "Got basswood seed from Hawthorne's place on left side of road," he wrote in his pocket diary, next to his note that the brown cottage of the Alcotts was surrounded by evergreens and boxwood. Then he turned in the other direction, away from the fireside poets and Concord sages and toward the national center of power, Washington, D.C.

The Raymond Excursions guided tour to Washington that Burbank joined in Boston was a natural choice for a single man of thrifty ways who was also, perhaps, looking for company. Transportation (by steamer and train) to and from Washington was included ("ring three times for water," Burbank scribbled in his diary), the hotel was reserved (the Willard, $4.50 a night), and the tour price included a tastefully decorated book that printed the dates, the itinerary, and the names of every member of the group. Burbank had a wonderful time.

As he traveled first to New York and then to Washington, Burbank enjoyed the musicians on the steamer deck, the traveling companions, the basket lunches, and the views. He also carefully copied the names of seeds and bulb dealers he saw advertised on signboards along the train route and in magazines he gathered at stops in Long Island and in Philadelphia, with particular attention to those who dealt in lilies. He occupied himself picking out the seeds from a quart of Nova Scotia huckleberries he had bought in New York, adding them to his hoard of botanical gatherings. He happily visited the White House, sat in on a Supreme Court session during the Bell Telephone patent case, bought a souvenir knife and a napkin ring, and took carriage rides with the new friends he made on the tour. He visited the Patent Office, still one of the capital city's most imposing buildings. He made a point of stopping at the Department of Agriculture, where he was delighted to receive some new varieties of seeds and wrote home to his mother that he would be back for more.

The federal distribution of free seeds had grown into an enormous enterprise by then, with congressmen sending millions of packets to their constituents every year, but Burbank, unlike many more traditional seed sellers, did not object to this government-sponsored competition with his trade. Burbank's enterprise was very different from anything the Department of Agriculture had in mind. The biggest difference wasn't a matter of scope or scale or operational structure (though it is an interesting mental exercise to compare the lumbering reach of a federal agency, with all its redundancies and distractions of regulations, records, corruption, and reform, to the very different inefficiencies of a sole practitioner trying to do it all himself, especially one who is notoriously bad at keeping notes). Smaller, quicker, more creative, and free of oversight, Burbank's new business was based on the premise that what he offered was not available elsewhere at any price. He would use his seeds from the Department of Agriculture as the raw material for a vastly improved product that would easily command a premium price. Or at least that was his hope.

Everywhere he went, the desire for additions to his seed collection colored Burbank's activities. He was forever gathering botanical specimens, buying unfamiliar herbs at curbside markets, taking samples of flowering oxalis from near the bridge across the Potomac and seeds from the asters outside Mount Vernon. Going to the president's reception meant less to him than his repeated excitement, recorded in his letters, at picking up "oceans of plants and wild seeds," "some very rare seeds," "a great quantity of rare wild and cultivated seeds," "some rare ferns," and "a lot of low blueberry plants . . . as I see they vary some."

He liked his fellow travelers, especially the families with pretty daughters. He wrote down the names of his new travel companions in his notebook, marking the ones he particularly liked with his special crosshatch mark of approval, and continued to do so on his train ride back to California. "Mabel H. Smith. Delano. Kern County. #" is entered in his diary between the description of the Dutchman's pipe and the sumac seed in Fort Riley, Kansas. He never forgot his business, but Burbank was in a sociable frame of mind.

There was one part of the trip that did not go recorded, however, in either his diary, his letters, or any of the many authorized accounts of his life published during the next fifty years. Somewhere during his journey, probably on the train west from Chicago, he met a young Denver widow named Helen Coleman. She came to Santa Rosa. He went to Denver. Two years later, in 1890, they married. It was a disaster.

What went wrong? Of this there are even fewer details, though it's not hard to imagine sources of friction when a bachelor over the age of forty marries and brings his bride home to live with his mother. The newlyweds quarreled. Dishes were broken. After Helen slammed a door in Luther's face and gave him a black eye, he accused her of assault and moved into the second story of the barn. When he finally sued for divorce in 1896, after six miserable years, Luther brought in neighbors to attest that Helen had attacked him. Helen called his mother, Olive, a vile serpent and said, "Luther and all his family were a nest of cats and snakes and low-lived dogs." He gave her a generous settlement of ten thousand dollars and expunged her from his life.

In the following years, Burbank continued to live in Santa Rosa with his mother, in the small frame house he had bought in 1884. He rode his bicycle and drove his buggy back and forth to Sebastopol, served on the Santa Rosa library board, worked hard on writing his catalogs and harder on developing his new plant introductions. Olive lived until 1909, the constant companion to the middle-aged man who was once again her bachelor son, a famous breeder who would remarry after her death but never have children of his own.

It's worth contrasting all that we know about this much-recorded figure and all that remains a mystery. We know what Burbank's grades were in 1865 and what he spent on an umbrella in 1872. We know he bought a writing desk before he left Massachusetts and some railroad stocks that did not make him rich. We know he disliked oyster stuffing in his turkey, was very fond of onions, and had grave doubts about the health of children who did not eat meat. We know what he charged for his plants, how he paid his workers, what he wrote to scientists and to schoolchildren, and what he had to say about the evils of traveling salesmen and the awesome wonder of Yosemite Falls.

And yet there are so many things we don't know about Luther Burbank. We don't know how the shy child became the confident plant inventor of Santa Rosa, and then the sage who inspired a sense of calm and affection in everyone he met. We don't know the full story of that charming scamp, his little brother, Alfred, who seems to have vanished for years after bringing Luther to Santa Rosa, only to reappear early in the twentieth century giving interviews in which he claimed his brother's plant inventions as his own. And how do we reconcile the stories of Burbank's handsprings on the lawn with his own accounts of frequent illnesses and fairly regular retreats to a nearby health resort managed by Dr. W. P. Burke, who modeled his health regime on Kellogg's famous sanitarium at Battle Creek, Michigan?

As for Burbank's romantic life, there is again too much and too little information. We know that while he was married to Helen Coleman he spent a great deal of time at his nursery in Sebastopol, where, years later, an acquaintance would tell an interviewer that Burbank's "normal male sexual drives [were] a subject of lively interest among men he hired during the vigorous middle years of his working life," whatever that was supposed to mean. Another unnamed informant recalled that in the 1890s Burbank was interested in Dr. Alice B. Stockham, a gynecologist turned writer of sex manuals who went to India to study tantric sex and promoted a system of delayed orgasm she called Karezza. One should add that Stockham also wrote of the wise silences of nature and used language very much like Burbank's own pronouncements on the reproduction of plants.

It is hard to know what to make of such information or whether to give it any credence at all, beyond acknowledging that Burbank's status as a famous bachelor for much of his life, a man who produced no children but had a strong interest in the theory and practice of both human and vegetative breeding, has always made people wonder about these things. The only fact of which we can be certain is that during the years his first marriage was falling apart, Luther Burbank produced a dazzling series of new plant creations that transformed the plant-breeding business and brought him international fame as the man who could train nature to do his bidding.

NEW CREATIONS

IN

Fruits and Flowers,

JUNE, 1893.

KEEP THIS CATALOGUE FOR REFERENCE.

You will need it when these Fruits and Flowers become standards of excellence.
Supplementary Lists will be published from time to time.

BURBANK'S EXPERIMENT GROUNDS,

Santa Rosa, California, U. S. A.

Office and Residence:
204 Santa Rosa Avenue.

Cable Address:
" Burbank, Santa Rosa, Cal."

Marketing the New Creation

From the vast chaos of commingled species, forms have been created
and segregated which will produce great and unsuspected changes
in fruit and flower culture.

—Luther Burbank, *New Creations in Fruits and Flowers*, 1893

In 1893, three years after his marriage and almost twenty years
after he arrived in California, Luther Burbank published the
work that catapulted him to a new level of national and international celebrity. It was not one of the multivolume descriptions of
his plant experiments or the biographies and autobiographies written by a legion of ghost writers, and certainly not the book on child
rearing he would later publish to much acclaim. All of those would
appear in the coming century, and all would depend on the reputation he was about to achieve. What made the locally successful
nurseryman of Santa Rosa into Luther Burbank, the world-famous
plant inventor, was a fifty-two-page catalog called *New Creations
in Fruits and Flowers*.

It was a perilous time to be launching a new business. After
years of speculative overexpansion, the U.S. economy experienced
a financial panic followed by a depression—the second worst in
American history—that would last for the next four years. The
cost of freight was rising, as was the number of unemployed workers. Banks were failing and farmers, as usual, were the first to feel

the pain of limited access to credit. California fruit had enjoyed its own, more local boom in the 1880s and went through a parallel bust. From September 1892 to October 1894, the price of a box of California pears fell by 50 percent, and half the prune and plum trees in the state were cut down to prevent a glut on the market.

On the other hand, the trials of commercial agriculture and the decline of the California orchard business in particular may have convinced Burbank to turn his attention to the wider national market of home gardeners, who could be reached through the catalogs of retail sellers. Also, 1893 was the year of the World's Columbian Exposition in Chicago, the altogether magnificent celebration of what most people agreed were four centuries of glorious improvement of the new world first introduced to Europeans by Christopher Columbus in 1492. At the exposition, an estimated twenty-seven million visitors were exposed to extraordinary displays of exotic fruits and flowers, constant assurances that progress in all fields was leading the way to a future of gracious living, and clear evidence that the marketplace for even the most perishable goods now stretched around the world. The age of the frontier may have ended (as Frederick Jackson Turner declared to the American Historical Association when the group met in Chicago in conjunction with the Columbian Exposition), but the spirit of invention was showing no sign of decline. And if the wilderness was being settled, it stood to reason that all those new arrivals would be in the market for mail-order plants and seeds.

THE LUSH SEDUCTIONS of garden catalogs have a long history, but the second half of the nineteenth century saw a rapid expansion in the trade as a result of ever-increasing demand. As population moved west, many farmers and gardeners were separated from sources of seeds and of information, and catalogs provided both. At the same time, an expanding middle class moved to that other new invention, the suburbs, and took up gardening. The rising business in flower seeds, rosebushes, and ornamental shrubs marketed to this segment of the population was a testament to the growing presence of leisure, land, and discretionary income in quantities sufficient to turn gardening from a means of survival into a hobby.

Serving these new customers were more merchants of plants and seeds than ever before. In the United States census of 1850, 8,479 people identified themselves as gardeners, florists, or nurserymen. By 1880, the number of people in the garden trade had grown nearly sevenfold, to 56,032, and had been increasing in the years since.

The postal service was also helping the plant business. In 1860, Joseph Hold moved from the Patent Office to become postmaster general, and he immediately began campaigning for new postal rates that would make mail cheaper for everyone, and much cheaper for dealers in horticultural products. In 1861, seeds and cuttings in packages under eight ounces were, for the first time, accepted by the U.S. mail. Two years later, more sweeping changes effectively created the mail-order business in plants. Starting in 1863, a year after the separate Department of Agriculture was established and the Homestead Act sent thousands of settlers into the frontier and away from long-established seed merchants, domestic mail was divided into three classes. First class was for letters, second class for newspapers and magazines, and third class, the cheapest rate, for other printed material, including catalogs. The new uniform postal rates now applied regardless of distance; what was even more important was that the new regulations specifically allowed packages containing up to four pounds of seeds, cuttings, bulbs, roots, and scions to be shipped as third-class mail. Thirty years before other catalog retailers were able to send goods long distances at low prices, the postal service had helped the seed sellers and nurseries market to the nation.

Wider markets also meant wider competition, of course, and by the 1890s plant sellers went to great lengths to make their catalogs stand out, particularly with their illustrations. Sellers vied for the largest catalogs, the most extensive offerings, the most complete planting instructions, the cheapest prices, and the most alluring premiums, particularly for early or prepaid orders. Cheaper paper and improved techniques of printing led to catalogs that were much larger and more vivid than the simple price lists of earlier times. James Vick, who entered the seed business after a career as owner and publisher of a popular garden magazine, the *Horticulturalist,* commissioned beautiful color drawings for his catalogs; the illustrations were so popular he then offered them for sale as prints suitable for framing. Peter Henderson, the influential authority whose *Gardening for Profit* was advertised in the back of Darwin's *Variation of Animals and Plants Under Domestication,* had introduced five-color lithography in his catalogs as early as 1871. The John A. Salzer Seed Company routinely used eye-catching cartoons that mocked its own exaggerated claims while still advancing them. A typical advertisement for "the most wonderful cabbage in the world" showed awestruck farmers peering up at a gigantic head of cabbage, atop which smiling elves painted a billboard that was an ad within an ad.

Burbank's *New Creations* catalog was different. Instead of hundreds of fruits, vegetables, shrubs, and flowers, it promoted very

COURTESY OF THE BAILEY HORTORIUM, CORNELL UNIVERSITY, ITHACA, NEW YORK

few plants, many of them offered only as a single specimen of a novel variety. Here are the total offerings of the 1893 *New Creations in Fruits and Flowers:* two hybrid walnuts; one mammoth chestnut; four kinds of quinces; ten different plums and prunes; twenty-one hybrid and crossbred berries; six roses; four callas; a tall, large-flowered lily and a dwarf variety with multiple flowers on a single stem; an assortment of gladioli bulbs; one variety of myrtle; one poppy; one cross between a petunia and a nicotiana that Burbank called a nicotunia; two potatoes; an ornamental crossbred tomato; and a begonia-leaved squash. Burbank also mentioned a few experiments too new to be described, much less priced, including the plum-apricot hybrid that would later be named the plumcot.

The modest number of listings was more than balanced by the extravagant claims Burbank made for his plant inventions. *New Creations in Fruits and Flowers* was a trumpet blast announcing the arrival of a new force that had mastered nature. Had the Garden of Eden itself been up for sale, the prospectus might have read something like this publication. Like the first Creator, Burbank, too, was bringing forth a new order out of chaos, and putting more time into the effort: "twenty years in which I have been actively engaged in this new work, . . . the most extensive of its kind which exists or has ever existed in this or any other country."

Although he didn't quite say so, the implication was that while the first Creation was good, Burbank had made it better, going back to improve the stuff of nature with some marvelously useful adjustments to better suit current needs and desires. At his bidding, the walnut tree had been made to grow faster and to become more prolific and the rose to smell more fragrant. Under his touch, the plum had been taught to grow plumper while the hard, sour quince became softer and sweeter. No fruit was too small to escape his watchful eye or benefit from his care, he boasted. "No one will question the claim that I have made more and greater improvements in Blackberries and Raspberries during the last fourteen years than have otherwise been made during all the past eighteen centuries."

Burbank's language was exultant, his prices astonishingly high (at least for garden catalogs), and his merchandise at times seemed to be growing somewhere on the far side of credibility. His new quinces "are in all respects the greatest advance ever made in improving this fruit." His "more than half a million hybrid seedling

Lilies are producing profound surprise and admiration." His "aerial potatoes" grown on Burbank vines grafted onto a Ponderosa tomato plant promised a new era of aboveground tubers that would set nature upside down.

That was the goal. Nature needed to be shaken up, and with it the world of plant selling. Exaggerated claims were nothing new in the world of marketing, of course, but Burbank's offerings were different both in the kinds of plants he was selling and in the way they were being sold. His new creations were offered on an exclusive basis, with the buyer acquiring all stock and all rights, including the privilege of naming the plant. Since quantities were limited, often only a single plant and a few budding branches, the value was in their rarity. These were not twenty-five-cent seed packets or ten-dollar sacks of seedling potatoes; they were the foundations of vast future markets for the retailers who would continue to propagate and sell the plants for years, and Burbank charged accordingly. The cheapest thing in the catalog was a compact, heavy-blooming seedling rose, referred to only as H. 813, for the bargain price of $150 (the equivalent of three thousand or four thousand dollars today). The most expensive was a hybrid plum provisionally named "Golden," its stock consisting of "one original tree, twelve small ones, and some grafts in old trees," all for three thousand dollars. Most of the new plant varieties were priced between three hundred and two thousand dollars. The two new walnut trees—the Paradox that grew so fast and the Royal that produced such superior nuts—were so valuable Burbank insisted their prices could only be disclosed upon direct inquiry.

New Creations in Fruits and Flowers looked different from other garden catalogs, too, including the ones Burbank had put out for his own Santa Rosa Nursery. Those earlier catalogs were little more than price lists printed on rough pink or yellow paper, decorated with stock engravings of lilies of the valley, apples, smiling babies, and pretty young girls—none of which had anything to do with what Burbank had to sell. Claims as astonishing as the ones he was now making required photographic evidence.

The photographs in *New Creations* were not like the usual gorgeous portraits of perfect fruit and impossibly profuse flowers that filled (and still fill) the pages of other catalogs. Apart from an attractive pyramid of tomatoes that appeared on the cover, the illustrations seemed entirely suited for a textbook or a scientific treatise—one that focused on a very rarified world of man-made botanical marvels. Hybrid fruits, nuts, and berries were shown next to their parent plants to emphasize how much bigger they were, or photographed against a ruler to prove their size. Instead of displaying his raspberries, Burbank lined up fifteen different examples of the woody canes on which they grew to show their extreme variations in color, thickness, and size of thorns. Although the catalog offered only four Japanese quinces, the illustration showed thirty-five different crossbred quinces with no identification beyond the note, "A species so variable and with so many possibilities in the way of acid, should produce some valuable varieties." Twisted and misshapen tubers, the antithesis of the large, smooth Burbank potato, were proudly displayed as the offspring of a potato grafted onto a tomato vine. An early version of the stoneless plum, one of Burbank's most famous creations, looked eerily like an image from a surgical manual, the fruit cut in half to show the vacant space where ordinary fruits would have a stone.

Almost a decade before scientists became aware of genetic traits, Burbank's catalogs noted the effect of what are now called dominant and recessive qualities, which he described as both a valuable curiosity and a sign of the master breeder's skill. A cross of the Crystal White blackberry and Shaffer's Colossal raspberry, for example, produced a single plant whose value was increased by the fact that it was difficult to predict what its fruit might be: "thoroughly distinct Raspberries, thoroughly distinct Blackberries, or any conceivable combination of both." The following year, Burbank would introduce his "Iceberg" blackberry, a rebuttal to "the impression . . . entertained by some, that no White Blackberry could be as productive and hardy, with berries as early, abundant, large, handsome and delicious, as the best black ones." Burbank described his discovery in terms that unknowingly illustrated Mendelian laws of inheritance. The new berry, a cross of a productive black Lawton and the weaker, less abundant Crystal White, produced only blackberries for the first two generations of crosses, and then produced a single bush of pale, almost transparent fruit, "the canes bending in various directions with its load of delicious, snowy berries . . . at least as large, earlier, sweeter, and more tender and melting throughout, though as firm as the Lawton is when ripe."

The flowers in the *New Creations* catalog, like the fruits, nuts, and vegetables, were very different from the ordinary stock available at the time from nurseries, and like the other plants, they were also very expensive. A calla lily with handsome golden variegated leaves, the only such specimen among "hundreds and thousands" Burbank had raised from seed, could easily be multiplied by cuttings; in the words of the *New Creations* catalog, it was "as easily grown as potatoes." Easily grown by a professional nurseryman, that is; the price of $1,500 for five plants was the kind of investment no amateur would ever make.

Burbank had spent years developing his flowers, and he was very conscious that he was selling not just a plant, but a head start in research and development. In what would become a frequent type of transaction, a breeder from western New York purchased Burbank's entire initial stock of gladioli, used them for further experiments in hybridization, and became the nation's leading expert in gladioli. Burbank would continue working with the gladiolus well into the next century, varying his offerings for a market that was always eager for something new, but that initial sale demonstrates how the results of his experiments were seized on as the foundation for many other breeders' work.

And yet flowers are not really the same as fruit. Producing new lilies may involve processes that are very like those for producing new potatoes, but the justification for the enterprise is different. The potato is necessary for physical survival. The lily nourishes our soul, and also our competitive yearning for whatever is most new and fashionable. Although the 1893 *New Creations* catalog offered only two lilies, it promised future specimens as tall as six feet or as short as six inches, some with upright flowers and some with nodding heads, some with dark green leaves of a woolly texture and others with leaves that were pale, polished, and sharp, all in a spectrum of colors. Their only common trait was their distinctiveness: each lily was different from anything ever seen before. Here is Burbank's description of his field of hybrid lilies: "Can my thoughts be imagined," he asked, "after so many years of patient care and labor, as, walking among them on a dewy morning, I look upon these new forms of beauty, on which other eyes have never gazed?" Buying Burbank's lilies offered an experience not available since Eden.

The *New Creations* catalog introduced one more departure from traditional marketing. It was openly hostile to the retail customer. The first words on the first page were "This catalog is not for public distribution." A page later, Burbank interrupted his introductory essay with a boldface announcement: "My Grounds Are Not Open to the Public." On a following page, he reprinted a newspaper account of his work that ended with the warning: "He doesn't want present notoriety. *He doesn't want visitors;* he has not one second to spare to them; he is the busiest man in the United States; he doesn't want correspondence, except on strictly business and scientific matters; *he has nothing for sale,* or to offer for sale, except such things as may be found in his published list of novelties mailed free each autumn to all who wish it."

Every restriction served to enhance his reputation as a creator of scientific and horticultural marvels. Seven years before the publication of *The Wizard of Oz,* Burbank was creating his own Emerald City, a special place that was both lushly green and closely guarded. The important difference from Baum's wizard was that Burbank, boastful as he may have been in touting his wares, was no humbug. Many of the plants offered in the *New Creations* catalog were significant improvements over existing varieties, and many of them are still widely cultivated, demonstrating very unusual lasting power in a business that depends on a promise of constant new introductions.

Still, the best new creation was Burbank himself. The first *New Creations* catalog and all the annual editions and supplements that followed over the next twenty years provided a single, continuous vision of ceaseless progress and invention, with the steady unveiling of new marvels fashioned from the raw material of nature but greatly improved by the hand of man. One man. Luther Burbank. The front pages were crowded with testimonials, not to the business or the individual products for sale, but to the creator. "Luther Burbank [is] the greatest horticultural experimenter in America, if not in the world," wrote an admirer from Ohio. A customer in New Zealand confirmed the judgment: "Fruit growers throughout the world are indebted to you for your indomitable energy and perseverance in producing and introducing so many new and rare fruits. You will hand down to posterity an enviable name and reputation."

The *New Creations* catalog also included long excerpts from articles about Burbank that had appeared in prominent farm and garden journals over the preceding few years. As soon as he had returned from his eastern trip in late 1888, he had started inviting the press to call at his experimental grounds. He hired a photographer from Santa Rosa to make a visual record of the most remarkable new plants he was growing, images on glass plates that were used and reused for well over a decade in the many newspaper and magazine articles, scientific lectures, and even government publications that started coming out about his work. Burbank's methods might be secret, but he wanted news of his results to get around.

The excerpts reprinted in the *New Creations* catalog featured Luther Burbank, the garden master who could make plants conform to his will. In November 1889, the *American Florist* had published a rapturous discussion that was typical of the new reports:

> Mr. Burbank has devoted a life's work to the growing of new things, and has had wonderful success in gaining hybrids between distinct species, of hundreds of fruits and flowers, many of them between species that ten years ago a man would have been considered "a dead gone crank" if he had intimated that such hybrids could be obtained. . . . [N]early every known fruit and

flower that can be made to grow "in this California climate" has been manipulated, species ripped up, broken up, and "taken through a course of sprouts" until a botanist would not recognize the results.

Soon after, a correspondent named D. B. Weir had taken a tour of the nearly forty acres of experimental grounds and published his equally wonderstruck impressions in the *Pacific Rural Press*. "Mr. Burbank," Weir reported, "has proved that all life on this earth is akin; that every form can be made to 'break,' no odds how seemingly obdurate it may seem, and when once 'broken,' it may be carried in any direction at will by time, skill and patience." Much of this, too, was reprinted in the *New Creations* catalog, along with excerpts from an awestruck profile of Burbank that had taken up the entire front page of the *Rural New Yorker* on April 12, 1890, describing extraordinary successes with berries, roses, lilies, fruit trees, nuts, and olives, the huge variety of plums Burbank had developed, and the one great potato that had first brought Burbank's name into the agricultural news.

Not everybody was convinced, of course. Some of the seed sellers and nurserymen who received Burbank's *New Creations* catalog were offended at the blasphemy of a mere plant breeder calling himself a creator of new life, and doing it in language that so clearly echoed the book of Genesis. Others scoffed at his boasts and doubted Burbank's plant inventions were as big, as new, or as unique as he claimed. Many retailers were propagating their own plants, each eager to assert his own claim to be the provider of the biggest, the newest, the sweetest, the cheapest, and the altogether best of plants and seeds, and they dismissed Burbank's descriptions as the exaggerated fantasies of a competitor.

Certainly the language of *New Creations* was unrestrained and the image of Burbank himself, loudly proclaiming his ability to make nature do his bidding, revealed a vainglorious streak that weighed against the gentle modesty that was remarked on in almost every visitor's description. The more astute retailers, however, wasted little energy deciding if their feelings were hurt or if it was unseemly for a breeder to offer himself as a potential celebrity. They recognized that in branding himself as a creator of botanical wonders, Burbank was adding a great deal of extra value to anything of his they sold. When commercial houses bought a Burbank plant, they were buying his personality as well as his stock, grafting the master's fame onto their own catalogs. The eye-popping prices he was asking surely would be repaid in all the publicity they garnered. The price *was* the publicity, at least in part, and if the plants were any good, they would be well worth the investment. These companies wanted Burbank to be a wizard so they could sell his magical discoveries. A closer look at three large retail plant sellers who invested in Burbank's creations—John Lewis Childs, Stark Bro's Nurseries, and Burpee Seeds—reveals how the market for new plants was itself evolving.

JOHN LEWIS CHILDS was one of Burbank's earliest and most enthusiastic customers. Like Burbank, Childs had abandoned farming in New England to seek bigger prospects—in his case, to become a commercial flower grower in New York at almost the same time Burbank was taking up market gardening in Massachusetts. At seventeen, Childs was an apprentice to C. L. Allen, a grower of seeds and flowers in the tiny village of East Hinsdale, New York, in a part of Long Island less than twenty miles from

Manhattan but then still largely undeveloped. In 1875, Childs went into business for himself, renting land and building a small greenhouse. Over the next twenty years, while Burbank was juggling the demands of a retail nursery with the call of his outdoor laboratory, Childs established a profitable catalog business selling plants as well as seeds.

A fervent believer in advertising, Childs had established his own printing plant in 1892, the better to produce his catalogs, and founded a garden magazine, *Mayflower*, that eventually reached a circulation of half a million copies. His business was so large and successful that by 1893 the area around his nursery became known as Floral Park, although it wasn't formally incorporated as a separate town until 1908. By then he had several hundred acres devoted to bulb gardens, seedbeds, green houses, a demonstration garden, a rail spur for shipping, and a retail store for customers, all laid out on streets named for flowers. Fittingly, Childs himself would be the first president of Floral Park; later officeholders accepted the more modest title of mayor.

Already aware of Burbank's work, Childs had come to see his gardens during earlier visits to California. The first *New Creations* catalog of 1893 included an account of Childs's buying trip to Santa Rosa the previous year. As Burbank told the story, in the yarn-spinning vernacular that was one of his favorite literary voices,

a member of one of the largest nursery and floral firms in the United States, who had traveled over three thousand miles to see my grounds, after leaving the railroad station, overtook an old gentleman who had for years worked for me, and inquired of him if he knew Burbank. He replied: "Course I do. He used to have a big nursery, but sold it out, and now he raises acres and acres of stuff, and every summer has 'em all dug up and burned. I wouldn't give a hundred and fifty dollars for the whole kerboodle."

Of course the point of Burbank's story was that "the gentleman from the Atlantic shore" was smart enough to ignore the codger's opinion. Childs spent nearly seven thousand dollars on specimens listed in the first *New Creations* catalog, and later boasted that he made the money back a hundredfold in reselling offspring of the plums, berries, lilies, tomatoes, and chestnut trees he bought.

Clarence Stark of Louisiana, Missouri, was in the business of selling fruit trees, and he shared Childs's opinion that it was more efficient and more profitable for a retail seller to let someone else take on the chore of product development. By the time Clarence arrived in Santa Rosa in 1893 to inspect the wonders advertised in the *New Creations* catalog, his family's nursery had had a long and somewhat checkered history. His grandfather, James Hart Stark, had crossed the Mississippi River from Kentucky to Pike County, Missouri, in 1816, bringing his wife, their infant son (the first of nineteen children by three wives), and a saddlebag packed with scions of Jeniton apples. Stark grafted those original scions onto the sour but sturdy stock of local wild apple trees, starting his first commercial orchard. Over the next half century, the family business expanded to five locations, making it one of the largest orchard suppliers west of the Mississippi, but the earlier financial panic of 1873 had left William Stark, James's son, with only one nursery.

When William Stark died in 1880, his three sons took over the family business. Clarence was the company president, in charge of acquisitions and advertising; Edgar was vice president in charge of production; and W. P., called the office manager, was in charge of sales. Changing the company name to Stark Bro's Nurseries, they expanded the family business as energetically as their grandfather had done. They purchased land in Colorado and Virginia to extend the range of their orchards and collaborated with the Great Northern Railroad to encourage orchard fruit growing (and shipping) in the state of Washington. Forward-looking businessmen who embraced just about every marketing innovation of their highly commercial era, they advertised in circulars, through catalogs, on barn sides, and in national weeklies and magazines.

When Luther Burbank released his *New Creations* catalog, Stark Bro's Nurseries was once again recovering from a financial crisis. The business had almost failed when credit markets began to collapse in the Panic of 1893, and the brothers were reduced to paying workers in scrip before they were able to reorganize in August and sell stock in their newly incorporated company. Clarence Stark was looking for a new sensation to rekindle sales when he came to Santa Rosa to inspect Burbank's wares. He paid $3,000 for the Golden plum, another $2,000 for the A.P.-318 prune, $800 for the Van Deman quince, and $300 for limited rights to the Doris plum.

Like Childs, Stark expected that both the quality and the fame of Burbank's creations would allow him to resell them in quantities and at a price that would bring a profit in spite of the acquisition costs. For proof of superior quality, the company advertisements emphasized how many plants Burbank destroyed (as many as twenty million, according to his catalog) before he achieved the one worth keeping. What really caught their customer's eye, though, was their focus on the price they had paid for his rare and valuable fruit. Changing the name of one of Burbank's plums from

Golden, which described the color of its fruit, to Gold, a reference to its price, Stark Bro's advertised it in *Harper's Weekly* under the headline: "Gold ($3,000) Plum—The chiefest among, not 10,000 but 20 MILLION!"

A child of science, sprung from crossing our hardy fruitful American plums and the beautiful and exquisite plums of Japan. "It is four times larger than its parents, and tree wreathed and

COURTESY CLAY AND SALLY LOGAN AND LOUISIANA
AREA HISTORICAL MUSEUM, LOUISIANA, MISSOURI

smothered with gloriously handsome golden globes—nothing on earth as beautiful or good." No marvel, then, that such a jewel of purest ray serene is worth a small fortune; nor that we were glad to pay full $3,000 for a single tree!

Washington Atlee Burpee, born in 1859, was already the country's leading garden merchant when he came to Santa Rosa to shop in Luther Burbank's gardens. He had spent his childhood breeding exotic chickens in his parents' yard in the days when the line between family farm and family home was not so clearly drawn as it was to become. By the time he was ten, Burpee was publishing articles in poultry journals and running a mail-order business in baby chicks. Selling chickens led to selling chicken feed, which led to selling vegetable and flower seeds. In 1876, the year Philadelphia was hosting the Centennial Exposition to celebrate the hundredth anniversary of the Declaration of Independence, seventeen-year-old Burpee decided to open a business there, abandoning poultry for garden seeds and taking full advantage of favorable mail rates to spread his catalogs across the country.

Unlike Burbank, Burpee liked to travel, especially to visit potential suppliers. His favorite method of developing inventory was to search out promising new varieties, buy exclusive rights from the discoverer, and grow them for several years in the experimental fields of Fordhook Farm, his country home outside Philadelphia. There he would continue the breeding process, selecting for improved vigor and size and also, most of the time, engendering enough of a difference that he could claim the improvement as his own. In 1894, Burpee's big new product had been iceberg lettuce, which for better or worse continues to be the leading variety grown in the United States.

In 1899, Burpee was in Santa Rosa, hoping to acquire something he had no intention of selling as his own creation. Like Stark, Childs, and the many other companies that paid for the exclusive right to sell a Burbank cultivar, Burpee was buying more than a plant, no matter how beautiful and novel it might be. He was also paying for the special aura that came with the name of Luther Burbank, the man who by then was widely thought to have a unique understanding of the secrets of nature.

Burpee's first purchase, a rose with large, fragrant pink blossoms that he named the Burbank rose, was the beginning of a long commercial relationship between the two men. Although they had never met before, they were distant cousins, a fact that both used for additional publicity. Burbank's mother, Olive Burpee Ross Burbank, was still alive and sharing her son's frame house at 204 Santa Rosa Avenue. At eighty-three, she was beginning to slow down a bit, but she was more than happy to talk to the growing number of reporters about the Burpee-Burbank family link—yet another reason she was confident her famous son had acquired his gardening talents from her.

IN THE GARDEN BUSINESS, it is impossible to underestimate the importance of the grower's reputation. What is being sold is at best a pledge of future results, brightly colored little packets of promises. Then as now, a buyer had no way to know if a bare rootstock would grow into a sturdy, fruitful tree, if a seed would yield as bountiful a crop as the catalog promised, or if it would even develop into whatever plant was listed on the label. James Vick, a pioneer in color printing who was famous for his catalogs' beautiful pictures of flowers, also included illustrations of the large facility in Rochester, New York, where he processed orders. The pictures of the facility were meant to assure customers that their requests would be quickly and accurately filled, a particularly important point in the garden business, where it was entirely possible for the planting season to be lost if a customer received an incorrect order. As critics of the federal free seed program often pointed out, many of the packets sent out from Washington at taxpayer expense contained inferior seeds that failed to germinate. Commercial houses had to do better.

The Burpee company motto was "Burpee Seeds Grow." Short and simple, it addressed the doubts customers had about paying for products they wouldn't even see until long after they could be returned. Stark Bro's Nurseries had a similar motto, "Stark Trees Bear Fruit," often emblazoned on the silhouette of a lumbering bear, which made a memorable pun and looked particularly striking when painted on the side of a barn.

The slogans spoke directly to the buyers' fears, but they also highlighted an important feature of the increasingly intricate relationship between plant breeders and the retail sellers. Catalog giants like Burpee and Stark liked the fact that Burbank kept away from all the advertising gimmicks they so enthusiastically employed. They wanted him to be famous, and they wanted him to be pure, honest, and altogether above the commercial fray.

As Burbank and his customers knew perfectly well, he was not the only source for market novelties. There were professional plant explorers, working for the Department of Agriculture or as private agents, who combed the world for undiscovered varieties and brought them to the attention of the market. Another popular and even cheaper way of outsourcing the hard work of product development was to hold a contest.

The same year Stark Bro's made its first purchases of Burbank's "new creations," for example, it held a Fruit Fair to which amateur growers were encouraged to submit their best fruit. The winning entry was a crisp apple with an unusual five-pointed tip, probably a natural cross of Bellflower and Winesap. It had been submitted by an Iowa farmer named Jesse Hiatt, who had found it growing in his orchard. Growers call this kind of unexpected addition to their farm or garden a "volunteer" and usually rip it out, but Hiatt discovered that the unknown, out-of-place apple tree was too sturdy to eradicate. By the time it had begun bearing fruit, he was sure he had come upon something wonderful, and he entered it in the Stark Bro's contest. When Hiatt won the prize money, his victory included ceding all rights to Stark Bro's, which re-named Hiatt's discovery the Delicious apple and made it into a best-selling variety.

The current condition of the Delicious apple, globally available but rarely as delicious as the ancestor that inspired its name, is the result of further breeding that enhanced appearance and storage life at the expense of flavor. Too many Delicious apples today taste like a mouthful of crimson-covered cardboard, but rumor is that there are still some descendants of the original tree out in Iowa, growing near those storied bridges of Madison County.

Burpee used contests even more aggressively than Stark, especially to promote the sale of existing varieties. He offered cash prizes for growing the largest Cuban Queen watermelon, the most pods on a Creaseback pole bean, or the best of whatever else he was introducing that season. The very motto of the company was the winning entry in an advertising contest, which was another kind of promotion it was impossible to imagine Luther Burbank

$500 FOR ONE TREE

Our Japan Plum "J"

—Is One of Millions

(No longer "J," but "H.")

━━━✦━━━

It was selected by Luther Burbank, the originator of improved Japan varieties, who says, **"In the hedge row of seedlings and numbered "J" was the most vigorous, most productive, handsomest, most uniform and best flavored of any Japan Plum I have ever seen . . . I do not know of any fruit that will keep longer."**

Is it any wonder that we were ready to pay the large sum of **$500 for the one original tree** of this variety? Leading Pomologists have suggested that it be named **Hale**, in honor of its first extended plant here at the "Elms" and its future introduction by us.

G. H. & J. H. Hale,

The Elms

South Glastonbury, Conn.

Advertisement, Hale Nursery (n.d.)

conducting. Burpee also pioneered the practice of offering premiums for early orders; in the future, the premium would often be a packet of Luther Burbank seeds.

Contests were always good for publicity and sometimes led to enormously profitable products like the Delicious apple, but they didn't add the same prestige as Luther Burbank's name attached to a plant in a retailer's catalog. In boosting Burbank's reputation, his customers were bolstering their own status, too. His name added an extra layer of value to any product, as the two words "Luther Burbank" became a standard for both novelty and quality in the crowded marketplace for plants.

The commercial interests that bought and resold Burbank's inventions fostered his growing reputation for unequaled insight into the mysteries of innovative plant breeding, but it wasn't simply publicity that created his newfound fame. The vast and reliable crop of new introductions that sprang for years from Burbank's gardens was the product of his unmatched skill as a hybridizer and his equally remarkable talent for selection. And as Burbank himself worked to enhance his reputation, aided by commercial sellers and his many admirers in the popular press, the glowing reports of his achievements attracted the attention of a very different group of botanical enthusiasts. A new breed of research scientists was about to vault over the garden fence, eager to submit both Burbank and his products to more rigorous examination.

PART II

UNDERSTANDING THE GARDEN

MR. BURBANK IN HIS GARDENS AT SANTA ROSA, CALIFORNIA, EXPLAINING TO VISITORS SOME OF HIS PLANT WONDERS

Luther Burbank

THE HIGH PRIEST OF HORTICULTURE WHO HAS WORKED MARVELS IN
TRANSFORMING AND IMPROVING PLANT LIFE AND PRODUCTS

Cover of *Success Magazine*, July 1905.
COURTESY LUTHER BURBANK COLLECTION,
LIBRARY OF CONGRESS

THE PHILOSOPHER IN THE ORCHARD, THE SCIENTIST IN THE PEA PATCH

The statements made to the number and variety of Mr. Burbank's productions are so astounding that some might be supposed to consider them as so many flowers of rhetoric, such as we are accustomed to from the other side of the Atlantic, were they not authenticated by competent observers of established repute.

—*The Gardener's Chronicle*, London, 1897

Wickson Hall at the University of California campus at Davis houses the Department of Pomology, which studies the science of fruit growing. A practitioner of pomology is a pomologist, not to be confused with a thremmatologist, who is a propagator of plants and animals. These are just two of a large number of new words invented during the nineteenth century to identify the agricultural pursuits of people who had previously been obliged to go about their business without a specific title. "Agronomist" was another new name, used to differentiate an expert in the science of soil management and crop production from his more humble associate, the farmer. So was "taxonomist," which referred to the person creating the classifications and categories into which plants (and animals) could now be sorted.

The biggest new word of all was "scientist," introduced with considerable debate in the 1830s. Before then, there had been "natural philosophers," "men (and doubtless a few women) of science," "savants," or simply people who studied the workings of the natural world without troubling themselves about what title came with the job. William Whewell, master of Trinity College in Cambridge, England, invented the name "scientist" at the urging of poet Samuel Taylor Coleridge, who complained of the inadequacy of the existing terms. Whewell was extremely good at putting a name on new discoveries, and he provided much of the new vocabulary needed to discuss the emerging experimental knowledge of the age. Among his other inventions were the words "physicist," "anode," "cathode," "ion," "consilience," "catastrophism," and "uniformitarianism." Even with Whewell's obvious talent for nomenclature, it took several years for "scientist" to be accepted by the very people it described. By the end of the century, however, the word had achieved universal acceptance, and the profession had expanded greatly, reflecting the growth of academic institutions.

In the forty years since 1859, when Darwin and Wallace had pushed the concept of evolutionary change to the front of every conversation about the natural world, scientists had struggled to understand not just *why* those changes came about, but *how*. Competitive advantage, natural selection, survival of the fittest, and all the other new ideas that had entered the world of scientific discourse alongside the theory of evolution did nothing to explain the internal sources of those subtle variations that meant so much. If those sources could be understood, perhaps they could be controlled. And if they could be controlled, it would revolutionize the garden.

Plants seem simpler than animals—at least, a clover appears

less complicated than a camel or a kangaroo—but their reproductive processes remained far more mysterious to the scientists who were trying to understand them. The mating of animals, especially domestic animals, was familiar and even fairly easy to control. But plants? It was not until the early years of the twentieth century that the internal mechanics of plant reproduction began to be understood. Well into the nineteenth century, there were significant differences of opinion on both how to keep a favored variety from changing and also how to improve it.

For some time, scientists had been trying to understand what happened when plants were crossed, or hybridized. They also wanted to know why hybrid plants often reverted back to one or another parent form after the first generation or after many generations. Most of all, they wanted to know why and how plants would suddenly acquire what seemed to be entirely new characteristics, mysterious aberrations too sudden and too extreme to be explained by the gradual process of evolution. This last category, a plant that had suddenly changed its nature, was called a *sport*, short for *sport of nature*, but the expanding ranks of scientists dearly hoped to be able to find an explanation that went beyond the idea that the forces of creation were just playing games. The presence of such sudden divergences seemed, for a time, to discredit the Darwinian idea of a more gradual process of incremental evolutionary change. Perhaps more information would help.

In the midst of their confusion, both professional scientists and the general public turned to Luther Burbank. Many people were discussing evolution in abstract terms, but Burbank was out there taking Darwin's theory and quite literally testing it in the field, seeing if he could accelerate and guide organic change. His successes in breeding new plants had been so conspicuous that it seemed he must know the answer to how plants evolved and how humans might control the process.

THE SUMMER OF 1899 witnessed two significant gatherings of plant scientists, held at almost exactly the same time. On July 9, fifteen agents from different state Agricultural Experiment Stations arrived in Sebastopol to tour Burbank's grounds. Two days later, on July 11, the Royal Horticultural Society in England opened the first International Conference on Hybridisation and Cross-Breeding, with sessions in both London and Cheswick. Despite the obvious differences in size, formality, and declared ambition, both events were part of the new effort to pin down what it was that controlled plant variation. And both meetings represented a rare moment when research scientists were turning to commercial plant breeders for information.

In 1898, the *Yearbook* of the Department of Agriculture had included a long article on "Hybrids and Their Utilization in Plant Breeding" that contained many admiring references to Luther Burbank and photographs that came directly from his catalogs. The visitors to Sebastopol in 1899 were eager to see these wonders for themselves. Burbank had been dreading the interruption to his work, but when the agents arrived, he was an enthusiastic guide. He showed them the massive numbers of plants he was working on, pointing out the trees on which he had grafted hundreds of different buds for comparison. The research scientists walked through fields of lilies and rows of cacti and into the orchards where they were invited to bite down into the yielding center of a stoneless plum, straight through to the soft, bitter-tasting kernel at its heart. They saw thousands of daisies, part of a

still-unfinished experiment in hybridization involving four different parent plants. The visitors were very impressed with the huge
variety of plums Burbank was getting, and especially with a new
hybrid between a plum and an apricot, the latter a fruit that was
notoriously hard to cross. They were puzzled to learn that Burbank
kept notes on the flavor, size, and appearance of his fruit but not
necessarily of all the particular crosses that had gone into a favored
hybrid. Even more bewildering was his insistence that after a single generation of cross-pollinating by hand, followed by his own
keen-eyed selection from the resulting hybrids, there was no need
to guard against further uncontrolled crosses.

The Agricultural Experiment Station agents, trained to evaluate soil, test the viability of seeds, compare fertilizers, and recom-
mend specific crops for specific conditions, did not know quite
what to make of their visit. Professor Samuel B. Green took notes
for the group, recording Burbank's thoughts on irrigation, grafting,
and cross-pollination. He praised the new fruits and flowers on
which Burbank was working, paying particular attention to the
plum-apricot crosses, the stoneless plum, and a yellow variant of
the common white calla lily. As had become his custom, Burbank
asked for a typescript of Green's report so he could make correc-
tions. Later, in ink, Green added another note he had apparently
not submitted to his host: "Mr. B. believes that thought vibrations
influence plant variations and that plants vary more readily for
one person than for another." Green and his fellow agents were
unsure just how to apply this information to their own work.
The sense of a mystic oneness with nature, a philosophy that made
Burbank very different from his more commercial promoters and
competitors in the world of plant selling, was about to set him
apart from his new scientific colleagues as well.

At the meeting on the other side of the Atlantic Ocean, things were equally puzzling, though the questions were couched in different terms. The Royal Horticultural Society had been founded in 1804 at the suggestion of John Wedgwood, son of the famous pottery magnate Josiah Wedgwood, and it had existed for decades as an elite forum for amateur and professional horticulturalists to share their interests and findings. Recently, however, the Horticultural Society had grown to some five thousand members as the swelling ranks of university scientists, agricultural agents, and commercial plant breeders sought information on new developments in their fields.

Representatives of most of the major British seed sellers had been invited to the International Conference on Hybridisation and Cross-Breeding because they, like Burbank, had the most experience in the topic being discussed. From the United States, a member of the Department of Agriculture's Plant Breeding Laboratory went to London, along with a representative of the American Association of Agricultural Colleges and Experiment Stations, the very group that had sent a different delegation to Luther Burbank's experimental grounds. Liberty Hyde Bailey came from Ithaca, New York, where he had already established a reputation as a widely published expert on all aspects of the garden and would soon become dean of the College of Agriculture at Cornell University. Burbank had been invited to attend, but he considered a cross-country trip followed by a long ocean voyage unthinkable during his busiest season.

At the London conference, William Bateson of Cambridge University urged the professional plant breeders in the audience to make detailed notes of their hybridization experiments, successes and failures alike, to provide the statistical information needed to establish a scientific understanding of their discoveries. A few months later, several other scientists announced that Gregor Mendel, an obscure Austrian monk who had died in 1884, long before his work received any scientific recognition, had already compiled such records. What followed was a considerable upheaval in the world of plant breeding, and particularly in its academic branches.

The long neglect of Mendel's work has become a favorite tale in the history of science. Copies of Mendel's 1866 monograph, the pages still uncut, are rumored to have lain hidden in many important libraries, from Darwin's home bookshelves to the stacks of Harvard University. Whether or not those stories are true, it is indisputable that the garden-plot experiments of a small-town monk and schoolmaster living in what is now the Czech Republic, writing in German and publishing in the obscure journal of his local natural history society, simply did not get noticed.

Primary credit for the belated recognition of Mendel's importance goes to Hugo de Vries, the well-known, well-liked, and very well respected Dutch botanist who was a professor at the University of Amsterdam and director of the botanical gardens there. De Vries, like many biologists of the time, felt that the Darwinian account of evolution failed to answer a number of important questions about the sources of plant variations. The chief rival theories, both of which Darwin had specifically rejected, were neo-Lamarckism (named after French biologist Jean-Baptiste Lamarck), which held that species evolved in response to specific environmental needs, gradually acquiring characteristics that became hereditary, and saltation (from the Latin *saltare*, to leap), which argued for the role of spontaneous, discontinuous variations that produced new species. De Vries preferred to call these sudden changes *mutations*, which is of course the term now used.

De Vries had been in London in July 1899 for the first International Conference on Hybridisation and Cross-Breeding. Afterward, he returned to Amsterdam and continued writing his treatise *Die Mutatinstheorie* (*The Theory of Mutation*), based largely on his experimental observations of the evening primrose. Quite unexpectedly, a colleague who knew of de Vries's project sent him a paper that he thought might be of interest. It had been written by the still-unknown Mendel and had been languishing on his own bookshelf since its publication thirty-four years earlier.

De Vries immediately recognized the importance of Mendel's "Experiments in Plant Hybridization" in answering why and how specific characteristics would disappear and reappear in plants over the course of several generations. Starting with simple but meticulous observations from hybridizing generations of ordinary garden peas, Mendel had demonstrated the existence of independent units of inheritance (the word "gene" would not be coined for several years). He had shown, in what later came to be known as the law of segregation, that organisms combine hereditary units from each parent, some of which might be dominant and others recessive, but that the units of inheritance did not blend into a middle ground, as had been commonly supposed. Mendel had also concluded that the inheritance of any particular trait did not influence the inheritance of any other, which was later called the law of independent assortment. This meant, for example, that no amount of hybridization by itself would create pink flowers from a combination of red and white parents, and the appearance of either color would have no effect on the flower's size.

De Vries's articles about Mendel, and the almost simultaneous attention to Mendel by Carl Erich Correns in Germany and Erich von Tschermak in Austria, are generally described as "the rediscovery of Mendel." That is something of a misnomer, however, because it suggests that the record of Mendel's experiments with hybrid peas was known, then lost, and then, well, rediscovered. Perhaps the world of science needed thirty-four years to understand the larger significance of what Mendel had recorded in his garden in Brno. When de Vries published the first article about Mendel in 1900, the work that had been universally ignored in 1866 was embraced by a new generation, and nowhere earlier than in the world of commercial plant breeding. If careful observation could determine which were dominant traits and which recessive, and hybridization could coax one or another trait to appear, plant breeding could be wrenched from haphazard guesswork and brought into much more controlled production.

FROM SEPTEMBER 30 to October 2, 1902, a second International Conference on Plant Breeding and Hybridization convened in New York City to discuss the many changes to scientific knowledge and its practical applications that had become apparent in the three years since the first conference in London. Experts from many places gathered to discuss if and how the new theories of stable internal characteristics could be applied to the business of breeding plants.

The list of participants was full of people in newly created positions that reflected the rapid changes in the field of plant breeding itself. The head of the conference's advisory committee was the director of the U.S. Department of Agriculture's Bureau of Plant

Industry, which had been established the previous year to oversee the expanding field of agricultural research. Professors and government agents, many of them very recent converts to the study of plant heredity, came to the New York conference from universities and new government research centers in England, Scotland, Ireland, France, Canada, Barbados, and across the United States. They were there to consider the implications of Mendel's work and, equally important, to discuss its commercial significance. Not every person in attendance was convinced of the validity of the newly rediscovered theory, but they were all aware that it was a topic of great importance.

The call for Luther Burbank to contribute to the proceedings was even louder than it had been in 1899, but once again, Burbank was in the midst of a number of projects that seemed far more urgent than a cross-country trip that would take at least two weeks of his time. He had returned east in 1900, visiting established customers like John Lewis Childs on Long Island and Burpee in Philadelphia and meeting new potential buyers, but he hated the trip and swore it would be his last. "So keep my bob, if I ever travel and visit as much again I hope to be sent to a lunatic asylum," he wrote home to his mother. "I never did such hard, cruel, disagreeable work as visiting by rail in short time, sitting up every night in hot, stuffy rooms till past midnight in perfect misery to rest a little, but no rest." Besides, unlike the professors and extension agents who were flocking to New York, Burbank felt he already understood what he was doing. He would write a paper, though, and send it along.

The 1902 New York conference did in fact come at a busy time for Burbank. He was working on new plums and poppies, trying to create a yellow rose that wouldn't fade to white as the blossom opened, and developing so many new lilies and amaryllis that he had to issue a separate catalog to list them all. After almost ten years of work and multiple generations of hybridization, Burbank's cross of the familiar prune plum, Petit d'Agen, with the tiny, almost stoneless fruit that grew wild in France had produced a stoneless plum that retail nurseries would soon market as the Miracle plum.

Looking to the future, Burbank had high hopes for the new varieties of cacti growing in the plots behind his house and on rented grounds in other drier parts of California. Another big seller was Crimson Winter rhubarb, a cultivar that promised to extend the growing season for the "pie plant" that was still every cook's and gardener's favorite sign of the beginning of spring. Burbank had imported seeds of the new rhubarb from Australia and improved it through selection in his own gardens before introducing it in 1900; three years later, the *Los Angeles Times* would call it a "big boon for small ranches," while grateful growers dubbed the profitable new crop "the mortgage lifter." Once again, though, like the hybrid plums of a decade before, a single new introduction that represented years of effort was gathering more attention than all the others. In 1902, it was a flower.

How to Make a Plant:
Complex Hybrids

When he was feeling boastful, Burbank liked to claim he could make plants to order. Start with an ideal, he said, and then work to achieve it. One of his ideals was a large-flowered, pure white, long-stemmed perennial daisy. It took him years to get what he

Burbank Scrapbook 1902.
COURTESY LUTHER BURBANK COLLECTION,
LIBRARY OF CONGRESS

wanted. Some modern nursery catalogs list the Shasta daisy as a native of Europe, naturalized to the United States. They are wrong. The Shasta is a complex hybrid developed by Luther Burbank from a multigenerational cross of four different flowers. The simplest of blossoms, it marked the highest complexity of his art.

Burbank's first step in creating the Shasta daisy was to cross *Chrysanthemum leucanthemum*, the short-petaled oxeye daisy that grows wild across much of the United States, and *Bellis perennis*, the low-growing English daisy with larger, sparser flowers and a stubby stem often covered with what Burbank dismissed as "numerous unsightly leaves." He cross-pollinated hundreds of flowers, sowed the seeds of the next generation, selected for the best examples, and sowed them again. After several generations, Burbank selected the best of these hybrids and crossed them with pollen from *Chrysanthemum lacustre*, the German daisy, eventually producing a flower larger than any of the parent plants but still not the dazzling white blossom Burbank had in mind.

For several more years Burbank planted out the hybrids, selecting for whiteness and saving those seeds for the next generation. Then he obtained seeds for the small-flowered, large-leafed *Chrysanthemum nipponicum*, the Japanese daisy, which had brilliant white petals. After planting the new daisies, he applied their pollen to the latest round of hybrids and tested the resulting seeds. Finally, in 1901, one of the hundreds of resulting flowers met the criteria he had set at the beginning. Unlike the oxeye daisy (called marguerite in Europe, prolific weed throughout the world), the new daisy had longer petals, taller stems, a less invasive growing habit, and a much better smell. Unlike the English daisy, it had a straight stem with few leaves. Unlike the Japanese daisy, it had a very large flowering head.

Burbank named his new flower after the snowy peak of Mount Shasta, in northern California, and decided to sell the seeds himself as well as distribute them through other dealers. To gardeners around the world, it was the ideal flower: simple, modern, inexpensive (seeds cost as little as ten cents a packet), easy to grow, and yet with a remarkable pedigree that included an international list of ancestors, all gathered together in Santa Rosa for years of painstaking attention from the celebrated Luther Burbank. When he began to advertise his newest creation, the response threatened to overwhelm the local post office. Orders flooded in from private gardeners, from foreign seed sellers, from gardeners for royal es-

COURTESY LUTHER BURBANK HOME & GARDENS, SANTA ROSA, CALIFORNIA

tates, and from children who were encouraged to start their gardens with this flower that seemed the model of innocent beauty. Burbank continued to work on the Shasta daisy, introducing new variations every year, and the orders never ceased.

In the summer of 1902, Burbank finally sat down to write "Some of the Fundamental Principles of Plant Breeding," the paper he would send to the second International Conference on Plant Breeding and Hybridization. Although he had given talks at smaller gatherings of professional and scientific societies, this was the largest scientific meeting he had ever been asked to address, and he was proud of his contribution. His paper was published later that year as a small, square booklet with attractive art nouveau decorations on its lavender cover, and he included parts or all of it, word for word, in subsequent books for the next twenty years.

A 1902 letter from Burbank's longtime secretary, May Benedict Maye, to his sister Emma describes how "the Boss" went about the composition of "Some of the Fundamental Principles of Plant Breeding." It reveals the hectic flitting from task to task that was, unfortunately, Burbank's normal mode of operation. In his first *New Creations* catalog, Burbank had described his grounds as "chaos, utter chaos; a workshop, the birthplace of new vegetable forms." Visitors who toured the gardens always remarked on Burbank's calm serenity and patience, but a peek inside his office showed "utter chaos" as a less biblical, more literal description.

In her letter, Maye wrote that on Sunday there was a stream of visitors that started before breakfast. On Monday there was a rush to hybridize new plants in preparation for a trip to San Francisco on Tuesday. Preparing a new catalog took up most of Wednesday, along with mail from job seekers and visitors and seed companies clamoring for new exclusives as they readied their own catalogs. "Then the photographer must be taken to Gold Ridge to take photographs of things there. Then essays; he wrote one and got it off early in the week and now is engaged on another for the Plant Breeders' conference to be held in New York. Just as he gets all his notes spread out and going smoothly, here is an interruption—the man to cut the hay, another one comes to show him a . . . flower that has appeared in his garden, thinking, because he had never seen it before, that Burbank will be surprised to see it. . . . Then back again to the essay—another interruption. The mother wants to see him; no one else will do."

The paper would probably never have been finished if Judge Samuel Leib hadn't invited Burbank on a family trip to the Sierra Mountains that allowed him the time to work on it in relative isolation amid magnificent surroundings that evidently deeply influenced his thinking. When Burbank returned from the mountains in early September, he sent his essay off to New York.

THE HOST OF THE second International Conference on Plant Breeding and Hybridization was the Horticultural Society of New York, a group that was in many ways the American equivalent of the Royal Horticultural Society, host of the London conference. Founded in 1818 as the New-York Horticultural Society and incorporated under its new name only in 1900, the society's membership reflected the diversity of its nineteenth-century origins. It was a mix of amateur and professional plant lovers—seed sellers, commercial nursery owners, amateur garden enthusiasts, head gardeners for large estates, the wealthy people who employed those head gardeners and paid for their membership, botanists, botanizers, book and print collectors, and natural history buffs. The list of patrons for the 1902 conference was the American equivalent of a royal charter, a roster of the commercial and financial elite of New York City, starting with banker J. P. Morgan and including Frederick Vanderbilt, who offered a Hudson River boat trip to his estate in Duchess County as a diversion for participants.

The Horticultural Society did not have its own building, and the sites for the conference were themselves a bridge between past and future ways of introducing new ideas. Some of the conference sessions were held at the American Institute of the City of New York, on Third Avenue and Sixty-third Street in Manhattan, a grand hall built in the middle of the previous century for public expositions that had once been important showcases for both artisans and inventors. Other sessions took place in the recently opened Museum Building of the New York Botanical Garden in the Bronx, a ten-year-old institution whose mission was the development and dissemination of scientific knowledge. It wasn't quite the same as shuttling between a fairground and a laboratory, but it wasn't entirely different either.

The conference began with an address by William Bateson, the Cambridge professor who had already become a leading advocate for what was being called "Mendelism" and who would soon propose the word "genetics" to describe the field. Speaking on "Practical Aspects of the New Discoveries in Heredity," Bateson introduced his listeners to the new understanding of dominant and recessive traits, explained the fixed nature of gametes, and discussed the possibility of calculating in advance the results of hybridization.

Burbank's paper was also read on the conference's opening day. In light of his international reputation as the world's most fearless and successful hybridizer, the audience might have expected him to describe such signal achievements as his work developing the Shasta daisy or the plumcot, which had so impressed the judges at the Buffalo International Exposition in 1901 that they created a special gold medal to award to the fruit that fit no established category. The conference attendees might likewise have looked forward to a discussion of the almost thirty varieties of plums Burbank had already introduced, the start of over one hundred new varieties that would lead many people to judge Burbank's plums his greatest contribution to agriculture. These were the feats that made headlines in newspapers and magazines around the world, and that brought a stream of visiting experts to his experimental grounds.

What they heard, presented on Burbank's behalf by the president of the Horticultural Society, covered none of those topics, though it did include some impressive predictions of the profits to be made from improved plant varieties. Mostly, "Some of the Fundamental Principles of Plant Breeding" was an expression of the natural mysticism that Burbank had cherished since he was a young man. Burbank knew about Mendel and kept up with journals like *Popular Science Monthly*, then a leading source of new scientific information, but he did not think the new debate was adding anything to prior knowledge. He also rejected the tendency of the new Mendelians to ignore the importance of selection and, implicitly, the possibility of infinite change. To Burbank, talk of dominant or recessive traits was just another way of discussing the hidden qualities of plants, which in his opinion were better described in terms of the universal forces of creation than by the marshaling of statistics.

Loyal to what he had learned from Darwin, Burbank maintained that changes in environmental conditions could provoke internal change in plants (a position that today is once again gaining credence but which was very strongly repudiated by the early converts to Mendelian genetics). In a statement he would repeat many times over the course of his career, Burbank insisted that the building blocks of heredity were as susceptible to change as the organisms that contained them. "Every plant, animal, and planet occupies its place in the order of nature by the action of two forces: the inherent constitutional life-force with all its acquired habits, the sum of which is heredity; and the numerous complicated external forces or environment."

Burbank's insistence on the role of environment in evolutionary change is often dismissed as stubborn neo-Lamarckism, a simple-minded and wrongheaded belief in the inheritance of acquired traits. Whether or not this description is fair to Lamarck, it is something of a distortion of Burbank's ideas, which were often expressed in ways that are hard to sort out. Based on his personal observation that at least some forms of hybrid plants were able to reproduce from seed without reverting to prior types, Burbank was convinced that not all hybrids were sterile, suggesting that acquired changes could be inherited. He was also sure that a transfer to a new environment could provoke changes in a following generation that would remain evident in future plants. What Burbank meant came less from Lamarck than from what might be called a theory of the survival of the unfittest.

To Burbank, every life form contained myriad qualities that could be made to surface if the organism was jolted out of its usual development, whether by the shock of relocation, hybridization, or even electric current. Under ordinary circumstances, most of these previously unknown qualities would go unnoticed and would die out in a single generation, like the vast majority of biological oddities. Those changes could be supported by the grower's nurturing care, however, which included music, touch, or even thought. Under the right conditions, protected from the brutal hazards of natural selection, unexpected treasures could be preserved. Burbank did not believe plants understood language or would "behave" in different ways under different treatment, as some of his more sentimental followers liked to say, but he was convinced that the strict Mendelism that was being introduced, in which a specific plant had a limited number of potential traits or fixed qualities that could be shuffled but never changed, was too reductive to be true.

Burbank's innovative methods and his long list of striking results gave him great standing in the emerging field of scientific breeding, but the way he chose to explain his ideas undermined his stature among the very scientists who had hoped to learn from him. Unlike Darwin, who cataloged discrete incremental advantages in a world ungoverned by any overriding design, Burbank described an animate, almost sentient universe in a vocabulary that came less from science than from a natural philosophy that was rapidly being dismissed as irrelevant to modern ideas. His habit of talking to his plants, a seemingly sentimental gesture that many visitors to his gardens noted with varying degrees of surprise, was part of a larger conviction that there were forces (sometimes he described them as magnetic, sometimes as electrical, most often as vibrations) that allowed every organism to respond to every other.

The results of Burbank's crosses were essentially the same ones Mendel would have predicted, as shown in the emergence of the "Iceberg" white blackberry after repeated crossings between dominant black and recessive white parent stock, but Burbank preferred to describe his work in the language of persuasion. Approached correctly, he said in his paper for the second International Conference, plants could be convinced to change. The way to do this was to "perturb" the plant, shaking it out of its complacent sameness so it would remember some of the old characteristics that had been buried under more recent acquired traits. As Burbank explained in "Some of the Fundamental Principles of Plant Breeding," a gifted and dedicated plant breeder could stir up this deep, productive internal dismay in an organism through artificial crossing. In fact, this was simply another way of describing the process Mendel had observed, but Burbank resisted that association. What he was more willing to emphasize was the social value of his operation:

> With better and still better fruits, nuts, grains, and flowers will the earth be transformed, man's thoughts turned from the base, destructive forces into the nobler productive ones which will lift him to higher planes of action toward that happy day when man shall offer his brother man, not bullets and bayonets, but richer grains, better fruits, and fairer flowers.

In a nod to practical considerations, Burbank projected the economic benefits "for one man to breed a new rye, wheat, barley, oats, or rice which would produce one grain more to each head, or a corn which would produce an extra kernel to each ear, another potato to each plant, or an apple, plum, orange, or nut to each tree." Such seemingly small increases would produce "annually, without effort and without cost, 5,200,000 extra bushels of corn, 15,000,000 extra bushels of wheat, 20,000,000 extra bushels of oats, 1,500,000 extra bushels of barley, 21,000,000 extra bushels of potatoes."

It's not at all clear where Burbank got these numbers, but everybody at the conference agreed with his point—that more productive plants would have enormous benefits. They were all there to learn how to manage just this sort of highly profitable plant improvement. The economic potential of new and better plants was not really the subject of "Fundamental Principles," however. The cosmic wonder of the universe was Burbank's topic, and the real fundamental principles were those that underlie all of creation. His closing paragraph seems inspired more by the end of Thoreau's *Walden* than by anything that Mendel, Darwin, or any other scientist had to say.

"These lines were penned among the heights of the Sierras," he wrote, "while resting on the original material from which this planet was made. Thousands of ages have passed, and it still remains unchanged . . . far away down the slopes stand the giant trees, oldest of all living things, embracing all of human history, but even their lives are but as a watch-tick since the stars first shone on these barren rocks, before the evolutive forces had so gloriously transfigured the face of our planet home."

"Some of the Fundamental Principles of Plant Breeding," with its strange transitions from visions of mystic harmony to calculations of the profits to be gained from new plant varieties, shows how Burbank straddled two very different intellectual traditions that ran through the nineteenth century, both of them with origins that go back much further in history. One of these traditions passed through the work of Sir Charles Lyell, the geologist whose work on fossils made it difficult to believe in the traditional time line of biblical creation, and Darwin, the keen observer of what he came to call evolution. It circled back to include Mendel, the careful tabulator of generations of peas whose work in genetics was neglected for almost half a century, and continued on to de Vries, Bateson, and their many colleagues and followers. This is the line that triumphed in the twentieth century, fanning out to cross the work of nearly every academic and laboratory biologist for the next hundred years. It is the line of observation, of careful experimentation, and of a fervent belief in the powers of logic, reason, and proof.

Burbank's plant creations came out of this tradition of closely observed experiments, but the man himself was also deeply influenced by another line of scientific thinking, one that considered the earth and all that lives therein as united in a large, mostly harmonic system of interrelationships that could not be separated into manageable segments for laboratory study because the parts could only truly be understood as they related to the whole. This was the natural philosophy of Alexander von Humboldt, of Emerson and Thoreau, of John Muir, and, in important ways, of Luther Burbank. It was also the science of mystical thinkers like Emanuel Swedenborg and William Blake, philosophers like William James, practitioners of nonwestern systems of meditation, and followers of varied fashions in pseudoscience. Professional judgments of Burbank's work swung from reverence to scorn, depending on where the observers placed him and to which scientific traditions they themselves adhered.

What kept the debate over Burbank going was the continued array of plants emerging from his gardens in Santa Rosa and Sebastopol. As the participants at the New York conference returned to their businesses and scientific institutions, most embraced Mendelism and championed a view of fixed genetic inheritance that was, for a time, almost as rigid as the pre-Darwinian insistence on a static universe. But the second International Conference on Plant Breeding and Hybridization was neither the beginning nor the end of efforts to uncover the scientific principles of Luther Burbank's work. After all, the very important question of how Burbank got his results—and how others could imitate him—was still to be resolved. If Burbank himself wasn't going to answer those questions directly, there were other people close at hand who were willing to act as his interpreter.

Whenever humanity calls, Mr. Burbank stands ready to respond, and it may be said for his work that his best introductions are yet to come. It requires much time and close attention to properly segregate, classify, test and propagate, and after having secured the desired improvement the work increases in value and results in geometrical ration as time progresses, one life affording only a good beginning for others to build upon.

American Florist 1901

Souvenir postcard, Santa Rosa.

Courtesy Luther Burbank Home & Gardens,
Santa Rosa, California

CALIFORNIA BOOSTERS AND
THE IVORY TOWER

The *San Francisco Chronicle* advocates the seizing of Luther Burbank
at his home in Santa Rosa and placing him in a chair at Stanford
University. Mr. Burbank's manipulation of plant pollen with its re-
sultant creation of new and astonishing varieties rivals Edison's jug-
glery with the electric current. . . . The main thing is to get the recluse
away from his practical experiments long enough to tell people what
he has done. —*Los Angeles Times*, June 7, 1901

The elaborate effort to transform Luther Burbank from gifted
commercial plant breeder to disinterested scientist occupied
scores of people and absorbed many thousands of dollars in the
first decade of the twentieth century. It was propelled in part by
the force of scientific inquiry that was descending on the formerly
modest world of plant breeding, but another powerful impetus was
the desire on the part of several influential people to celebrate
Burbank's achievements and, at the same time, bolster California's
reputation as an intellectual center.

There is no simple way to unravel the separate strands of science, self-promotion, boosterism, commerce, and intellectual excitement that twined around Luther Burbank at this time, but the
tangle almost certainly starts with two separate champions, Edward J. Wickson and David Starr Jordan. The University of Cali-

fornia in Berkeley, where Wickson taught, was a public institution funded by a government mandate to promote the pursuit of agriculture, which included plant breeding. Leland Stanford Junior University, thirty-five miles south of San Francisco in Palo Alto, was a private university whose founding president, Jordan, had been a student of Louis Agassiz and had a lifelong interest in botany and evolution. Without quite collaborating, both Wickson and Jordan led the effort to make Luther Burbank into a recognized leader of modern science, a flattering project in which the self-taught plant breeder was at least a somewhat willing participant.

THE FIRST THING you notice in images of Edward Wickson is the mustache, a luxurious handlebar affair with waxed and pointed tips that overshadows a trim little beard, balances his balding forehead, and makes him easy to pick out in group photographs of a century ago. There he is, escorting distinguished foreign visitors around the botanic garden that flourished on the Berkeley campus when that was the state university's only campus and the Berkeley hills, now crowded with expensive houses, were still undeveloped land. There he is, presiding over the meeting of the California State Floral Society, delivering a speech to the California Teachers Association, and lecturing to Berkeley undergraduates on California horticulture on Tuesday and Thursday afternoons. And there he is again, sitting on a fallen tree trunk next to Luther Burbank, interviewing the wonder worker of Santa Rosa for a series of articles that appeared in *Sunset* magazine beginning in 1901.

Born only six months apart, Burbank and Wickson had both come to California in 1875, Wickson from upstate New York and the same mixed landscape of agriculture and small industry that

Burbank had known in Massachusetts. A graduate of Hamilton College, Wickson combined a classical education with an interest in the dairy industry, and he became one of the many nineteenth-century journalists who covered the farm beat. He had been a reporter for the Utica (New York) *Morning Herald* when a fraternity brother invited him to California to join a San Francisco concern that published a popular farm and garden journal called the *Pacific Rural Press*. He settled in Berkeley, rose to become editor of the *Pacific Rural Press*, and remained in that position until his death in 1923, writing articles, tending to circulation, providing answers to readers' queries on a wide range of agricultural and horticultural topics, and publishing a number of encyclopedic books about California crops and growing conditions that remain extremely useful texts. A tireless writer, Wickson also contributed articles to other journals on everything from the management of the modern dairy to the future of farming in Palestine, and he drafted outlines for future books on the back of scrap paper the way other people doodle.

This would seem to be a full career, but what is remarkable about Wickson is that he continued his extensive editorial duties even after joining the Berkeley faculty in 1879. He started as a lecturer on dairy husbandry, a subject that required more practical experience than laboratory training, and he retained his preference for wisdom gained in the field long after he became a full-time member of the faculty. When Wickson was named dean of the College of Agriculture in 1905, despite the opposition of the university president, it was a tribute to his enormous popularity among California legislators and farmers.

Burbank and Wickson had known each other since at least the late 1880s, when Wickson was head of the California State Horticultural Society and Burbank submitted roses to the society's shows, and they had known *of* each other almost from the time they arrived in California. The *Pacific Rural Press* was the first place Burbank advertised in 1877, paying more than thirty very hard-earned dollars to push his Burbank potato, and Wickson was among the many editors to whom Burbank sent samples of his plums and walnuts in the years before the *New Creations* catalog of 1893. Always happy to promote a superior product of California agriculture, Wickson provided long and laudatory descriptions to Burbank's work in both the *Pacific Rural Press* and in his books. He had so many good things to say about the Perfection plum, a large heart-shaped fruit with greenish-yellow skin, that Burbank rechristened it the Wickson plum in his second *New Creations* catalog in 1894, the name by which it is still sold today.

In 1901 and 1902, Wickson was not promoting any particular Burbank fruit or flower. He was introducing Luther Burbank as a popular inventor who was also a scientist and, equally important, a model of the modesty, purity, and practical acumen that Wickson identified as the mark of true greatness. And he was doing it not in an agricultural journal but in *Sunset*, the magazine that most completely expressed the vaulting aspirations of their adopted state.

By the start of the twentieth century a lot of people were singing the siren song of California, and many special interests were trying to call the tune. One of the loudest was the voice of the Southern Pacific Railroad, which founded *Sunset* in 1898 to "chronicle the world of the West over which the dawn of future commercial and industrial importance is just beginning." Put more plainly, *Sunset* existed to persuade people to take the train to California, travel around once they got there, settle down and start a company that depended on shipping, and invite their friends from other parts to board the train and pay a visit. It also strove to balance on its pages the somewhat antithetical claims that California was at once a wide-open land of boundless opportunity and a civilized place that was already a center of artistic, economic, and intellectual achievement.

Wickson's profile, "Luther Burbank: Man, Methods and Achievements," appeared in *Sunset* in four installments from December 1901 to June 1902, several months before the second International Conference on Plant Breeding and Hybridization. It was the first serious attempt to elevate Burbank's scientific standing in the academic world of breeding plants, and it was not a simple job. By 1901, the title of "scientist" was no longer just an occupational or vocational category. It was a badge implying a certain kind of training (at a university), a certain kind of setting for conducting research (in laboratories or experimental fields with institutional affiliations), and a certain way of recording one's work (in laboratory notebooks and academic journals).

Burbank conformed to none of these definitions of the modern scientist. Neither did Wickson, but he never aspired to be anything other than a teacher and a writer, the disseminator of other people's discoveries. Wickson knew that if he wanted to claim Burbank as a scientist, he would have to redefine the term, and so he did. It was easy to praise Burbank as a lone inventor, always a beloved national type, but to make him a part of the new world of professional science required a good deal of rhetorical hocus-pocus.

Beginning with what were already conventional boasts about the size and value of California agriculture, Wickson quickly moved to the assertion that Burbank's work would make California a leader in science as well as commerce. He attributed Burbank's lack of a scientific library to his prodigious powers of retention, which allowed him to memorize books he thus had no need to own. The absence of laboratory equipment led to a comparison to David, the biblical hero who conquered Goliath with nothing but a slingshot and a smooth stone. As Wickson wrote in his inimitable way, "He cast aside the elaborate armament of his scientific brethren lest it should impede his movements." As spelled out in Wickson's articles in *Sunset*, Burbank was a scientist because of his years of study and because of the penetrating mind that allowed him to see the laws of nature behind the individual plant. Quoting a Berkeley professor of botany, Wickson assured his readers that "we have, at Santa Rosa, a laboratory for the study of variation on a gigantic scale and a magnificent array of facts and discoveries of great value to science."

Wickson praised Burbank's creations for their higher yields, extended seasons, unusual sizes, exotic colors, increased ability to survive the rigors of long-distance shipping, and all the other qualities that endeared him to commercial growers, but he insisted that these market improvements, while significant, were only part of the story. According to Wickson, California agriculture, as embodied in Luther Burbank's many plant improvements, was a force of social good that transcended mere economic development. The Burbank potato, which by then dominated the California potato industry, was a vehicle of world-saving nourishment. Burbank's roses, cannas, lilies, and gladioli brought grace and nobility to a land of abundance. Wickson was equally insistent about the inspiring purity of Burbank's soul, which made him the representative not just of California agriculture, but of the best spirit of California itself. The inescapable conclusion for anyone reading the *Sunset* articles was that better fruits and more beautiful flowers would come from better breeds of plants, that these better breeds were the product of scientific knowledge, that the plants of the future were going to be developed and grown in California, and that Luther Burbank was leading the way. In 1903, Wickson's articles reached more readers as the Southern Pacific Railroad reprinted them in a book it distributed to libraries and individuals across the country.

This was all very flattering, and it seems to have gone to its subject's head. When Burbank had moved to Santa Rosa in 1875, experimental farming was still something he could imagine doing in his front yard, and the pressing necessity had been to get a garden, not a college degree. Twenty-five years later, however, Burbank had begun to feel his work entitled him to recognition from the growing rank of scientists whose practical experience in plant breeding was nowhere near his own. One way of claiming his place among the new men of science was by contributing to scientific meetings like the 1902 second International Conference on Plant Breeding and Hybridization. Another way was by becoming a professor himself.

RAILROAD TRACKS SEPARATE commercial Palo Alto from the campus of Leland Stanford Junior University. The tracks remind us that Leland Stanford Senior made his fortune in the transcontinental railroad before serving as governor, senator, breeder of racehorses, and endower of a major institution of higher learning created in memory of his beloved only son. On October 1, 1891, the new university had held its opening day ceremonies in front of the hundred-foot-high Memorial Arch that stood at the entrance to the campus, set on an eight-thousand-acre site that had been the Stanford farm. The university's founding president, David

Starr Jordan, had rallied his first group of students and teachers with a vision of "a school which may last as long as human civilization. . . . It is hallowed by no traditions; it is hampered by none. Its finger-posts all point forward." Two years later, in 1893, Leland Stanford Sr. died and Luther Burbank published his first catalog of *New Creations in Fruits and Flowers*. For the next decade, both Jordan and Burbank worked to establish their respective enterprises. By many measures Burbank had been more immediately successful, and Jordan soon joined the ranks of those seeking to bring Burbank's achievements to campus.

Like Wickson, Jordan had grown up in the farm country of upstate New York, though he had no interest in the practice of farming and was himself a distinguished scientist. A member of the first class to graduate from Cornell University, New York's land grant college, he earned an MD and a PhD as he embarked on a career in natural history studies (from wildflowers to fossil fish) and academic administration that included his appointment, at the age of thirty-four, to the presidency of Indiana University. Arriving at Stanford when he was forty, Jordan immediately took to his unofficial position as California booster. For the next twenty-two years, he combined the roles of university president, respected researcher, and promoter of the manifold wonders of the Golden State.

Jordan met Burbank through their mutual friend Samuel F. Leib, the San Jose judge and Stanford trustee who took Burbank to the Sierras in the summer of 1902. Leib was one of the many professional men in the area who were also investing in farms and ranches, and he had sought out Burbank some time in the 1890s after reading about him in the *Pacific Rural Press*. As Leib described their first meeting, "A friendship sprang up between us which makes us like brothers." Leib and Burbank visited and corresponded for years, sharing news of promising tree varieties, the adventures of Leib's children, business opportunities, and the ever-fascinating topic of their respective ailments.

Jordan soon became another Burbank admirer, advocate, and friend, eager to hear what the plant breeder had to say on botany, evolution, and the future of agriculture in California. Jordan had a wife and six children, a household menagerie that included parrots and monkeys, and a career that encompassed teaching, fundraising, faculty recruitment, scientific publications, and a full calendar of ceremonial and administrative duties. His daily life could not have been more different from Burbank's, but they maintained a friendship based on their shared interest in plants (Burbank was often sending Jordan new specimens, particularly of fruit trees and cacti), and their shared respect for the older, more philosophical language of natural history that had been the model of their early years.

The Stanford president knew that Burbank was not a conventional scientist, at least by the new standards of the twentieth century. He had already arrived in Palo Alto when Burbank had addressed the American Pomological Society in 1895 on "How to Produce New Fruits and Flowers," instructing his somewhat surprised audience of professional nurserymen and representatives from the pomological division of the Department of Agriculture to "listen patiently, quietly and reverently to the lessons, one by one, which Mother Nature has to teach. . . . She conveys her truth only to those who are passive and receptive." Jordan had read "Some of the Fundamental Principles of Plant Breeding" and had toured the grounds in Santa Rosa, where he very probably heard Burbank's theories on the power of music, voice, and thought vibration over the growth of plants.

Jordan's own academic credentials were impeccable, but he was of the firm opinion that there were many ways of being a "scientist" and even more ways of teaching. He had learned botany by walking his father's acres in upstate New York and had spent several summers on Penikese Island, off the coast of Cape Cod, exploring marine life in outdoor classes led by the charismatic Louis Agassiz. If Burbank could come to Stanford and talk to students about what he was doing, Jordan was sure it would be a valuable educational experience.

On October 7, 1904, Burbank accepted the invitation to join the Stanford faculty as lecturer on evolution. It was the most generous of arrangements. Burbank could have whatever title he liked, lecture whenever he liked, and get paid by the lecture. There were no papers to read, examinations to grade, or other academic duties. On Wednesday, November 16, Burbank began his new career as a professor, taking the train and ferry from Santa Rosa to San Francisco and then another train to Palo Alto. He was going to meet the twenty students in Jordan's class on evolution and speak to them on the topic "Heredity." Knowing Burbank was not an experienced speaker, Jordan had assured him the class could be as informal as a conversation. Still, Burbank must have felt nervous about his new venture and the daunting prospect of standing before students who were, at least on paper, more educated than he, and he prepared a formal lecture.

In the fall of 1904, after many delays and financial struggles that followed Leland Stanford's death, Stanford University was finally beginning to look like a real campus. The Memorial Chapel had just been dedicated, and the Memorial Arch provided a gateway to Palm Drive, the tree-lined colonnade that led to the main campus. A marble statue of geologist Louis Agassiz presided over the Inner Quad with its companion statue of naturalist Alexander von Humboldt. President Jordan had his office there, near the lecture hall where his class met, and the two statues served as guardian spirits of precisely the sort of outdoor, observational science he wanted to preserve from the rising emphasis on laboratory work.

Like the members of the Pomological Society and the participants in the second International Conference on Plant Breeding and Hybridization, the students who attended Burbank's lecture heard a presentation that entirely rejected the mechanistic view of science. Instead of discussing Mendelian inheritance or Darwinian evolution, Burbank described all of nature as an intricate web of vibrations and magnetic forces where "all motion, all life, all force, all so-called matter are following the same law of heredity found in plants and animals, a forward movement toward attractions through lines of least resistance." His lecture, like his earlier speeches and papers, seemed more closely related to the Transcendental philosophers of his youth or the contemporary interest in spiritualism than to current ideas about heredity, his supposed topic.

The next month Burbank gave another lecture that was very similar. He also sent Jordan an unpublished paper that went into greater detail about his "Theory of Force and Matter," a system of vibrating energies that Burbank had been attempting to chart for several years, and which Jordan confessed he did not at all understand. By October 1905, the start of his next series of three monthly classes, the format had changed. At Jordan's urging, Burbank brought some of his lantern slides to Palo Alto, projected them on the classroom wall, and answered questions related to the images. "Here are two sets of walnut leaves," Jordan observes in the transcript of one lecture. "Tell us about that." After Burbank does, Jordan asks again, "Tell us about the Shasta daisy." This approach continued through the entire class.

Burbank's comments, if not exactly conventional discussions of plant genetics, were much more technical than the lectures of the year before. He gave straightforward descriptions of how a cross was made, what qualities he looked for in his selections, and how long it took to find them. Jordan's questions kept him focused on the details of his work with plants rather than his theories of the larger meaning of life. But now and then Burbank's deeply personal view of nature asserted itself and he could not keep himself from describing the lantern slide images in anthropomorphic terms. Jordan asked, "These poppies are quite far apart [in appearance], are they not?" And Burbank answered, "Yes, and I suppose that is why they cannot agree upon the seed. They can agree on the matter of bloom, but on the seed questions the life forces of the plant find themselves at variance."

In January 1905, Jordan published a long essay in *Popular Science Monthly* called "The Scientific Aspects of Luther Burbank's Work," which included many of the results with hybrids that had been appearing since the late 1880s, as well as more recent descriptions that may have been influenced by Burbank's interest in astronomy and electricity. Using Burbank's own archaic variations of terms that were often applied to planetary orbits but seldom to garden plants, Jordan quoted Burbank as explaining that "by [crossing] we get the species into a state of perturbation or 'wabble,' and take advantage of the 'wabbling' to guide the life forces into the desired habits or channels." This was confusing, but no more so than Burbank's assertions, which seem to be seconded by

Jordan, that mutations are only extreme examples of evolutionary change and that grafts are another form of hybrid.

The following year, Jordan's Stanford colleague Vernon Kellogg, a professor of entomology, took up the effort to boost Burbank's scientific credentials with a follow-up article in the October 1906 issue of *Popular Science Monthly*. According to Kellogg, the economic impact of Burbank's plant inventions obscured his scientific contributions. From this perspective, the myriad varieties of plums and prunes, the new kinds of berries, walnuts, roses, and all the other fruits and flowers that were so profitable for California growers were in fact a distraction. "It is obvious," Kellogg insisted, "that there must be a large accumulation of data of much scientific value in its relations to the great problems of heredity, variation and species-forming. Burbank's experimental gardens may be looked upon from the point of view of the biologist and evolutionist as a great laboratory in which there is being produced a great mass of valuable data."

At this point, we have to wonder why they were trying so hard. Nobody was struggling to make the president of the Burpee Seed Company into a scientist, after all, or calling James J. H. Gregory's potato fields a great laboratory of unrecorded information. And California had other plant breeders and a growing population of professional plant scientists. Why was it Burbank who was seized upon as the hero of the new science of California crops?

At least part of the answer lies in Burbank's strangely winning personality, a quality that many people tried and failed to describe to their own satisfaction. David Starr Jordan wrote in his "Scientific Aspects" article that "Burbank's ways are Nature's ways, for Burbank differs from other men in this, that his whole life is given to the study of how Nature does things." Vernon Kellogg attributed Burbank's success to "the inherent personal genius of the man." David Fairchild, who traveled the world for the USDA in a position with the glamorous title of plant explorer and met a good many celebrities along the way, compared Burbank to Tolstoy, "in that, when one was with him, one felt the strange force of his simplicity and his profound confidence in his own abilities." The effect faded on leaving the master's presence, Fairchild continued, but everyone who met Burbank came under his spell, and even those who later grumbled that they had been misled or even hypnotized agreed he had a mysterious quality, both in his personality and in his work, which hinted at something very important just beneath the surface, waiting to be revealed.

Burbank's great personal charm was bolstered by his almost irresistible story. In the search for a man of genius who could embody both the aspirations and the achievements of California, and particularly northern California, no other candidate rivaled Luther Burbank. To David Starr Jordan and quite a few other people of his generation, Burbank's success as a plant breeder verified the value of coming from "good stock," in this case a line of French and Anglo-Saxon ancestors that could be traced back to the earliest days of Pilgrim settlement in New England. Like Edison, Burbank also fit the extremely popular image of the self-made man of genius. And last but not at all least, he had left Massachusetts for California, enacting exactly the transfer of influence his local supporters wanted to promote.

There was another even more specific reason for promoting Burbank's qualifications as a scientist. The assembled professors were eager to prove the plant inventor was a scientist because they wanted him to win a prize they felt would bring great credit to them all. The new Carnegie Institution of Washington, D.C., was supporting major investigations into fundamental science, and many people wanted Luther Burbank to bring one of those grants to the Golden State.

"Gigantic Gargantuan Ponderosa Bigissimus Growths the Eastern Mind
Associates with the Mystic Genius of Burbank."
Country Gentleman, February 25, 1914.

THE CARNEGIE INSTITUTION
SEAL OF APPROVAL

It is Mr. Burbank's natural desire for experiment that has led him into this novel and delightful work . . . his experiments are so extensive and he tries so many things for the mere zest of it, that he does not make money . . . some philanthropist could render a good service to mankind if he would endow this experimental garden and allow its proprietor to devote his whole energy to research.

—LIBERTY HYDE BAILEY, *The World's Work*, 1901

Andrew Carnegie, the Scottish immigrant who had risen from bobbin boy in a Pennsylvania cotton mill to become one of the richest men in America, saw himself as only a steward of the great wealth he had amassed from coal, oil, and steel. While he may have turned a blind eye to the quotidian welfare of the labor force that enabled him to make his fortune, he felt it was his duty to devote much of his wealth to philanthropic causes. In 1901, he had decided to use some of his millions "to encourage in the broadest and most liberal manner" scientific studies directed toward the improvement of mankind.

To do this, he proposed an independent research center, something like the new Rockefeller Institute in New York, but with much better funding. Ten million dollars in gold bonds seemed like an appropriate endowment for what would become the Carnegie Institution of Washington, D.C. Unlike the similarly named Carnegie Institute of Pittsburgh, which began in 1900 with Carnegie's offer of one million dollars to help the city of Pittsburgh establish a place where machinists, mechanics, and other skilled workers could get technical training, the Carnegie Institution of Washington, D.C., was to support research conducted by people who had already demonstrated scientific expertise.

As soon as word of the new Carnegie Institution spread, a number of distinguished people began to campaign for Luther Burbank to receive a grant to fund his work. Most of them were affiliated with California universities, either as presidents, deans, or members of the board of trustees, but they did not accept the growing distinction between academic and applied science. They promoted Luther Burbank because they admired the results of his efforts—superior knowledge turned to practical ends—and they wanted to foster his innovative experiments. They also felt that if the inventor of new fruits and flowers could be recognized as a scientist, it would grant a special cachet to the growers and shippers who sold his products, to the new universities that were still struggling to assert themselves as intellectual centers on a par with those in the East, and to the entire state of California.

In 1903 and 1904, the campaign for Luther Burbank to receive a Carnegie grant intensified. At the University of California, Edward Wickson joined with Eugene Hilgard, the founding dean of the College of Agriculture, and Benjamin Ide Wheeler, the university president, to support Burbank's candidacy. At Stanford, Jordan championed Burbank and urged his nomination to Judge William W. Morrow, a San Francisco lawyer active in Stanford affairs who was also a trustee of the Carnegie Institution.

Another Burbank advocate was Liberty Hyde Bailey, widely considered to be the country's leading authority on botany. During this period, Bailey was refusing repeated invitations to leave Cornell for the University of California, but he did spend time in Berkeley starting in 1901, and had made it a point to visit Santa Rosa. Bailey, a gardener as cautious as Burbank was enthusiastic, was not persuaded that the Mendelian revolution was going to provide an instant improvement to the art of plant breeding, and he was also not entirely sure that all of Burbank's predictions of plant improvement would come to pass. Like most visitors, though, Bailey was stunned to see the sheer number of different plants Burbank had under development and the variety of species he was working on at once. Returning to New York, he described Burbank's efforts to improve the world through plant breeding in multiple articles that carried the judicious weight of science while clearly laying out the case for a grant in support of Burbank's work.

Other champions came from even farther away. Hugo de Vries, the best-known "rediscoverer" of Mendel, accepted an invitation to lecture at Berkeley in the summer of 1904 but confessed he had come to California largely because he wanted to meet Luther Burbank and see his gardens. Like Bailey, de Vries was thoroughly charmed by Burbank and astonished by the massive numbers of different hybrid specimens he had growing on his grounds. Burbank loaded his new friend with photographs of his creations and actual samples of leaves, flowers, and nuts, all of which were used to illustrate the lectures on Burbank's hybrids that de Vries gave in different European cities after his return from California. De Vries also wrote a glowing report, "A Visit to Luther Burbank," that was published in *Popular Science Monthly*. If Hugo de Vries, leading

Dear Sir:

Yesterday I had a glorious day delivering an address on your hybrids and methods before a distinguished audience at the Hague, the capital of our country. It was illustrated by all the photographs you so kindly sent me. . . . There was also the photograph of your residence and garden given me by the Southern Pacific Railway Co. The dried leaves and flowers you gave me, when fresh, on both my visits, especially those of the walnuts and poppies. Also the nice samples of nuts you sent me, which attracted much attention. I feel very much indebted for your friendship in procuring me the means of so delightful an address.

Yours very truly,

Hugo de Vries

expert on genetics and mutation, considered Burbank a serious scientist, it would seem hard to argue the point.

Even with this flow of endorsements, however, Burbank was not an obvious candidate for a Carnegie Institution award. The first president of the Carnegie Institution was Daniel Coit Gilman, a dedicated champion of disciplined academic science and arguably the central figure in the rise of the American university as a research center in the late nineteenth century. Gilman had studied at the University of Berlin in 1855 and returned to the United States determined to impress the stamp of German academic standards on the raw clay of American intellectual life. His entire career had been devoted to promoting a rigorous definition of academic science that was very different from anything that Burbank could ever be imagined doing.

Gilman had served for a brief time as president of the University of California in the formative years before the school even had a campus, and he recalled with special pride his battle against state legislators who wanted the new university to teach subjects he considered merely useful, rather than academic, including most of the agricultural curriculum. At Johns Hopkins University, another new institution where Gilman had been the founding president, he had proudly introduced to the United States the German system of graduate seminars, formal research, and publication in professional journals as the proper forums for the advancement of knowledge. When Gilman came out of retirement to found yet another pathbreaking research center, serving as director of the Carnegie Institution for its first two years, it was not his intention to relax his high standards.

The first nomination of Burbank for funding from the Carnegie Institution was rejected, but a year later, his supporters prevailed. On December 29, 1904, shortly after R. W. Woodward took over from Gilman as director, the Carnegie Institution announced a grant to Luther Burbank of the enormous sum of ten thousand dollars a year "for the purpose of furthering your experimental investigations in the evolution of plants." Although the period was not defined, Burbank was led to believe the grant would continue with annual payments for the next ten years.

This was the largest grant the Carnegie Institution had made to an individual, and it came with a significant share of internal dissent. With or without Gilman, the board of trustees was very hesitant to give so much money, or indeed any money, to a self-taught commercial plant breeder with no formal academic training in biology, botany, or much of anything else.

They were ignoring the fact that Burbank's bootstrap education also described their founding benefactor, who took an active interest in the institution that bore his name. Unlike academic scientists and administrators, many of them concerned with asserting a new and hard-won status as professionals, Andrew Carnegie saw Burbank as an original thinker who was blessedly untainted by the cautious concern for precedent and proof that could hamper useful invention. Carnegie was not afraid to tell his trustees that he "worried about men of science interfering with the work of a genius." Elihu Root, Theodore Roosevelt's secretary of war and a member of the board of trustees, agreed. He preferred Burbank's "extraordinary and exceptional faculty," he said, to "the careful, scientific way."

The trustees compromised. Instead of the unconditional financial support his advocates had hoped would free Burbank from the pressures of deadlines and market demands, the Carnegie money came with a stipulation: the intuitive genius of Santa Rosa was to be observed by a trained biologist with academic credentials, who would prepare a report to be published by the Carnegie Institution. It took over a year to find an acceptable candidate for this delicate task. Burbank had not been expecting to have anyone trailing him around or writing down what he was doing, and most people with the skills to translate his operations into the proper discourse of academic science were far enough advanced in their careers that they were reluctant to take on the job.

Meanwhile, in a consequence as inevitable as it was unintended (at least by the grant makers), the Carnegie Institution's recognition of Burbank's work functioned like an official seal of scientific authenticity attached to a gilded ribbon of humanitarian genius. As far as the general public was concerned, Burbank's popular identification as a wonder worker of science was now confirmed. As soon as the grant was announced, long before the official process of observing and recording Burbank's work began, the man receiving this singular honor became the subject of countless articles in newspapers and magazines.

Journalists delighted in offering highly exaggerated descriptions of Burbank's powers of plant invention. He could make plants to order, the newspapers announced. He was breeding cold-resistant bananas that would grow in Boston and lure farmers back to the abandoned fields of New England. His flowers would bloom forever, and a single fruit from Burbank's trees would be large enough to feed an entire family. And those were the serious reports.

The satires were better, and they continued for years. Cartoons were the favorite form. Luther Burbank was breeding a tree that bore shamrocks for St. Patrick's Day, or giant fruits and flowers that towered over New York City's Madison Square and threatened to crush the porters at the docks. He could teach a mango to do the tango, invent new trees under which songwriters could place their same old courting couples, or even, in the caption of a cartoon from the *Chicago Record-Herald* of August 1, 1905, "evolve from the common garden variety of grafter a new and distinct type of financier, fingerless and pocketless." *Country Gentleman,* a magazine published on oversized paper, accompanied a long cover story about Burbank with a full-page cartoon by the popular illustrator Harrison Cady. Elaborately detailed, the illustration showed a crowded landscape where enormous plants of every kind dwarfed barns, houses, railway cars, garden fences, and, of course, human beings. The caption read "Gigantic Gargantuan Ponderosa Bigissimus Growths the Eastern Mind Associates with the Mystic Genius of Burbank."

Satiric poetry was also popular. "In Luther Burbank Land," printed in the *Los Angeles Times* on November 28, 1905, proclaimed in one stanza,

> *The pear and the tomato,*
> *The pickle and the plum,*
> *Now fraternize as brothers,*
> *And I have planned some others—*
> *I've grown a sweet potato*
> *That gives us chewing-gum,*
> *Paired with the pear-potato,*
> *The pickle and the plum.*

The January 1908 *Harper's Monthly* published a satire in a similar vein, "A Burbanker," that consisted of lines and lines of punning doggerel describing new crops like celery bred to carry its own saltcellars.

Another immediate result of the Carnegie grant was a significant increase in precisely the kinds of gawkers and tourists that Burbank had always tried to discourage. The number of letters arriving from around the world asking for garden advice seemed to multiply with every delivery, and so did the requests to be allowed the enormous privilege of working for Mr. Burbank in his fields, his gardens, his greenhouse, or anywhere else he might be kind enough to provide a job. For years, Burbank had been complaining of how intensely busy he was. In his *New Creations* catalog in 1893, he had proudly quoted a journalist who called him

XXXVII

HERE I was fortunate to catch
Luthe Burbank, in his cabbage patch,
Teaching a tractable young Mango
The proper way to do the Tango.

Harper's Weekly, February 29, 1914.
COURTESY LUTHER BURBANK COLLECTION,
LIBRARY OF CONGRESS

"the busiest man in the United States," and many of his letters consisted of messages saying he was too busy to write. During the hectic early years of the Carnegie grant, when he was besieged by visitors and inundated with mail, Burbank printed postcards warning people to "ask no questions which you think can be answered elsewhere." The Santa Rosa Chamber of Commerce began to feature his name in promotional literature, and in spite of all Bur-

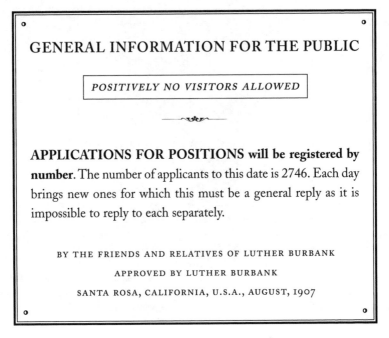

bank's attempts to discourage the merely curious, the result was caravans of tourists who expected a tour of his gardens as part of their trip. People joked that the Wizard of Santa Rosa could cross an eggplant with a milkweed to make an omelet bush, but they were determined to see for themselves the man who had mastered the secrets of nature.

As the crowds increased, Burbank's friends persuaded him to put up a large sign that advised "Private Grounds: Positively No One Allowed" over the gate of the white picket fence that surrounded his Santa Rosa garden. He printed tickets charging the considerable sum of five dollars for a brief visit with the great man, though they were not actively marketed; the object was not to make money but to thin the crowds. Tourists who wanted to visit Gold Ridge Farm, in Sebastopol, were told it would cost even more: $2.50 per quarter hour, $5.00 per half hour, and $10.00 per hour. By way of comparison, one could spend the entire day at the St. Louis Exposition of 1904 for fifty cents.

Still the visitors came, lured by newspaper features, magazine articles, books, picture postcards, and the ever-enticing Burbank catalogs. Some arrivals were too important to turn away. Starting in 1905 and continuing for the next twenty years, Burbank's guest book was a catalog of prominent people who found themselves in San Francisco and happily extended their journey to meet the famous garden genius to the north. Helen Keller, Jack London, the king of Belgium, and a constant stream of poets and actors and opera stars arrived at Burbank's door in Santa Rosa. Burbank's close friend Samuel Leib sent a letter begging him to make some time for the Prince de Croy, who was eager "to meet Mr. Burbank, the most prominent man of the world in the improvement of flowers and fruit." By then he was already receiving letters from Baron Rothschild's director of gardens, addressed to "the most celebrated grower of fruits and flowers," whose great kindness "is as well known in the whole world as your skill in the territory of Gardening and Agriculture." When Burbank heard that Hugo de Vries was returning to Berkeley in 1906, he wrote to his friend, "I am happy as a clam at high tide to think you are coming again, just simply delighted. I would rather see you than all the kings and queens that walk the earth." By then, royal visits were starting to be a fact of life, not a figure of speech.

Ordinary tourists didn't bother to write. They just showed up and leaned over the fence, trying to catch a glimpse of the wizard at work. Perhaps they came *because* of the very restrictions that made it hard to see their hero. The image of Burbank shielding his seedlings from prying eyes had enormous appeal. The fences, the warnings that no one would be admitted, even the printed reply cards announcing that Burbank was far too busy to answer mail—all of it enhanced his reputation as a solitary and dedicated genius.

Burbank was not really solitary, but he certainly had little time for such a crush of visitors and correspondents. As he understood it, the purpose of the Carnegie grant was to relieve him from the financial uncertainties of business so he could concentrate on developing his new creations without worrying about a steady flow of sales revenue. That did not mean, however, that he planned to close his business.

New generations of plumcots were demanding his attention, and he was thinking of renting some additional land for cacti to see how they would respond to different conditions. He was working on a time-consuming commission from J. H. Empson, a California vegetable canner who had asked Burbank to breed a new variety of green pea that would remain small and sweet throughout its growth, so it could be harvested by machine to compete with the French *petit pois* picked by hand every day in season. In 1905, Burbank was getting ready to introduce the Burbank cherry, the Alhambra plum, a large white asparagus that had no name as yet, and several new varieties of amaryllis, dahlia, and clematis for the flower garden. Many other plants were at earlier stages of development, to be introduced in future catalogs.

Burbank wanted to be recognized for his knowledge of plant biology, but he also wanted to be an inventor of what he called economic plants—new varieties that would have an advantage in the market and a useful place in the consumer's kitchen and garden. When he received the first payment from the Carnegie Institution, he did not use the money as a scientist would. Instead of investing in equipment, setting up a laboratory, or cutting back on his plant introductions, he expanded his enterprise. He bought more land, paid more scouts in other countries to send promising new seeds and plants, and hired more workers for the gardens and greenhouses in Santa Rosa and Sebastopol.

He also made plans to build a new house across the street. For the first time since moving to California, the fifty-six-year-old plant inventor and his mother, Olive, now ninety-one, would have a home that was separate from his place of business. The grounds and greenhouse would still be used for plant-breeding experiments, and the old house would become purely an office, with room at last to sort and store the papers that for years had been tucked in drawers and jumbled into haphazard piles. And he posed for a new photographic portrait. It was not vanity, or at least not entirely so, but a response to the rising demand. The number of newspapers asking for his picture had increased greatly since the Carnegie Institution had anointed him as that rarest of specimens: a successful businessman who was also a certified genuine scientist.

And then, just as Burbank's status as an expert in the science of plant breeding was starting to be celebrated, he took another professional detour, away from both the narrow path of academic research and the broad road of commerce. In 1905, he began to draw upon his experience as a student of nature for lessons in the raising of children.

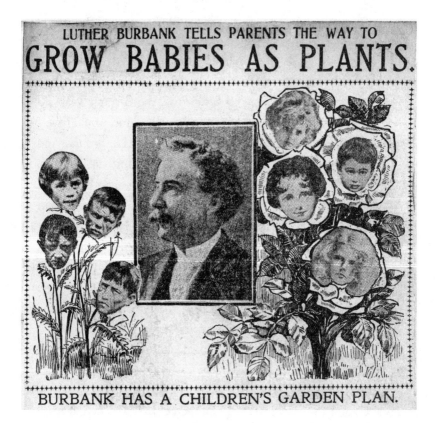

New York *Evening Journal*.

THE TRAINING OF THE
HUMAN PLANT

If we had paid no more attention to our plants than we have to our
children, we would now be living in a jungle of weeds.

—LUTHER BURBANK, 1906

The modern effort to apply the principles of selective breeding
to human society began in England with Francis Galton, a
cousin of Charles Darwin. Galton, a champion of the use of statistical methods, coined the term "eugenics" in 1883 to describe a
program of intervening in reproductive choices to improve heredity and discourage the continuation of what were considered inherited flaws ranging from deafness to criminality. From the
beginning, the parallels to selective breeding of domestic plants
and animals were obvious. The American Breeders' Association,
founded in 1903 by members of the American Association of
Agricultural Colleges and Experiment Stations to apply the new
science of genetics to agricultural science, soon had a Committee
on Eugenics. David Starr Jordan of Stanford was the committee's
head, and Luther Burbank was made an honorary member of the
association at its first meeting.

In hindsight, it is abundantly clear that the "hereditary" weak-
nesses that eugenicists reported from their studies often were the

result of economic and social deprivation or projections of the prejudices of the viewer. In the early years of the twentieth century, however, many intellectuals and activists on both sides of the Atlantic viewed the eugenics movement as an engine for positive social reform. The Rockefeller Foundation and the Kellogg Foundation each sponsored research on human genetics (an even newer and more bewildering field than plant genetics) with the aim of promoting eugenic programs in areas that included medicine, law, and education.

Another emerging center for eugenics research in the United States was the Station for Experimental Evolution at Cold Spring Harbor, New York, on the north shore of Long Island. In 1904, when the study of genetics was still in its earliest stages, the Cold Spring Harbor center began to be supported by grants from the Carnegie Institution of Washington, D.C., which was also providing funds to extend and record the breeding experiments of Luther Burbank.

Burbank was never really an active eugenicist, and in future years he would specifically criticize the movement's oversimplified and often erroneous view of heredity. He was fascinated by the debate, however, and made a thorough study of several books on human improvement given to him by David Starr Jordan in 1904. The first notice of this new interest in eugenics came at the banquet in his honor hosted by the California Board of Trade in September 1905. When he accepted the invitation, Burbank had warned the dinner's sponsors that any speech he made would be "brief, and not to the point." He lived up to his word. While the other speakers celebrated the ways Luther Burbank embodied the best of science, commerce, and humility, Burbank gave a talk that captured the headlines of all the San Francisco newspapers the following day. His topic, a subject he said he had "plunged into" recently, was the emotionally charged question of nature versus nurture as it applied to children.

Burbank's speech established a case for what might be termed the liberal fringe of the eugenics movement. In taking up the question of human improvement, Burbank did not want to limit or guide fertility. He recoiled from the idea. Instead, he defended the wonderful possibilities of human hybrids and urged his audience to embrace the vast experiment in "crossing" that the United States provided. Since chance had already mixed and transplanted the American population on a scale that even Burbank could not match, he thought it was time for society to take the next step and create an environment in which children, like plants, could be protected and improved. That was what he did in his own gardens, and that was what society should do, too.

After some pleasantries at the beginning of his talk about his own roughness as a speaker, Burbank warmed to his subject, speaking with a simple eloquence that was very different from the language of his scientific lectures. "I was brought up in a family like most of you," he began, "and my eyes have always been wide open when something appeared which promised to be useful to myself or others. Among other things, flowers and children never escape my notice." But the effort to improve plants could be frustrating indeed, Burbank continued, while "children respond to ten thousand subtle influences." And the best influence was close familiarity with the ordinary wonders of the natural world.

"Don't feed children on maudlin sentimentalism or dogmatic religion," he urged his listeners. "Give them nature. Let their souls drink in all that is pure and sweet. . . . Let nature teach them the lessons of good and proper living, combined with an abundance of well-balanced nourishment. Those children will grow to be the best men and women. Put the best in them by contact with the best outside. They will absorb it as a plant does the sunshine and the dew."

Six months later, *Century* magazine, the widely circulated successor to *Scribner's Monthly*, published an expanded version of Burbank's speech as "The Training of the Human Plant," a title that was offered and received with complete seriousness. It appeared the following year as a book, also called *The Training of the Human Plant*. Both as an article and as a book, Burbank's application of garden wisdom to the human sphere was widely read and enormously popular.

The Training of the Human Plant offers many sound observations, a good number of questionable assumptions about human inheritance, and two very striking imperatives. The one that is most often remembered, and the one that made Burbank a hero of home-schooling advocates, was his belief that formal education should not start until the age of ten, lest a child's innate love of knowledge be stifled by the rote memorization of facts. The second imperative, an idea that is as powerful and, sadly, as neglected today as it was a century ago, was his call for a national system to provide nonsectarian financial relief to those who could not afford the wholesome food and healthy environment needed to make their children strong. Spending money on children was not charity, Burbank pointed out, but an investment in the shared future of the entire country.

"The nation, or the commonwealth, should take care of the unfortunate," he told his audience. "It must do this in a broad and liberal and sane manner, if we are ever to accomplish the end sought, to make this nation rise to its possibilities. Only through the nation, or State, can this work be done."

Unlike the vast majority of people who wrote about children who were physically or mentally challenged, Burbank categorically rejected the kind of extirpation he practiced in his garden. He recognized that in society, as in the garden, unregulated "crosses" would lead to poor results as well as good ones, but there would be no human equivalent to the famous bonfires where he destroyed inferior plants. "Go to the mother of an imbecile child and get your answer. No; here the analogy must cease," he insisted. "Where is the man who would deal with such Spartan rigor with the race?" Nor did Burbank favor forced sterilization or even the "better breeding" programs advocated by David Starr Jordan, among others. Burbank instead insisted, "What we should do is strengthen the weak, cultivate them as we cultivate plants, build them up, make them the very best they are capable of becoming."

And then he gave the prescription that became the most popular, most quoted passage in *The Training of the Human Plant*, a wonderful evocation of the joys of his own childhood wandering the fields and woods of nineteenth-century New England. "Every child," Burbank wrote, "should have mud pies, grasshoppers, water-bugs, tadpoles, frogs, mud-turtles, elderberries, wild strawberries, acorns, chestnuts, trees to climb, brooks to wade in, water-lilies, woodchucks, bats, bees, butterflies, various animals to pet, hayfields, pine-cones, rocks to roll, sand, snakes, huckleberries and hornets; and any child who has been deprived of these has been deprived of the best part of his education."

It's always difficult to calculate the influence of a book, even a popular manifesto like *The Training of the Human Plant*. It seems strange that readers would welcome instructions on how to raise children from a childless plant breeder, even one who had a well-known name and had just been given an enormous and highly publicized grant to support and encourage his scientific work. Fame certainly helped Burbank find an audience, but the enduring popularity of *The Training of the Human Plant* had little to do with either the Carnegie Institution or the contemporary interest in eugenics. Its real influence came from the inherent hopefulness of Burbank's message. No child was incorrigible. Love, sunshine, wholesome food, and freedom were more powerful than authoritarian programs of religion or education.

The Training of the Human Plant tapped into a huge reservoir of popular emotion centered on both the value of home and the wisdom of nature. The parents of America, particularly the mothers, responded to Burbank's message with gratitude and admiration, as did progressive reformers. Few people were willing to go quite so far as to keep children from school until they were ten, though some admirers certainly did so. More often, Burbank's recommendations encouraged classroom lessons based more on experience and less on rote recitation for children in the early years of school. Leaders in progressive education embraced Burbank's ideas and used his book to promote plans for nature-centered schools, parks, playgrounds, fresh-air camps, schoolyard gardens, and nutrition programs for the poor. Jacob Riis, author of *How the Other Half Lives* and a leading advocate of better conditions for the children of urban slums (and not by any means a supporter of eugenics), admired Burbank and visited him when he was in California in 1909.

After the publication of *The Training of the Human Plant*, Burbank came to be regarded as a special advocate for children and even more of a popular hero than he had been before. In California, mothers' clubs launched a successful campaign to have his birthday, March 7, honored as Arbor Day. Across the country, scores of schools, parks, and nature-study clubs began to be named for the famous horticulturalist and advocate of natural education. Even the city of Burbank, California, which is named for a Los Angeles dentist, has a Luther Burbank Middle School.

In *The Training of the Human Plant* and the many speeches and interviews about child rearing he gave in following years, Burbank transformed the application of scientific methods to human reproduction from a disturbing premonition of stringent social control into an invitation for every child to realize his or her best potential. In the process, the skilled inventor of new and better plants was declared a sage who taught how to apply the solaces of nature to the human soul. While the world of science was still trying very hard to discover what it was Burbank knew about plant breeding, other groups were also turning to him for the special wisdom that came from the garden. And they all were trying to get it in writing.

Luther Burbank pollinating poppies in Santa Rosa.

∘ 11 ∘

LEARNING FROM LUTHER BURBANK

"How can and will Burbank live as Pliny lives, as Herbert Spencer lives, as Darwin lives? *By telling his story as they have done.*"

—OSCAR E. BINNER, 1910

On April 18, 1906, just as the *Century* magazine issue with "The Training of the Human Plant" was appearing in mailboxes and on library tables across the country, a massive earthquake shook the San Francisco Bay area. Ruptured water mains and gas lines soon contributed to an uncontrollable fire that consumed much of the city of San Francisco. On the Stanford campus, the Memorial Arch, with its frieze depicting "The Progress of Civilization," was reduced to rubble, and the statue of Louis Agassiz fell from its perch on the zoology building and lodged headfirst in the ground.

Many of the large brick buildings in downtown Santa Rosa were toppled, but Burbank's home, like most of the town's frame houses, was damaged but not destroyed. In what some admirers took as a sign of a divine dispensation, the glass plate negatives recording Burbank's plant creations were the only ones that survived unbroken in the downtown Santa Rosa photographer's studio where they were stored. When concerned queries came in from across the country, Burbank gave interviews, issued statements, and wrote letters to schoolchildren (his newest admirers) assuring everyone that he and his grounds were unharmed. "The clock jumped off the shelf . . . and the house was shaken up and down and sideways just as you would shake a lot of marbles in your hat," he wrote to an elementary school class in Chicago, but "not a leaf was broken off, not a tender plant was injured." Very similar assurances (minus the marbles) went to the directors of the Carnegie Institution.

An earthquake was not enough to stop Luther Burbank, and certainly not enough to impede the important mission of finding and recording the secrets of his success. A few weeks later, when much of Santa Rosa was still littered with debris and almost all of San Francisco was a smoking ruin, a group from the Carnegie Institution came to California. One of the visitors was George Harrison Shull, the young man the Carnegie trustees had at last chosen to learn Burbank's secrets and set them down in a way that met the new requirements of scientific discourse. During the summer of 1906, and for intervals over the next five years, Shull left his own research on plant genetics at the Carnegie-supported Station for Experimental Evolution in Cold Spring Harbor to try to clarify and record Burbank's methods.

Almost immediately it became clear that there were at least three big problems with the Carnegie Institution's plan to translate Burbank's work into the language of academic science. The first was that his gifts, scientific or not, were not the sort that constituted a describable and replicable system. The Carnegie Institution wanted to capture what Burbank saw when he selected one twig from another or imagined the fruitful, beautiful merger of two seemingly unrelated plants, but this would prove to be a very elusive goal. Burbank's triumphs as a breeder of new plants, the result of long and patient effort, depended on an extraordinary eye and a creative imagination that were hard to describe and almost impossible to duplicate in the way that scientific standards demand.

The second problem was that Burbank didn't want to share his knowledge. The emerging model of scientific research assumed an open exchange of ideas, with discoveries announced at conferences, published in journals and books, and spread even more widely through classrooms and other educational forums. There were no trade secrets, because the scientists were not engaged in trade. They were salaried professionals, supported by universities, government research centers, and privately funded institutions like the Rockefeller Foundation or the Station for Experimental Evolution. Burbank, however, belonged to the commercial side of scientific investigation, where new understanding is expected to lead to new products and processes. He wanted a patron, not a shadow, and he certainly had no interest in giving his methods to Andrew Carnegie or anyone else so they could profit from his hard work.

The third problem with the Carnegie Institution program for recording Burbank's work in scientific form was that George Shull was exactly the wrong person for the job. A generation younger than Burbank, Shull approached plant biology as a profession, not an adventure. He had graduated from Ohio's Antioch College in 1901 and earned a doctorate at the University of Chicago in 1904, only two years before arriving in Santa Rosa. From Chicago, he had gone to the Station for Experimental Evolution, where he was working on ways of tracing the genetic heritage of individual plant specimens. Shull was an extremely talented researcher and had a good deal of insight into Burbank's character, which he admired, but he found the older man's operations quite removed from anything he could call scientific method.

Burbank fully believed he belonged among the ranks of scientists (not to mention philosophers and educators), but he preferred to think of himself as a scientific inventor like Thomas Edison, not a laboratory investigator like George H. Shull. And he always worried about theft, of both his products and his ideas. If his methods were recorded, the special gift that separated him from other breeders might somehow be deciphered, making it possible for his work to be appropriated and reproduced on a much larger scale by anyone who had enough money to finance the process. It was one thing to help investors like Dutton and Leib go into the plum or walnut business using his special techniques to mass produce their orchards, but it was quite another to use his experimental grounds as a blueprint for someone else's production facility. Independent genius would be no match for capitalist clout, and the multitudes Carnegie envisioned as benefiting from Burbank's work would very likely do so as customers of the few who had learned how to duplicate Burbank's experiments on a larger scale.

Were his fears warranted? Yes and no. The trustees of the Carnegie Institution and Andrew Carnegie himself often spoke among themselves of the importance of deriving economic benefits from Burbank's work. By this they almost surely meant economic benefits to society, through the discovery of better, more productive plants. But it is also clear that they were not at all concerned about the economic benefits to Luther Burbank beyond the generous but finite payments of their grant. It was only natural for a commercial inventor to be ambivalent about sharing his methods and processes, even with a research center that was paying him a generous stipend.

AFTER A MONTH OF OBSERVING the master breeder at work, Shull submitted a preliminary report that would be, in fact, the only formal record to come from his years in Santa Rosa. In his report, Shull attributed Burbank's successes to a combination of ordinary methods and a vivid but limited imagination. "The general methods used by Mr. Burbank are very simple," he wrote, "consisting almost solely of cross-fertilization and selection. In most cases, when he wishes to cross two plants, self-fertilization is prevented by the removal of the anthers before they open. The pollen is then applied in one of several ways: (a) By brushing the stigmas with the freshly opened anthers, e.g., Oenothera [the evening primrose of de Vries's experiments]. (b) By brushing about in one flower with a camel's hair brush and then in another flower, e.g., Cactus. (c) By collecting unopened anthers in a watch-crystal or a tin box lid and drying, then applying to the stigma by the finger or a brush."

Looking at the scribbled mess of the nursery notebooks, with their inscrutable codes and enthusiastic but highly unscientific notations like "the best," Shull ignored Burbank's deep knowledge of taxonomy and the obvious care with which he memorized his crosses and selections. He dismissed Burbank's private system of notations as an absence of records and discounted Burbank's extraordinary ability to locate any plant in his vast experimental gardens and give a concise oral history of its development, since it was not something that was written down. This last feat—Burbank's

seemingly total recall of everything growing on his many acres—
was often noted in accounts of tours of his grounds. Casual visitors
found it impressive and scientists who struggled with their own
much smaller test plots resorted to highly unprofessional words
like "uncanny" and "mysterious" to describe Burbank's familiarity
with his plants.

Shull was not a believer in supernatural talents. In his report,
he reduced Burbank's achievements to four main points: the sen-
sitivity that allowed him to notice minute variations, the "quick
and vivid imagination" that enabled him to leap from those minute
variations to a vision of a transformed plant, the persistence to
keep with the project and continue pursuing his original vision,
and the concentration to keep all his different goals and projects
in his head. To Shull, who never really became close enough to
Burbank to know how he spent his time, the plant breeder seemed
to have little interest in the breaking news of science or the pursuit
of fundamental knowledge. Burbank's greatest innovation, Shull
decided, was the enormous scale of his experiments, and his greatest genius was in anticipating what the market would want. Other
observers found these to be very admirable achievements, but to
Shull they were the antithesis of modern science.

The more questions Shull asked about the specific steps that
went into making any particular plant, the more annoyed Burbank
became. And the more annoyed Burbank became, the more doubtful Shull grew that there were any scientific methods to record.
They maintained a polite relationship that even had moments of
mutual admiration, but each found the other trying to be around.
Shull wrote to Washington complaining that Burbank was not
giving him enough time, and Burbank wrote (more briefly) complaining that Shull was impossibly demanding and verbose.

In addition, Shull was a student of Mendelian genetics at a time when it was felt that to follow Mendel you had to reject Darwin. Shull took Burbank's admiration for Darwin and his indifference to statistical records as additional proof of his lack of scientific insight. He was ready to admit Burbank's genius for the mass production of plants, but that was about all he could see that constituted news.

It is interesting that Shull paid almost no attention in his report to hybrid cactus, a highly commercial crop that was absorbing a great deal of Burbank's time during this period, and gave no notice at all to *The Training of the Human Plant*. In truth, he seems to have been embarrassed about his Santa Rosa assignment, which he rarely mentioned later in his career. Instead of regarding Burbank's commercial successes as proof of the value of his contribution, Shull felt that an interest in what were called "economic plants" signaled a lack of seriousness unless it was also a contribution to pure knowledge, and he wanted to make sure his contact with the plant breeder did not stain his own emerging professional reputation. Burbank, for his part, found the whole arrangement very uncomfortable and instinctively shrank from Shull even when he sincerely believed he was cooperating.

Shull did have cause for complaint. He asked for technical explanations and instead was handed scrapbooks full of newspaper clippings that were long on enthusiasm but conspicuously short on reliable facts. He wanted interviews and was given hurried, off-putting promises that Burbank would be available another day. What most astonished Shull, though, and angered the directors of the Carnegie Institution, was that Burbank had made a unilateral decision that if there was going to be any attempt to record his work, there might as well be several.

. . .

THE CARNEGIE INSTITUTION'S PROJECT was not by any means the only effort to learn from Luther Burbank, or to publish the results. By the time George Shull arrived in Santa Rosa, the attempt to understand and record Burbank's wisdom had become a well-established business. Emma's scrapbooks of newspaper clippings bulged with articles by and about her brother, often the same piece reprinted in several different places, jammed together every which way in an unattributed, undated, only roughly chronological patchwork of adoration. By 1906, however, newspapers had been eclipsed by more substantial accounts.

Edward Wickson had started the Burbank literary industry with his articles in *Sunset* beginning in 1901. In 1904, a journalist named W. S. Harwood had published a hugely laudatory magazine account of Burbank's work that he soon expanded into a book called *New Creations in Plant Life*, which appeared in 1905. Harwood combined Burbank's optimistic projections of the future productivity of new plant varieties with his own faulty arithmetic to produce very exciting but impossibly exaggerated statements of how Burbank plants would soon cover the earth. David Starr Jordan had already published the first article in *Popular Science Monthly* that in 1909 would form part of *The Scientific Aspects of Luther Burbank's Work*.

Liberty Hyde Bailey and Hugo de Vries were only two of the several other scientists who had also published their own descriptions of Burbank, his gardens, and his work. Now the Carnegie Institution seemed to feel its grant included the right to gather material for its own published book on Burbank's methods. Each account was colored by the intellectual capacities and commercial calculations of the author, and Burbank, unable to control this flow of information, seems to have concluded he might as well let them all happen at once and collect whatever profits he could from the process.

The result was a circus of competing authors, all operating in the small arena of Luther Burbank's gardens. In the summer of 1906, when Shull arrived in Santa Rosa to start gathering scientific information, Harwood was back seeking additional interviews for a revised edition of *New Creations in Plant Life*, which would be reprinted at least three times over the next two decades. Harwood had been writing about Burbank before the Carnegie Institution came on the scene, but what really shocked Shull was the news that Burbank had just signed an agreement with Dugal Cree, a Minneapolis publisher, for an illustrated ten-volume set of books about Burbank's work that would be sold by subscription to a popular audience. As Shull reported to his superiors with some incredulity, "Mr. Burbank informed me that the Cree books cannot in the least conflict with our work. He says that the 10 volumes will not contain as much 'meat' as ten pages of the Carnegie work." That was not a very comforting assurance, of course. It is hard to imagine how Shull and his superiors could have been anything but embarrassed by the vision of traveling salesmen peddling a multivolume illustrated history of . . . well, it wasn't clear what, but surely something that would diminish their own subsequent effort.

Cree himself went back to Minneapolis early on, after hiring a local minister to do the writing for his multivolume project and a junior professor from Stanford to check the science. At times there was the ludicrous situation of two or even three different writers simultaneously trying to get information from Burbank, who was himself trying to avoid them all and go about his work. George Shull was up early to waylay Burbank as he inspected his experimental gardens; William Harwood was back for new material for later editions of *New Creations in Plant Life* that promised to be no less exaggerated than the first; and William Mayo Martin, Cree's first writer, was ensconced in Burbank's original frame house, poring over piles of scrapbooks and catalogs.

Personal tragedy, too, clouded Shull's summers in Santa Rosa. He had married soon after he left Santa Rosa in 1906 and returned in the summer of 1907 with his very pregnant bride of eleven months. The baby died at birth, the mother a few days later. Shull bought a plot at the Odd Fellows Cemetery in Santa Rosa big enough for his wife and child and, later, himself, and never discussed his loss. He resumed work, but still Burbank wasn't giving him much time. In 1908 Shull was back again, and again in the summer of 1909, accompanied by his second wife. So were the other writers, and the ever-growing throng of reporters.

It was an impossible situation, and many people blamed Burbank for allowing his reputation and his work to be tarnished by what they perceived as a proliferation of unseemly commitments. Only a few years before, he had been lauded as a man of rare and special knowledge, a wonder-working humanitarian who was also a seemingly boundless source of new and useful products. Then, as often happens with cases of extreme infatuation, many of those early admirers tried to dismiss their former passion for Burbank and his works. By 1909, the effort to enshrine the plant breeder within the scientific pantheon was falling apart.

Burbank's last important scientific paper, "Another Mode of Species Forming," foreshadowed his fall from academic favor. The paper, read at the American Breeders' Association meeting in

January 1909 and reprinted in *Popular Science Monthly* in September, detailed Burbank's conviction that it was possible to create hybrids that were a distinct new species and that would breed true from seeds. Hugo de Vries, who just a few years before had been eager to study all of Burbank's creations, now rejected Burbank's evidence of "true-breeding hybrids" as little more than a recombination of traits present in the parent plants. Decades later, the effect that Burbank lacked the means to prove would be validated as polyploidy, the condition of having more than two homologous sets of chromosomes. When he presented his paper, however, his findings were dismissed and his reputation as a scientist discredited.

In the community of commercial plant sellers, too, Burbank was suffering a backlash from the earlier raptures over his work. He had recently introduced the Sunberry, a cross of two varieties of common nightshade—neither of them poisonous but neither very good to eat. The new berry tasted better than either of its parents, especially when cooked. John Lewis Childs, still one of Burbank's best customers, bought the rights for around three hundred dollars, bred great quantities on his grounds in Floral Park, renamed it the Wonderberry, and began an enormous advertising campaign built around Luther Burbank's name. Almost immediately the *Rural New Yorker*, which in 1890 had boosted Burbank's career by devoting its entire front page to his new achievements, started a campaign to discredit the Wonderberry. The so-called new berry, they said, was nothing more than black nightshade, a common nonpoisonous garden weed. That doesn't seem to have been true, though it is possible that Childs's stock may have become contaminated in the field. In any case, the attack was on.

Accusations, denunciations, and satires circulated through the agricultural press that had once been ready to promote and applaud anything that Burbank sent them. The 1909 Boston Flower Show judged the Wonderberry a failure, and Burbank's attempts to defend his hybrid led to new rounds of attacks. In July 1909, the Department of Agriculture surprised fruit canners by informing them that jam containing Burbank's plumcots would have to be labeled as mixed fruit, because the government didn't believe it was a true hybrid. The Pasadena Garden Club passed a resolution condemning Burbank's "nature-faking methods" and unseemly desire for publicity. The motion was led by a club member who failed to mention his true grievance, that he had not been paid for work he had done for one of the several companies trying to publish books about the plant breeder. Burbank, who still managed all his affairs with only the assistance of gardeners, secretaries, well-meaning friends, and his sister Emma, had no one with the skills to help him respond to these attacks.

The bad news continued. In December 1909, Olive Burbank died at the age of ninety-six. Emma was at her bedside, but Luther was in San Francisco on business and didn't make it back in time for her final moments. In all of her son's life, they had lived apart for only two years. A few weeks later, at the very end of the year, Burbank received a different shock, less personal but much more humiliating. Robert S. Woodward, president of the Carnegie Institution, wrote to inform him that the board of trustees had "determined to discontinue subsidies in aid of your horticultural work."

Woodward had been warning Burbank that he needed to drop his arrangements with other publishers and cooperate more fully with Shull's efforts. Now he deemed it "unnecessary here to set forth the reasons which have led to this action." Not long after,

David Starr Jordan, still president of Stanford University and still Burbank's friend, suggested that it might be better for everyone if Burbank no longer burdened himself with the obligation of giving lectures on evolution or maintaining a faculty appointment. Burbank's uncontrolled, undocumented experiments created some wonderful new plants, but they weren't leading to the kind of recordable knowledge with replicable results that is the goal of academic science.

Burbank was bitterly insulted by the termination of the Carnegie grant, although he tried to treat the cancellation as a welcome liberation. In January 1910, he wrote to Samuel Leib congratulating himself on getting out from under the Carnegie yoke. "I have greatly rejoiced to be let loose from this infernal arrangement," he wrote his old friend, a man who had worked very hard to get Burbank the grant in the first place.

> *I am happier than I have been for five years and my friends say I am looking better, and I am certainly gaining flesh. This being tied up with a lot of old antiquarian so-called scientific galoots has satisfied me that a man should run his own business whatever else he does and quit when he is not able to do so—then work for somebody else who can run their own business. The whole thing now looks ludicrous to me from beginning to end, and if you hear of anybody who wants to annex themselves to my institution, tell them that I am now up to snuff and you do not think it will be a "go."*

THERE ARE MANY WAYS to foster a greater understanding of plants. If you wanted to create a repository of unchanging botanical information, you could establish a herbarium, a vast collection of plant specimens like any one of the six that now make Harvard University's collected herbaria the largest at any university and one of the largest in the world. You could go further and found a hortorium, as Liberty Hyde Bailey did at Cornell University, "a place for the scientific study of garden plants, for their naming, for their classification, and their documentation" that included a herbarium within an even grander center of horticultural knowledge. You might decide to endow a free-standing institution like the Station for Experimental Evolution at Cold Spring Harbor, where research on plant genetics could be conducted very far indeed from the hubbub of the marketplace. You could found an entire campus for agricultural instruction and research like the University Farm founded in Davis, California, in 1905, championed by Edward Wickson and dedicated to the premise that the best place to promote new agricultural practices was in an academic environment, sheltered from the financial concerns that beset ordinary farmers.

If you wanted to sell the fruits of your knowledge, however, or just sell fruit, you would have to go out and mix in the somewhat dirtier world of commerce. In 1910, when the Carnegie Institution grant ended, Burbank was over sixty. Although his doubts about the rigid fixity of Mendelian inheritance and his insistence that hybrids could sometimes be considered distinct new species would eventually prove to be correct, he was no longer considered a member of the scientific community. Angry and annoyed, he went back to business. He still had a very grand international reputation and a large experimental garden that was expensive to maintain. So he began to sell himself.

Of course, *began* is not the right word, because Burbank the man had always been a big part of the Burbank brand. The early end of the Carnegie Institution grant was a sign that the world of science was moving on without Luther Burbank, but that did not mean the end of the public fascination with the man and his work. Quite the contrary. The information sought by the Carnegie Institution and the larger society of plant scientists was only one way of understanding the garden. Ordinary people still wanted to know all about Luther Burbank—what he looked like, what his gardens looked like, what kind of shovel he used, what hat he wore, what he thought about children, poetry, immigration, world peace, and any number of other things that a disinterested observer might think were outside his areas of expertise. Most of all, they still wanted to understand the secrets of his garden, and in terms they could comprehend.

No one was more sympathetic to this pent-up demand than Oscar E. Binner, a Chicago publisher who had bought out Dugal Cree's book contract and was determined to publish a lavishly illustrated, definitive record of Burbank's work. According to Binner, the books that Burbank had dismissed as containing less "meat" than ten pages of the Carnegie report were going to be essential reading for every farmer, orchard grower, lumberman, gardener, and student in the country, "as necessary as a plow, a hoe, a harvester, and a spade," while also becoming a tasteful addition to every public, private, and academic library.

Binner's dream was not just a set of books, but an association of Luther Burbank admirers who would purchase their volumes through advance subscription, support the enterprise with their membership dues, and have the opportunity, in return, to contribute their own editorial comments to the books before they went to press. In 1910, as though to replace the Carnegie Institution with a much larger circle of supporters, he designed elaborate invitations to join the Luther Burbank Society, printed in black gothic script with huge red-letter capitals, and mailed to a very long list of college professors, government agronomists, school principals, librarians, journalists, bankers, and other prospective buyers.

Binner, who had gotten his start in advertising, believed fervently in Luther Burbank's genius and in the commercial prospects of anything accompanied by lavish color illustrations. He spent over a year desperately trying to draw together the earlier drafts of the multivolume series Cree had started, the alphabetical files of notes on Burbank plants that George Shull had left in Santa Rosa, the occasional handwritten scraps Burbank would provide, the voluminous but rambling interviews compiled by company secretaries, and the often grossly exaggerated information contained in Emma's scrapbooks of newspaper clippings. He moved with his family from Chicago to Santa Rosa to supervise the project. He was willing to invest in any number of photographers, researchers, typists, stenographers, and writers to bring Luther Burbank's garden secrets to the waiting public.

Meanwhile, Burbank himself, still eager to pursue his lifelong calling as "evoluter" of new and better plants, continued to introduce a wide variety of them. He had returned to his gardens, the actual fields of his tangible triumphs, and he was putting his energy into what had always been his passion: accelerating evolution, perturbing nature, and nurturing the very best of the oddities that rose out of that creative tumult. In the years between 1910 and 1915, Burbank introduced dozens of new fruits, vegetables, and grains. He began working on wheat, oats, and at least seven different varieties of corn (Aurora, Burbank, Burbank Early Sweet, Burbank's World Wonder Sweet, Rainbow, and Select Orange). During these five years he also introduced a sunflower bred for

BURBANK'S EXPERIMENT FARMS, SANTA ROSA, CAL.
THIRD RHUBARB BULLETIN
"The Most Valuable Vegetable Production of the Century."

The great value of Rhubarb as a vegetable has always been its earliness, and a vast amount of time and labor has been spent during the last two centuries in efforts to originate a variety which would produce stalks even **a day or two** in advance of other early varieties. My New "Crimson Winter" Rhubarbs will produce marketable stalks **abundantly full six months earlier than any other Rhubarb. [1910]**

higher seed yield, a New Early Burbank tomato (now regarded as an heirloom variety), and several early versions of his rainbow chard, a vegetable so pretty it was also promoted as an ornamental plant. The giant Santa Rosa artichoke was a selection made from seeds Burbank had received from Victor Emmanuel III, the king of Italy and another member of Burbank's international coterie of garden admirers. And the evening primrose, the humble flower that was the subject of Hugo de Vries's research on mutations, became a favorite of home gardeners when Burbank introduced a variety whose blossoms were much larger than usual, reaching five inches in diameter, and pure white instead of the more common yellow.

Even if Burbank was no longer hailed as the man who could explain the secrets of genetics, he was still regarded by many as a potential solver of the world's agricultural problems. In 1912, a Colorado potato grower with the somewhat unfortunate name of Eugene Grubb, having completed a government-sponsored tour of European potato fields, published a call for greater potato production to prevent global starvation. His book, simply called *The Potato*, was dedicated to three men: James Wilson, the U.S. secretary of agriculture; W. C. Brown, president of the New York Central Railroad and sponsor of the book; and Luther Burbank, "the world's greatest plant breeder."

Burbank was also featured as the subject of a cover story in the November 1912 issue of *The Craftsman*, a magazine put out by the popular lecturer and philosopher Elbert Hubbard, a leader of the Arts and Crafts movement in the United States (and uncle of Scientology founder L. Ron Hubbard). Hubbard had established a community of artisans in East Aurora, New York, to produce work based on preindustrial ideals of craftsmanship, but he greatly admired Luther Burbank, the mass producer of agricultural miracles. *The Craftsman* story, "What One Man Has Done to Lower the Cost of Living: A Sketch of Luther Burbank, Increaser of Harvests," managed to combine almost all the popular perceptions of Burbank in one account, including the breathless claim that "scarcely a harvest will be gathered into barns this fall, or a feast spread on our national day of Thanksgiving, that will not have been directly or indirectly increased and benefited by the inspired vision and patient labor of a childlike and loveable, yet profoundly scientific, man living in a small corner of the Far West."

Meanwhile, Oscar Binner was still in Santa Rosa, pressing for more information for his books. In 1912, in what may have seemed like a way of persuading Burbank of his seriousness, Binner hired yet another writer: Edward Wickson, the man who had written the first long tribute to Burbank's work over a decade before. Like so many others, Wickson had toyed for several years with the idea of writing his own book about Burbank, so the project was a welcome opportunity. Binner's offer of several thousand dollars was another incentive, and the ever-prolific Wickson, about to retire from the University of California, assured the publisher that six months would be ample time to complete what was now projected as a twelve-volume set of books.

The job was enormous, and with it came the task of maintaining a voluminous correspondence with Binner, a man who easily matched Wickson in the flow of words. After several months of work, Wickson was shocked to learn that Binner had sold the Luther Burbank Society, with its glorious brochures and membership certificates, and returned to Chicago. The new owners promptly incorporated as yet another company, the Luther Burbank Press, hired their own writer to complete the series, and strenuously evaded Wickson's letters asking about payment. Trying to mend the resulting breach, Burbank insisted to Wickson that he had no control over what he called the Cree-Binner project, and very little knowledge of their operations. This was probably true, though in the same inadequate way that stockbrokers and movie stars from time to time explain their failure to pay income taxes by saying they had little actual knowledge of what their accountants were doing. Wickson blamed Burbank for the whole mess, and it was the end of their long friendship.

Luther Burbank, His Methods and Discoveries and Their Practical Applications finally appeared in 1914, having gone through at least six writers. The last author, and the only one who received any credit, was a writer identified as "Henry Smith Williams, M.D., LL.D.," whose chief qualification seems to have been that he had already completed a five-volume *History of Science*. Given their troubled history, the books are surprisingly readable, though often inaccurate and far from the required public-school textbook or salvation of the modern farmer that Binner had originally projected. They contained a competent assembly of just about everything Burbank had ever done, or thought, or thought of doing, combined with numerous complete flights of fancy, a great many eugenic-inspired asides about national character that seem to have been a favorite topic for Williams, and a healthy mix of the kind of useful garden instruction found in any beginner's guide. This was all patched together with many odd changes of tone that reflected the project's multiple authors, and interlaced with color photographs every few pages that often recorded uninspiring things like garden tools and seed bags. As promised, the members of the Luther Burbank Society received their twelve-volume set, autographed by Luther Burbank and bound in elegant tooled leather. Expenses had been high, though, and by 1916 the Luther Burbank Press had gone out of business, taking the Luther Burbank Society with it.

Surprisingly, the end of the Carnegie grant had not meant the end of the book the Carnegie Institution still hoped to publish. In theory, George H. Shull was still at work when the Luther Burbank Press books came out, though in fact he had made little or no progress beyond compiling notes on different plants growing at Burbank's experimental grounds. Shull was traveling in Europe when *Methods and Discoveries* was finally published, and he seemed to have greeted the news with both embarrassment and relief. He informed Charles Davenport, head of the Station for Experimental Evolution, that he did not feel there was any point in continuing his Burbank reports. Davenport replied with a one-word telegram: STOP.

In the future, Shull's own career would continue to prosper. He founded the journal *Genetics* in 1916, continued working at Cold Spring Harbor until 1917, and then became a professor of botany at Princeton, where he would remain on the faculty until his retirement in 1942. More than thirty years after he stopped working on the Carnegie report, Shull was still holding on to his personal notes from those years in Santa Rosa. In the 1940s, when a librarian at Berkeley asked if he would consider contributing relevant papers to their growing collection of Burbank material, Shull refused, saying they represented "a large personal equity" that he still intended to use. He never did, and he never returned to Santa Rosa until his death in 1954, when he was buried next to his first wife in the Odd Fellows Cemetery.

But that is not the end of the story of Luther Burbank and George H. Shull. For both men, the collaboration on a report for the Carnegie Institution had been a secondary project. What occupied the main part of their time were two entirely separate experiments, each of which had the potential to transform the future of food supplies. One was triumphant and the other became a footnote in agricultural history, but they deserve to be considered together.

THE SPINELESS CACTUS
A RESULT OF
MR. LUTHER BURBANK'S
WORK

· 12 ·

THE CORN PALACE
AND THE EMPIRE OF
THE PRICKLY PEAR

The Corn Palace in Mitchell, South Dakota, is a regular stop for travelers on their way to or from Mount Rushmore, three hundred miles west on Interstate 90. Tour buses stop at the Corn Palace because it is in the middle of a long road with few other attractions and also because it is, in itself, alluringly bizarre. A large building of vaguely Moorish design, the Corn Palace began in 1892 as a temporary edifice rising anew from the fields every summer, constructed from the very product it was meant to display. Since 1921 it has been a permanent building, but it is still decorated inside and out with mosaics made entirely from dried ears of corn of different colors, carefully arranged and nailed in place.

As the name suggests, the Corn Palace is the royal home of the local monarch, corn. Like Versailles, the palace of the Sun King, it is designed for show, and every element reflects the glory of the ruling vegetable. From streetlamps to trash cans, the town of Mitchell is festooned with decorative motifs in the shape of ears of corn, and the local stores and restaurants are relentless in their homage to the power and glory of this mighty crop. But unlike other South

Dakota tourist attractions—the World's Largest Pheasant, the World's Largest Hairball, the National Presidential Wax Museum, or the 563-foot-high memorial to Chief Crazy Horse begun by Korczak Ziolkowski in 1948 and nowhere near completion—the Corn Palace is not a monument to obsessive-compulsive behavior on a grand scale.

It is and always has been an unapologetically commercial structure, the last vestige of a kind of agricultural bragging house that was once fairly common. It was built to lure visitors, sell real estate, promote various political causes, and display the astounding variety of the local crop. The planners had been inspired by Iowa's even larger corn palace in Sioux City and the Blue Grass Palace in Creston, a turreted affair that was all about grain and had nothing to do with country music. In South Dakota, which seemed to have been particularly partial to this sort of thing, there was another Corn Palace in Gregory and a Grain Palace in Plankinton. Today the one in Mitchell is the sole survivor, a giant souvenir stand whose thousands of corn-themed products obscure the fact that corn has become both a more dominant and a less diverse crop since the Corn Palace was built.

What changed everything was the introduction of hybrid corn. And the person generally credited with the original research that led to hybrid corn was none other than Burbank's frustrated chronicler, George Harrison Shull. While Burbank was working in his large-scale Darwinian way, hoping to speed up evolution by raising "over a million seedling plants . . . each year for selection and for the study of variation from the effects of crossing," as he had boasted in a letter to the Carnegie Institution, Shull was doing his own research on what was beginning to be called plant genetics, concentrating his attention on corn.

In the early years of the twentieth century, farmers competed to raise the best corn. Even when saving their finest ears to use for seed, however, they had few ways of guaranteeing that future crops would repeat past successes. Corn is the most promiscuous of plants, given to spontaneous flings that made it impossible to be sure what kind of crop would emerge from last year's seed. Every stalk contains both male pollen in the tassels and female pistils hidden under the broad leaves, and the chance of limiting reproduction to a selected mix is as slim as the possibility of an entire summer of totally windless days. Given the normal course of events—including not just wind but also bees, rain, and any number of other unpredictable and anonymous agents—pollen from the male tassels will spread over great distances. Seven hundred feet is suggested as a minimum distance between plants to control cross-pollination, but in fact corn pollen can and will travel much farther.

Farmers had understood at least the rough mechanics of how to hybridize corn since the eighteenth century, but they did not know how to control that hybridization to create reliably good lines of seed. They also were aware of heterosis, or hybrid vigor, by which the product of a cross was often stronger and better yielding than either of the parents but then inexplicably declined in subsequent generations. Darwin had explored heterosis briefly in his 1876 study *Effects of Cross and Self Fertilisation in the Vegetable Kingdom*, noting the remarkable improvements that could result from hybridization (and providing much of the inspiration for Burbank's work). In 1877, William James Beal of Michigan Agricultural College managed what seem to have been the first controlled crosses between two varieties of corn, again producing noticeably better crops. Beal's method of hybridizing—removing tassels by hand from one of his corn varieties to control the source of pollination—has been used in various forms ever since, and detasseling corn remains a familiar summer job for teenagers in the Corn Belt, but it took George Shull and his successors to make Beal's work productive enough to be worth the effort.

In the years of the Carnegie Institution grant, Burbank cultivated a patch of teosinte, corn's ancient ancestor, in his garden in Santa Rosa, along with several kinds of modern corn, including a variety with rainbow leaves that attracted a great deal of publicity as an ornamental crop. Burbank was interested in corn because he was interested in everything; even today, biologists are unsure of the genetic and environmental factors that influenced the development of modern corn, and a century ago they were debating whether teosinte was even the correct ancestor. At the same time, Shull was spending the winter months in his laboratory at Cold Spring Harbor on a much more focused project: trying to trace the genetic inheritance of specific ears of corn by counting the number of rows of kernels.

Shull's contribution to modern agriculture—and it was huge—was to develop a way of creating consistent lines of hybrid corn that had, each generation, the famous "hybrid vigor" that led to astonishing increases in yield. His methods were the opposite of Burbank's. He cultivated a single species in carefully controlled situations, self-fertilized his corn for inbred purity, and then sheltered it from the kind of happy accident that Burbank was always ready to entertain. No bees here. No breezes. Not very good corn, either, though that was beside the point; the inbred line was going to be weak, but if he crossed two of these inbred lines, the next generation would be very strong.

Shull was the first to show how to produce reliably vigorous and consistent hybrids, an enormous breakthrough in the continuing search for more productive corn. He also grasped the commercial implications of his work. Inbreeding the parent lines was difficult and expensive—not something that farmers would do. Saving the seed of hybrid corn was possible, but it was guaranteed to produce decreasingly good results because of the loss of hybrid vigor. As Shull noted in a 1908 paper for the American Breeders' Association, the declining quality "[makes] it necessary to go back each year to the original combination, instead of selecting from among the hybrid offspring the stock for continued breeding." In other words, if farmers wanted the higher yields that resulted from heterosis, they would have to buy new seed every season.

After Shull announced his results with inbred lines of hybrid corn in 1908, he moved on to other research. The successful means of making hybrid corn on a commercial scale would be developed over the next decade by Donald F. Jones, head of the Connecticut Agricultural Experiment Station, who started with Shull's findings and added a second generation double-cross of the original hybrid, producing enough seeds to be marketed at an attractive price but still using inbred strains that would not grow true in the next generation. In 1926, Henry Wallace founded the Hi-Bred Corn Company after studying both Shull's and Jones's research. By 1962, over 95 percent of the corn grown in the United States was hybrid varieties.

In one of the many missed opportunities that make Shull's work with Burbank such a saga of noncommunication, Burbank had already observed that recrossing a hybrid in the successive generations would often "fix" its inheritance, but Shull had taken no notice of his finding. Burbank didn't explore the implications of Shull's research either, and may not have even known what it was Shull did in the winter months. In the future, hybrid corn would produce yields that would have seemed fantastic to a farmer in the first decade of the twentieth century, and much of that new corn would be used for cattle feed.

Grass-fed beef—like the analog clock, the acoustic guitar, and the gin martini—is a descriptive name that had to be coined after World War II to distinguish it from the newer product (digital, electric, vodka, or, in this case, corn-fed) that had suddenly become the norm. Over the past fifty years, corn has come to be the main source of cattle feed in the United States. Most cattle today are fattened up, or "finished," in feedlots. In recent years, as corn prices have risen in the wake of increased ethanol production and greater global demand, feedlot owners seeking cheaper alternatives have turned to barley, peas, soybeans, potato peelings, and even processed potato confections like hash browns and Tater Tots. Anything, it seems, is better than letting the beef out of the pen.

A hundred years ago, things were different. In those days, cattle grazed. Ranchers took their herds out to pasture in the summer and mowed hay to dry for feed during the winter, using corn and other fodder to supplement the hay. The expansion of cattle ranches into the desert regions of the American West, where grass did not grow, as well as to the arid stretches of South America, Spain, India, New Zealand, and Africa, raised real questions as to what all those animals would eat. Pumpkins had been raised for fodder when Burbank arrived in Santa Rosa, but he had a different idea. During the early years of the twentieth century, and particularly when George Shull was making regular visits to Santa Rosa, Luther Burbank thought spineless cactus might be the answer.

. . .

THE DEVELOPMENT OF SPINELESS CACTUS was a typical Burbank quest, taking a plant with limited economic value and making it useful and profitable by "persuading" it to undergo a rapid
and fundamental change. Ranchers already fed their cattle the
broad paddles of desert cacti during times of drought, but the
thorns, or spines, would tear the animals' mouths and lodge in
their tongues. Removing cactus spines from an animal's mouth was
a laborious process. So were the two other options: burning the
spines off with a kerosene torch or rubbing them off with special
abrasives. Since the desert was not a place with a lot of workers
available to do such intricate hand labor, it seemed like a very good
idea to get rid of the spines another way.

That was where the wizard hybridizer came in, at least according to the optimistic reports that filled the popular newspapers at
the height of the spineless cactus craze from 1905 to 1915. After
all, much of Burbank's reputation came from making plants relinquish what would have seemed to be an essential, defining char-
acteristic. If he could breed a white blackberry, a fast-growing
hardwood, or a stoneless plum, and had photos to prove it (an
increasingly important form of evidence), a spineless cactus seemed
a perfectly plausible addition to the list.

It was an experiment that had been going on for years. When
Burbank arrived in California in 1875, he had been entranced by
the many local varieties of cacti, some of which grew to enormous
size and many of which could survive in relatively cold climates. He
began to experiment, expanding his cactus nursery over the years
by his usual method of gathering plants from distant regions to see
if and how the change of environment might jolt them into faster

variation, then following this by massive hybridizing and selection. After his work started to attract national publicity in the 1890s, admirers began sending him unusual plants, including many different varieties of cacti. Professional plant hunters also knew of Burbank's interest, and by the start of the twentieth century he had cacti from all over California and from states as unlikely as Maine and as close as Arizona, as well as from Australia, Japan, Hawaii, Sicily, Africa, Mexico, and several countries in South and Central America.

Burbank was particularly interested in the prickly pear, or *Opuntia*, a fast-growing cactus species that had not only broad paddles but also edible fruit that had long been part of the diet of desert dwellers. He knew the spineless cactus would need some irrigation to grow in the driest regions, as well as fencing to protect it from desert animals in search of food, but those details were often ignored as glowing reports of his newest plant invention spread.

Today, breeding the thorns out of cactus so it will be better suited for grazing cattle seems like a very hard way to find a new source of animal feed, but a hundred years ago the possibility of a spineless cactus drew interest around the world. Government agents arrived from as far away as Russia and New Zealand to inspect Burbank's experimental cactus gardens. Brazil, Mexico, and Argentina all invited Burbank to advise them on cactus cultivation. John Rutland, an Australian plant retailer who spent several years in Sebastopol observing Burbank's work, was the earliest buyer, acquiring the rights to five different varieties of Burbank cacti in 1905. In South Africa, where Burbank had recently been voted one of the two most admired Americans (after Teddy Roosevelt), other buyers came forward, and initial plantings in India were reported to be doing very well. Prickly pear had already been

> It is very desirable that the cactus should take as soon as possible an important place in the agricultural regions where prolonged droughts make it very difficult to furnish stock with juicy food where it is almost indispensable during periods of great heat. Many of our colonies would find it greatly to their advantage to cultivate the cactus; and every possible attempt should be encouraged to disseminate it and perfect its culture in Senegal, Sudan, the greater part of Madagascar, in some districts of New Caledonia and Indo China.
>
> *Journal d'Agriculture Tropicale*, Paris 1904

Quoted in *The New Agricultural-Horticultural Opuntias*

introduced to North Africa from the western hemisphere as a source of both water and nutrition for cattle, and the spineless variety was soon planted in Algeria.

The high hopes for the spineless cactus grew out of genuine need, but they were also kept aloft by the pervasive get-rich-quick mentality of California itself. At the start of the twentieth century, when the film industry had not yet arrived in Los Angeles, the dream machine in the Golden State was agriculture. From grapes to olives to rice to cotton, growers were busy introducing exotic crops to a landscape that they continued to treat like an agricultural blank slate, a place where success could bring fabulous profits and failures could always be erased. Still, the introduction of new crops often required significant investments in draining, irrigating, terracing, tiling, or doing whatever else was needed to transform an untouched paradise into a working commercial garden. One of the charms of the spineless cactus was that it was a plant that seemed to be suited to existing conditions.

Enormously lucrative crop introductions could and did happen. In 1873, Mrs. Eliza Tibbets, a resident of the struggling three-year-old city of Riverside, California, received two orange tree bud stocks from the U.S. Department of Agriculture as part of the national seed distribution program. The buds were "sports" derived from an orange tree discovered in Bahia, Brazil, and the fruit proved to be thick-skinned, delicious, and conveniently free of seeds.

The new navel orange, as it was called, did very well when grafted onto local orange trees in southern California. Soon other planters were getting cuttings from Tibbets's orchard. By 1880, the year before Luther Burbank began sprouting almonds to jump-start the prune industry in Sonoma County, Riverside's Tom Cover had employed Chinese and Native American workers to graft seven hundred navel orange buds to citrus rootstock—a feat much smaller than Burbank's production of new plum trees but still a major expansion of the local crop. More orchards followed, transforming the scrublands east of Los Angeles into a national center of citrus production. By 1895, in spite of droughts and infestations, Riverside had the highest per capita income in California. There was ample reason to think that the spineless cactus could be the same kind of success.

In the United States, developing cattle feed for the desert was a national priority, and the Department of Agriculture actively supported Burbank's efforts. David Fairchild, the USDA plant explorer, arranged for Burbank to receive cactus varieties from Italy, France, and North Africa. The USDA greenhouse in Washington, D.C., where earlier explorers had deposited their trophies, provided other specimens. In 1905, an agent from the Department of Agriculture journeyed to Riverside to look for a location to set up a cactus experimental station, a precursor of the 1907 Citrus Station that eventually grew to become a campus of the University of California. The head of the Department of Nutrition and Foods of the University of California in Berkeley tested several spineless cacti there and declared them "to have nutritive powers three-fourths of alfalfa." Another location for experimentation emerged after soldiers from Fort Brown, Texas, were involved in the racially charged Brownsville Raid of 1906; President Theodore Roosevelt transferred control of the fort to the Department of the Interior, where it was used for years as an experimental garden for spineless cacti.

In the summer of 1907, just as George Shull and two other writers were descending on Santa Rosa to vie for Burbank's very divided attention, Burbank issued a special twenty-eight-page catalog devoted entirely to cacti, *The New Agricultural-Horticultural Opuntias: Plant Creations for Arid Regions.* It caused an immediate sensation.

During this period, while his reputation as a scientist was still unquestioned, Luther Burbank could hardly do or say anything that wasn't considered newsworthy, and one of the things he did very often was express his confident expectation that his new cacti would transform agricultural practices in the arid reaches of the world. As it turned out, though, the *Opuntia* was never quite as easy to grow or as nutritious as Burbank had hoped, and certainly not as useful a crop as later salesmen claimed. If Burbank hadn't been so very famous, the spineless cactus might have found a modest niche in the agriculture of desert regions. Instead, it became the center of a profit-making scheme that showed both the dangers of overpromotion and the frantic speculation in agricultural novelties a century ago.

The *New Opuntias* catalog of 1907 made great promises. The spineless cactus was going to rid the world of the scourge of famine. It was also "as safe to handle and as safe to feed as beets, potatoes, carrots or pumpkins," a list that gives some idea of the variety of popular cattle feeds before the advent of hybrid corn. Parts of the catalog sounded more like the setting of an adventure story than an appeal to growers: "Systematic work for their improvement has shown how pliable and readily molded is this unique, hardy denizen of rocky, drought-cursed, wind-swept, sun-blistered districts and how readily it adapts itself to more fertile soils and how rapidly it improves under cultivation and improved conditions." Cultivation and improved conditions were hardly what the desert offered, but these difficulties were usually overlooked in the general enthusiasm for the new product.

In September 1907, Burbank addressed the National Irrigation Congress in Sacramento, the state capital, describing his fifteen years of work on developing a cactus that would be productive, nutritious, and free of spines. The story was on the front page of the *Los Angeles Times* on September 6, 1907, and was widely reprinted elsewhere. "Of course my first object was to get a thornless [cactus]," Burbank told the assembled experts on desert conditions, "then next to get an individual which would produce a great weight of forage to the acre. That has been very well accomplished. I have now a cactus that will produce 200 tons of food per acre. Beets, carrots, turnips, cabbage, and almost anything cultivated in the soil, produces about twenty tons per acre for a good crop, while some of the older cactus will produce about 100 tons. My object is to combine this great production with great nutrition. Then, my opinion is, the cactus will be the most important plant on earth for arid regions and I have not the least doubt of securing that."

This seems an extraordinary boast, brimming with overoptimistic calculations, though we have to remember that if anyone at the time had been making predictions about future corn yields they would have seemed equally unlikely. Nor were there many rival crops for arid regions; the date palm was the chief competitor and it, too, was about to be introduced to California. Drip irrigation, desalinization, and other mechanical means of making the desert bloom were all in the future. In 1907, the prediction that cactus would be "the most important plant on earth for desert regions" was a bit hyperbolic, but not completely beyond the bounds of reason.

Interest in the spineless cactus was high at the University of California and at Stanford, as well as in Santa Rosa, San Francisco, and all the communities where Burbank bought or rented land to establish new cactus farms. Enthusiasm was higher still in Los Angeles, which was then a booming oil town struggling with water shortages and eager to establish its reputation as a gateway to agricultural development. Near the end of 1907, Burbank made the biggest single sale of his career: for twenty-seven thousand dollars, he granted rights to seven varieties of his cacti to the newly organized Thornless Cactus Farming Company in Los Angeles. That sale and another smaller order for additional varieties received a great deal of free publicity, adding to the widespread opinion that Burbank was a wonder worker whose creations would soon transform desert agriculture.

Then it got complicated. Luther Burbank—the world-famous plant inventor, the celebrated recipient of a prestigious grant from the Carnegie Institution of Washington, D.C., and the subject of a growing library of books and articles that insisted he was a scientist—still faced the same commercial problems that had confronted him when he developed his first potato in 1872. He couldn't patent his spineless cactus, he couldn't prevent other growers from reproducing their own stock from whatever they bought from him, and he didn't have the time or space to ramp up his own production to establish a dominant market presence before competitors arrived. What had changed, though, was that there were now many more people eager to help Burbank market his newest innovation. Unlike Burpee, Stark Bro's, Childs, or the other garden retailers who sold products from Burbank's *New Creations* catalogs in the 1890s, the new middlemen were not experienced plant growers themselves. Their expertise was in selling, and they dragged Burbank into a world of trouble.

The first group to approach Burbank was led by the Law brothers, promoters of patent medicines in San Francisco, who proposed to form a company named Luther Burbank Products, Incorporated, to market his cactus and other creations. After 1904, when Burbank thought he would be receiving ten thousand dollars a year from the Carnegie Institution for the next decade and dealing with George Shull for the indefinite future, it seemed a very good time to end his retail sales completely. Burbank signed a contract, almost immediately regretted it, decided he didn't really need a sales manager, and somehow persuaded his partners to let him out of the agreement before it even took effect.

Time passed, the Carnegie grant ended, and Burbank continued selling his cacti through catalogs that always contained warnings that stock was limited and would require care to propagate. George Shull delivered his paper on what he called "a pure-line method of corn breeding" at a meeting of the American Breeders' Association in 1908, but a commercial application of Shull's breakthrough work would not be ready until 1920. In the meantime, federal support for the spineless cactus remained high. In 1912, Senator John Downey Works of California was petitioning the Committee on Public Lands to grant Luther Burbank and his associates permission to acquire several sections of desert lands on which to grow spineless cactus. In the House of Representatives, Everis Anson Hayes, representing San Jose, California, read paeans to Burbank from authorities around the world and insisted that a photograph of his cactus fields be inserted in the *Congressional Record*, an unprecedented tribute.

That same year, a new set of investors proposed to take over the chore of promoting Burbank's spineless cactus and other new creations. Once again, this time without subsequent retraction, Burbank agreed to relinquish control of sales and distribution, receiving thirty thousand dollars as initial payment with a promise of fifteen thousand dollars a year thereafter. The new group incorporated itself as the Luther Burbank Company, not to be confused with the earlier Luther Burbank Products, or with the existing Luther Burbank Society, Luther Burbank Publishing Company, or Luther Burbank Press. The one principle that united all these commercial ventures was the conviction that any business named after Luther Burbank would succeed.

The Luther Burbank Company sold shares with a total worth of about three hundred and seventy-five thousand dollars. Everybody expected to get rich, but it didn't work out that way. Although the Burbank spineless cacti did well in Australia, India, and Africa, they never really succeeded in the United States. American cattle ranchers wanted faster results than the slow-growing cacti could provide, and they weren't ready for the irrigation and other upkeep the plants demanded. The bigger problem, though, was bad management. The directors of the Luther Burbank Company knew nothing about plants and, as it turned out, not much about business, either. They rented a needlessly large, expensive space in San Francisco, the former Army and Navy Store on Market Street, renamed it the Burbank Building, and used it as an elaborate showroom for agriculture displays. They opened an additional branch office in Los Angeles, managed by a man named Bingham Thorburn Wilson, author of *The Cat's Paw*, *The Tale of the Phantom Yacht*, and other novels whose very titles should have given pause to everyone involved. They spent a fortune on advertising, hired a large sales force, and told the salesmen to accept every order that came their way. Their mistakes of overexpansion were classic errors of start-up businesses in any field.

For a time, though, business seemed very good indeed. In 1913, a group of Canadian investors bought a hundred thousand plants from the Luther Burbank Company that they intended to propagate on newly acquired acreage south of Riverside, California, as part of a larger plan to enter the hog and cattle business. Another big order came from Texas. In October 1914, a buyer in Mexico City ordered enough spineless cactus cuttings to plant a thousand acres, which the *Los Angeles Times* noted "would take more than the entire Burbank plantation could supply at one time."

The *Times* reporter had spotted a problem that the Luther Burbank Company managers had somehow missed: limited inventory. The result was a cautionary tale of the perils of moving too fast on a product still under development. In 1915, having accepted too many orders for their stock, the directors compounded their problems through a fraud that would have been comical if it had not been so ruinous. They bought ordinary cacti, singed off the spines with blowtorches or rubbed them off with pads, and sent out the doctored slabs for planting. Of course the buyers discovered they had been deceived as soon as the newly planted cactus slabs started growing. Trust, that most important element in plant sales, had been destroyed. Although Burbank was not responsible for the sales company's errors, it had operated under his name, and his reputation among growers and in academic circles never fully recovered. In the future, Burbank would license his creations only to well-known garden retailers or sell them himself through his own catalogs of seeds, bulbs, and garden plants.

Over the coming years, the spineless cactus would fade from memory, an agricultural curiosity that never quite caught on. In little more than a decade, plant genetics had gone from an unnamed puzzle to an established area of academic research, and the inflated claims of the cactus marketers gave professional scientists yet another reason to dismiss Burbank's contributions. But no one in the growing army of researchers at land grant universities and Agricultural Experiment Stations, men and women who worked so successfully to develop improved strains of corn and wheat and other crops, would ever approach Burbank's stature in the popular imagination. Forty years after his arrival in California, even during the most public days of the failure of the Luther Burbank Company, the Wizard of Santa Rosa was still revered as the country's most famous inventor of beautiful and useful plants. Even George Shull, who experienced so many difficulties during his time in California, continued to admire Burbank. Many years later, Shull described him as "a man of the finest, cleanest character of any person I have ever known. I always felt that he was the sort of man who *deserved* to be a popular hero."

Thy Crowning years should speed most happily
Of work thou lov'st so full with bud and tree;
Labor o' love is light, its long hours bright—
Untiringly may'st thou thy tasks pursue
The world to benefit with marvels new;
Hand work with heart and brain—all toil [illeg]
Earth know fresh glories, beauties, new delights,
Rich, wondrous, rare wrought by thy patience's might;
Brought to perfection by slow, sure degrees!
Urged thou great Nature on to grace the leas,
Remold her shapes, expand, improve, combine
Best qualities into one flow'r or vine!
All centuries to come shall bless thy name
New world & old, with laurels crown thy fame;
Knowledge so deep hath source in the Divine!
"The universe salutes thee! Joy be thine!"

Acrostic poem sent to Luther Burbank by an admirer from
Oakland, California, in honor of his birthday, March 7, 1911.

PART III

POSSESSING THE GARDEN

Thomas Edison, Luther Burbank, Henry Ford, Santa Rosa, 1915.

THE MEETING OF THE MASTERS

The inventors of fire, electricity, magnetism, iron, lead, glass, linen, silk, cotton; the makers of tools; the inventor of decimal notation; the geometer; the engineer; the musician; severally make an easy way for all, through unknown and impossible confusions. Each man is by secret liking connected with some district of nature, whose agent and interpreter he is.

—RALPH WALDO EMERSON, "Uses of Great Men," 1850

On October 22, 1915, three men sat together on the front steps of Luther Burbank's house in Santa Rosa, posing for an informal portrait. They were all past middle age, relaxed and genial, healthy, well dressed, and clearly comfortable with themselves and their fame. They wore suits with vests and shirts with high starched collars, but they had taken off their hats and held them loosely between their knees.

Thomas Edison, the master inventor of the laboratory realm, smiled at the camera. Henry Ford, the master inventor of the factory, was saying something to his host, while Luther Burbank, the master inventor of the garden, listened to Ford but looked past him, as though seeing something in the distance.

Across the road in the experimental gardens, beds of cacti gave way to rows of poppies in colors shading from pale orange to dark red. Tall stalks of elephant garlic rose near stands of corn with multicolored leaves. In the greenhouse, amaryllis giant bulbs and multitudes of daisies were waiting for division. Reporters and cameramen had been on hand to record every step of the visit, but the moment everyone would remember was the three masters of invention relaxing on the porch steps on a fine October afternoon.

Edison and Ford had spent the previous day at the Panama-Pacific Exposition in San Francisco, where "Thomas Edison Day" had marked the thirty-sixth anniversary of Edison's first successful electric lightbulb. The exposition was the city's elaborate ten-month celebration of the opening of the Panama Canal—finally completed after ten years of construction and centuries of dreams—linking the Atlantic and Pacific oceans and shortening the voyage from New York to San Francisco by over five thousand miles. Controlled by the United States under a seventy-five-year agreement with the nation of Panama, the canal was not just a triumph of civil engineering but also a tangible assertion of American claims of global power. Having won the prize of hosting the exposition, San Francisco was using it to showcase the city's resurrection from the rubble and ashes of the devastating earthquake and fire of 1906.

In the six decades since the first modern World's Fair, the Crystal Palace Exposition held in London in 1851, international expositions had become expansive expressions of national pride and a popular way to display the abundance and superiority of new products. The Eiffel Tower, the Ferris wheel, and the ice cream cone had all made their first appearance at international expositions. In San Francisco, Ford Motor Works had installed an entire auto assembly line at the fairgrounds, which were illuminated with Edison electric bulbs.

By the time the Panama-Pacific Exposition had opened in February 1915, after years of planning, Europe was engulfed by war and thousands had already died in the trenches of France and on the beaches of Gallipoli, but in San Francisco visitors were welcomed to an alternate world of peace and plenty. One of the first buildings they saw as they entered the exposition, before they even passed under the Tower of Jewels that led to the rest of the grounds, was the Palace of Horticulture. A giant confection of domes and minarets, it set the tone for the exposition and established the overarching theme of California as a second Garden of Eden.

Inevitably, the exposition planners had approached Luther Burbank to ask for his participation. Surprisingly, the man who declined almost all invitations agreed to lend his support. In 1912, he had joined a delegation on a whistle-stop tour of California, Oregon, Washington State, and British Columbia to promote San Francisco's bid to host the exposition; he was the biggest celebrity on the tour, and the Canadian minister of agriculture came all the way from Ottawa to Vancouver just to meet the legendary genius of the garden. In 1915, Burbank again agreed to be part of the exposition, or at least to let his name be used. Depending on which prospectus you consulted, horticultural displays and the extensive landscaping of the entire exposition had been supervised, directed, designed, or just approved by Luther Burbank. Early programs promised that Burbank would maintain an office within the Palace of Horticulture and be available to answer garden questions, right alongside the changing displays of exotic hothouse plants and the demonstrations of olive oil production, although it is very doubtful this ever happened.

He had certainly been there on Luther Burbank Day, June 5, when he gave a speech about child rearing and was greeted by a throng of admiring nursery owners and seed agents from other countries. Burbank also went to San Francisco for Sebastopol Apple Day and gamely waved a wand over a gigantic redundancy— an enormous model of an apple made from dried apple rings that opened to reveal Miss Elva Howell, the Gravenstein Apple Queen. Burbank had been selling Gravenstein apple seedlings since the 1880s, and in 1890 he helped a Sebastopol farmer, Nathaniel Griffith, identify the unknown cultivar growing on his land. Griffith started an orchard that by 1915 had transformed Sebastopol into an orchard city, with the Gravenstein apple its signature crop. Whoever had dreamed up the event, it seemed designed to confirm the popular opinion that Burbank was a genial magician, and he participated in good spirit.

On the other hand, Edison Day at the exposition cannot have been an unalloyed treat for its guest of honor. Edison was never comfortable sitting still, and banquets were not his idea of fun. He prided himself on his taste for simple fare and had a series of firm (though frequently changing) theories on diet. Sometimes he ate only once a day. Sometimes he chewed every mouthful twenty times. Sometimes he only drank milk. At no time would he relish the kind of heavy, multicourse meal deemed appropriate for such an occasion.

Moreover, in a cruel irony for the man who had invented the phonograph, Edison was virtually deaf, unable to follow general conversation in a crowded room and completely incapable of catching whatever speeches were being made or toasts raised in his honor. At home in New Jersey he would bring a book to the table, but that was hardly possible at a banquet in his honor. In private, he would have his wife or an assistant shout into his ear, but that, too, was not really an option at the exposition. All in all, it must have been a very long day.

The next morning, after the exposition hoopla was over, Edison, Ford, and their many companions traveled north to Santa Rosa to visit Luther Burbank. They had been invited only a few days before, when Burbank went to meet their train at its stop in Sacramento, but Ford and Edison had immediately rearranged their travels to include this visit to a new acquaintance they regarded as one of their few peers. Even at that first brief encounter, it was clear how much the three eminences enjoyed one another's company. A railroad worker later recalled the event for Burbank: "I saw you meet Edison and he put an arm around you, then you met Ford. . . . Pretty soon you all went off together, and the last thing I saw you and Edison were arm in arm . . . with Edison bending down and holding his hand to his ear to make out what you had to say, and anxious not to miss a word." Their shared renown drew Edison and Ford to Burbank, but the immediate friendship suggests the three men had deeper bonds.

In an important sense, they all came from the same place. All had been born on farms, loved the outdoors, and distrusted what they considered "fancy" manners. All cherished the simple life of their early years, at least in nostalgic retrospect. None had liked school and each had left the classroom without completing his formal education. They shared the same restless energy. Burbank, a youthful sixty-six, loved to clown around with children and was still known to turn cartwheels on the grass. Edison, now sixty-eight, still posed for photographers pretending to nap on his laboratory table, as though to confirm his claim that he rarely slept except for such brief respites and had little interest in the world beyond his work. Ford, a relative youngster of fifty-two, liked to take rides in the country and stop the car to go skinny-dipping.

They were country boys, they were heroes, and they were all deeply conflicted about the new world they themselves were so very actively shaping. Self-made men, they prized concrete results over theoretical advances. Each insisted throughout his career that the motive of his work was to improve the lot of the common man, but they also shared a driving ambition and obsessive attention to detail that was only partially concealed by their down-to-earth demeanor. Different enough to feel no threat of competition from each other, they enjoyed the opportunity to reaffirm the ideas and accomplishments that made them at once so similar and so distinctive.

Nothing in particular happened the day they gathered in Santa Rosa. No inventions were perfected, no companies formed, no visionary enterprises announced. They talked about the war in Europe. Just a few months earlier, German submarines had torpedoed and sunk the British ocean liner *Lusitania*, moving public opinion away from the United States government's official neutrality. Ford, however, was an adamant pacifist, convinced that war was little more than a profit-making scheme backed by greedy "cosmopolitan" moneylenders. Indeed, to Edison's tolerant bemusement, Ford was using his trip west as a campaign for neutrality.

War meant the loss of lives and the diversion of resources to vital but nonproductive purposes. It also meant interruptions in international supply lines. In Santa Rosa, both Ford and another member of the party, the tire magnate Harvey Firestone, worried aloud that access to rubber plantations in Ceylon, India, and Malaysia might be cut off by submarines. Whether or not the United

States went to war, they were sure it was in the national interest to find raw materials nearer to hand and more closely under American control.

Burbank suggested they should try to find or breed an alternative plant source that could thrive right in the United States. Several years before, when dictating notes that would go into the twelve-volume *Methods and Discoveries*, Burbank had envisioned the economic promise of plants whose use had not yet been discovered: "Who will be the one," he had asked, "to produce a plant which shall yield us rubber—a plant growing, perhaps, on the deserts, which shall make the cost of motor car tires seem only an insignificant item in upkeep? And who, on those same deserts, and growing, perhaps, side by side, shall perfect a plant which can be transformed into five-cent alcohol for the motors themselves?"

It was the seed of an idea that would flower years later. More immediately, Firestone proposed that the men take an auto trip down the coast to San Diego, where another, smaller Panama Canal Exposition was under way. Ford and Edison agreed. It was the first of what would become an annual series of camping trips, to which Burbank was always invited. He never went, although his name was often part of the nightly conversation around the campfire. After several hours of excited, almost boisterous conversation, a tour of the garden, and a bit of playing with Burbank's little terrier, Bonita, the new friends made vague plans for future travels and firm promises to stay in touch by mail. On the surface, it was an inconsequential encounter, and yet it was a turning point for all three masters of invention in ways they would have been hard-pressed to explain. Each embraced the new friendship and used it as a way of defining himself.

Why were these men so important to each other? For Luther

Burbank, being welcomed as an equal by the country's great heroes of useful invention confirmed his identity as a practical businessman who delved into the mysteries of nature to improve and enhance human existence. The spineless cactus marketing company wasn't doing well and neither was the Luther Burbank Press, but these were men who had also known their share of failures. It was Edison, after all, who declared of his lightbulb experiments, "I haven't failed. I've just found 10,000 ways that won't work." Entry into Ford and Edison's circle, even more than the grant bestowed by the Carnegie Institution a decade before, was an affirmation of Burbank's proper position in the first rank of celebrated innovators.

Edison had burst into the public consciousness in 1879 in a dazzling gleam of incandescent light, and journalists had been calling Burbank "the Edison of the Garden" for almost as long, but in his writings and interviews before 1915, Burbank more often spoke of himself as a scientist plumbing the mysteries of creation, struggling with the mighty task of understanding nature and turning her secrets to useful ends. Now he was as likely to describe himself as an industrialist whose finished products happened to be new varieties of plants. Borrowing the language of the factory, he spoke of "speeding up" Nature's processes "in a wholesale way."

Burbank predicted that plant inventors would soon equal the feats of "Edison and Ford and the Wright brothers and Alexander Bell and Marconi and his followers and all the other great geniuses of chemistry and mechanics" to "double the working capital of the world." For years after the meeting in Santa Rosa, Burbank repeated the story of how he had advised "some of my friends in the rubber business" about dealing with the dangerous reliance on foreign sources for raw materials. And after forty years as a commercial plant breeder, he began to identify himself as a businessman in a way he had rarely done before.

Edison, in turn, was inspired by Burbank's talk of the chemical treasures to be found in plants. Keenly aware of his own very different status as the successful producer of patented and branded mechanical innovations, he could empathize with Burbank's plight as an inventor without legal protection for his creations. He could also identify with Burbank's struggles to be accepted by the more academic men of science; three decades had passed since Edison's announcement that he had discovered a mysterious quality he called "etheric force," but the later realization that he had been observing radio waves did not erase the memory of the scientific scorn with which his claim had been received.

For Henry Ford, the greatest innovator of methods of mass production, Burbank's work represented something else altogether. Ford was inspired by Burbank in the same reverent way the mothers' club members were inspired, taking the man himself as a model. He admired Burbank for reasons that had to do less with business than with his own nostalgia for a swiftly passing society marked by self-sufficiency and rural values. To the auto magnate, the garden master had an enviable purity. He embraced Burbank's experimental gardens, densely planted but still so small and close to his house, as a link to a way of life Ford's own inventions had done so much to render obsolete.

Ford was a collector of mentors and sages, the doers and thinkers of a slightly older generation whose work he admired. His greatest hero was Edison, but there were others in his personal pantheon, and he immediately placed Burbank in their ranks. Two years earlier, in 1913, Ford had gone after the reclusive nature writer John Burroughs. When Burroughs criticized the automobile as a noisy intrusion that marred the landscape, Ford had sent him a Model T with the suggestion that he use it as a way of getting closer to the natural world. At the age of seventy-six, Burroughs found himself whizzing through the countryside around his fruit farm in New York's Catskill Mountains. Soon he was visiting Ford in Detroit and at Edison's winter home in Florida.

Burroughs had repaid the unfamiliar delights of Ford's luxurious hospitality by introducing the automaker to the works of Emerson and Thoreau. These were already Burbank's favorite authors, a shared taste he and Ford discovered in the course of the Santa Rosa visit. It confirmed Ford's sense that Burbank embodied the best traditions of New England culture, untainted by the more recent immigrants whom Ford's xenophobic imagination saw as a threat to the "true" America.

Burbank never shared Ford's fear of foreigners or his paranoid convictions about hidden conspiracies of Jewish financiers. He had never shown much interest in national or international politics either, whether it was the American Civil War during his childhood or the current conflict in Europe. Now, however, he was put on Henry Ford's short list of important people who should be converted to the cause of pacifism. Several weeks after their meeting in Santa Rosa, Ford invited Burbank to board the Peace Ship, an ocean liner he had chartered to bring a large and miscellaneous assembly of notable people to Sweden, where they planned a peace conference to persuade the warring nations to end their conflicts and "bring the boys home by Christmas."

The Peace Ship was much publicized and much ridiculed, and even those who shared Ford's belief in the power of the grand gesture doubted he would get far. John Wanamaker, department store millionaire and former postmaster general, offered what he considered a more sensible alternative: that the United States end the conflict by buying Belgium from Germany for one hundred billion dollars. Burbank responded to Ford's invitation to board the Peace Ship with a telegram: "My heart is with you," a rather evasive message that could be read as a refusal, a statement of support, or a condolence note.

However Ford interpreted the telegram, it did nothing to mar his admiration for his new friend. Ford idolized Burbank as a man who somehow managed to preserve his connection to a better past, and he cherished their contact as evidence that success hadn't severed his own ties to nature, sincerity, and the craftsman's touch.

AMONG THE PHOTOGRAPHS TAKEN the day Ford and Edison visited Santa Rosa is a group portrait of all the guests who had arrived in Ford's private railcar and the people who had greeted them at Burbank's home. Mina Edison and Clara Ford are in the picture, as are Harvey and Idabelle Firestone, along with the gaggle of secretaries and assistants who accompanied Ford and his companions everywhere they went. Emma Burbank Beeson stands near her brother, a vigilant figure who seems to be protecting him from several unidentified people who worked for him at what he sometimes called the Old Home. In the back row is a tall, serious young woman with deep, dark eyes.

Elizabeth Waters had been living with relatives in Oakland, California, when she took a job as a researcher for the Luther Burbank Publishing Company and moved north to Sonoma County. After the research work was finished, she became Burbank's private secretary, bringing unprecedented order to his always voluminous correspondence. A few months later, in 1916, the managers of the Luther Burbank Press abruptly closed their doors, moving from Santa Rosa to New York and surprising shareholders of the Luther Burbank Society who had been expecting to receive more for their sponsorship than a handsome certificate and a set of books. That same year, the Luther Burbank Company collapsed into bankruptcy, with Burbank himself suing the cactus salesmen for ten thousand dollars due on his original contract. In the midst of these crises, Burbank's secretary became his supporter and his confidante. In December 1916, they married.

He was sixty-seven and she was twenty-eight. Still handsome, spry, and very famous, Burbank brought his much younger wife out of the background and into the center of a life that included sunny seasons in the garden, rainy winters of books and music, endless requests for literary projects, and a stream of interesting guests. He also gave her gifts of large sums of money, totaling at least ten thousand dollars. Betty Burbank looked after her husband's interests, helped him answer the mail and write more books, coddled him, talked baby talk to the dog, and gave his home a peace and happiness it had long lacked. She also brought a child—little Betty Jane, who was probably her brother's daughter—to the household of a man who had always adored children. He called Elizabeth "my friend sister wife sweetheart companion and helper" and "dearest bestest of all," and he wrote to her father in San Diego, "I have had some success in a small way with the Daisy, but my feeble efforts melt into insignificance compared to the wonderful girl you raised."

Burbank's miserable first marriage in 1890 had sent him into a frenzy of invention and promotion. His much happier second marriage in 1916 coincided with a new phase in his career, one that looked back to older values that had little to do with plant inventions. Burbank was no longer the young adventurer ready to re-shape nature, but neither was California any longer an untouched paradise waiting to be planted. A growing number of people were turning to the garden—and particularly to flowers—as a source of moral and spiritual wisdom. Once again, Luther Burbank was to become the defining spirit of a garden that was itself being redefined.

Burbank Golden Jubilee Celebration, 1923.

· 14 ·

THE GARDEN OF
BEAUTIFUL THOUGHTS

Is it not inspiring to realize that the very best things in the world, even on the material side, are within reach of us all, when we shall command the genius to make the most of our environment? And this genius, I insist, will prove to be the genius of democracy—the expression of a divine aspiration for a better, freer and ampler life on the part of the masses of men and women who bear our burdens in war and peace. Even so, there must be leaders and prophets, men of vision who see clearly a little ahead of their time, tall men who hear the whispers of the Infinite. Of such men, in this line of work, the incomparable leader and prophet is Luther Burbank.

—WILLIAM ELLSWORTH SMYTHE, *City Homes
on Country Lanes*, 1921

The paradoxical behavior that allows people to welcome industrial progress but also to yearn for a connection to untouched nature is expressed in myriad ways, from pictures of flowers printed on paper towels to helicopters that airlift skiers to untouched slopes. In the years after World War I, one of the great demonstrations of this kind of doublethink was the public embrace of Luther Burbank as both an innovative businessman and an embodiment of the values of the natural world.

Burbank was still claimed as a champion of botanical invention and scientific progress, and hailed as a leader in the growth of California agriculture, but now he was also a sentimental favorite whose very name lent luster to any group. Scientific groups like the American Breeders' Association, the National Forestry Association, the American Pomological Society, the California Academy of Sciences, and the American Museum of Natural History had all made Burbank an honorary member, but so did the Bohemian Club (an exclusive retreat for San Francisco's business leaders), the Boy Scouts, the Women's Christian Temperance Union, and the Loyal Knights of the Round Table. After 1910, Burbank was also identified with the environmental movement; John Muir, the patron saint of American environmentalism, admired Luther Burbank's work, and Burbank used his *New Creations* catalogs to endorse the fledgling Sierra Club, which he had joined as soon as he learned of the group. By the end of his life, Burbank was also a Mason, an Elk, a Lion, a Moose, and a Member in Excellent Standing of the Northern Pacific Railroad's Great Big Baked Potato Boosters Club.

Doubtless he cherished some of the honors bestowed upon him and regarded others as amusing, but what he thought was increasingly beside the point. Burbank's fame had become a commodity that could be separated from his plant inventions, and it was freely appropriated by any number of groups claiming him as a sympathetic patron: atheists, spiritualists, anti-immigrant glorifiers of "New England" virtues, educational reformers, philosophers of self-sufficiency, and promoters of California real estate all invoked Burbank's name to burnish their own endeavors. To the organizations that sought an association with the legendary Luther Burbank, what mattered was that they could elevate their own standing by claiming him as an affiliate of their cause. And to the throngs of tourists who continued to arrive in Santa Rosa, the fascination with Burbank persisted.

Often it was his own fault. Like many celebrities, Burbank sometimes found it hard to remember that the ability to command an audience does not necessarily mean you have something important to say. As his fame grew, he would sometimes modestly admit his sense of being a messenger of divine inspiration, if not a divinity himself. He entertained yogis and land- and water-use reformers and statesmen of opposing persuasions—each of whom, it seems, came away with the conviction that the unpretentious but very famous plant breeder from Santa Rosa shared his own particular way of looking at the universe. But most of all, Burbank was celebrated as the genius loci of the flowerbed.

BURBANK MADE HIS REPUTATION as a breeder of vegetables and fruits, but he had been enthroned as the spiritual keeper of the ornamental garden as early as 1894, when he presided over the first annual Santa Rosa Rose Parade. In the years after World War I, as the world of professional science became an increasingly rarified realm of equations and specialized vocabulary, the moral leadership of Luther Burbank was an even more treasured part of popular wisdom. Working behind his picket fence, tending his rows and rows of plants, now white-haired and perhaps a bit less frantic about asserting his scientific credentials, Burbank seemed to many observers to embody a more direct and accessible relationship with nature. With every season, his stature as a tangible link to the natural world was becoming increasingly important. The pilgrims making their way to Santa Rosa were not there because of Luther Burbank's contributions to scientific research.

They had come to see a sage who helped them reconnect with their own best selves.

After 1917, when it seemed so much of the past had been lost beyond recapture on the battlefields of Europe, Burbank was regarded as the grand old man of the garden. Meanwhile, a new generation was taking over the plant-selling business. Lloyd and Paul Stark, Clarence Stark's sons, were now in charge of Stark Bro's Nurseries, busy promoting another spontaneous apple novelty the company had bought from its discoverer and was promoting as the new Golden Delicious. W. Atlee Burpee had died in 1915 and his son David was now heading the company, reorienting it to reflect his own greater interest in flowers. John Lewis Childs still owned his nursery business, but he spent much of his time on state politics and on editing a birding magazine called the *Warbler*. Public demand for new varieties of plants for farm and garden was as insatiable as ever, but much of the research and development was now being done by university-trained biologists, many of whom were working at government-supported Agricultural Experiment Stations.

Santa Rosa was changing, too, as was Sebastopol, even as migrant workers continued to pick apples in the fall and the Children's Aid Society brought its charges up from San Francisco in the summer to camp in the strawberry fields and help with the harvest. In 1917, Henry Ford sent Luther Burbank the first Fordson tractor to come off his assembly line (along with a newsreel photographer to film the delivery), but it was automobiles that now lined the streets of Santa Rosa. Burbank's garden rows were becoming a rare patch of agricultural activity within the center of town.

There were now many more sources of plant information than

had existed when Burbank began his career. The new Department of Genetics at Berkeley, like its counterparts at other universities, was exploring the intricacies of inherited traits. Agricultural extension agents, funded by the Smith-Lever Act of 1914, were fanning out across the country to provide farmers and home gardeners with practical advice on the best methods of growing just about anything. The flower fanciers and suburban gardeners of America were devoted to Burbank, however, and he was still the individual most identified with horticultural wonders and improvements. While commercial groups tallied the millions of Burbank plums and walnuts harvested every year, home gardeners prized the novel colors of his hybrid roses, the delicious fragrance of his lilies, and the tall stems and clear white petals of his Shasta daisy. Nostalgia for the vanishing farmhouse surrounded by its garden led to a sentimental glorification of Burbank's Santa Rosa gardens—the humble plot where anything, it seemed, could grow.

Burbank continued to distribute several catalogs a year, each featuring both past successes and new varieties that represented years of hybridization and selection. But it was his stature as the human embodiment of natural wisdom that was becoming his most treasured contribution. In the years after his second marriage, requests for his presence and his approval came from across the country, just as requests for his daisy seeds and plum scions had filled the mail in earlier decades. Agents for the Chautauqua lecture circuit, the popular program for bringing great ideas to the intelligent masses, clamored for Burbank to give talks at all or any of their locations. When he refused, other speakers stepped in to meet the audience demand. Henry Augustus Adrian, identified on programs as "The Luther Burbank Man," toured the country for years lecturing on Burbank's life and works.

HENRY A. ADRIAN:
THE LUTHER BURBANK MAN

Thousands of people all over the country have desired to see Mr. Burbank and some of the wonderful work he has accomplished, and to hear more about it. Mr. Adrian has given thousands of people this opportunity, and describes the work more brilliantly, perhaps, than Mr. Burbank, himself, could do. Through all the world's long history new forms of plant life were produced only by the slow processes of nature. Mr. Burbank has shown the way to add almost without limit to the kinds of useful plants we now possess, and Mr. Adrian tells in a vivid manner how he does it and the results that are being accomplished. He also shows, in the course of a single lecture, the great value of this work to humanity at large.

Chautauqua prospectus of the 1920s.
COURTESY UNIVERSITY OF IOWA DIGITAL LIBRARY

Popular magazines continued to feature Burbank, with articles and full-page color advertisements like the one in the *Woman's Home Companion* entitled "Good News for Flower Lovers" that offered a packet of Burbank's "precious flower seeds" to magazine subscribers. The expanding network of local garden clubs, a reflection of the growing popularity of the garden as a gracious pastime for women, incorporated in 1923 as the Garden Clubs of America. They, too, looked to Burbank for inspiration and also for speeches. So did the readers of *Fruit, Garden and Home* magazine, which

Luther and Elizabeth Burbank with children
dressed as flowers, Santa Rosa, c. 1920.
COURTESY LUTHER BURBANK HOME & GARDENS, SANTA ROSA, CALIFORNIA

began publication in 1922 and grew to a half million subscribers its first year and to a million in four years, by which time it had changed its name to *Better Homes and Gardens*.

Many admirers followed the suggestion of William Ellsworth Smythe, who wrote in 1921, "To apprehend [Burbank] one must stand in his presence, as gentle as that of the poet Whittier and as spiritual as Emerson's." And, increasingly, they received an audience. After his marriage—to his secretary, after all—Burbank was also more gracious about the mail. Journalists and admirers wrote to him incessantly, asking his opinion on any number of topics, and he answered an astonishing number of the requests. He gave statements on the joys of music (he liked it, and so did his plants), the value of studying Latin (largely a waste of time) and daylight savings time (he was for it). He began issuing annual messages on his birthday, in the manner of European royalty, and joined in the Arbor Day programs at Santa Rosa's Luther Burbank Elementary School, where he and all the pupils were usually treated to a giant birthday cake as well. More and more often, too, he accepted invitations to parades and pageants, presiding over events like the Sonoma County Prune Festival or Potato Day in Stockton, which honored the moment that city established a new world record for potato production. All of this was photographed, of course, and often filmed, and circulated through the national media.

In 1920, Emma Burbank Beeson asserted her own claims on her brother's wisdom and his special affinity to both plants and children. In a prelude to what would become a regular stream of books about Burbank aimed at the youngest readers, she and two other former elementary school teachers put together a strange little volume called *Stories of Luther Burbank and His Plant School*. The experiments in plant selection and hybridization that the Carnegie Institution of Washington, D.C., had sought to record for the advancement of science and that the Luther Burbank Society had advertised as the salvation of farmers and gardeners were now reduced to a series of anecdotes and experiments that Burbank, in his Introduction, praised as "described . . . in a most pleasing form for the child."

Stories of Luther Burbank and His Plant School epitomized the sentimentality that was already running rampant over Burbank's reputation in the 1920s. Each chapter of the book featured an anthropomorphic plant that was "educated" by its teacher, Luther Burbank. In describing the work to find a crimson version of the familiar orange California poppy, for example, "These little *Eschscholt-*

zia maidens were being taught to change the color of their gowns."
The stoneless plum was identified as a descendant of "Half-pit, a
poor little French outcast," and "Little Beach," the small, sour
plum native to North American coastal areas. In the evening, as
the appropriately rootless schoolmates sat around a campfire, "Siberian bramble" confided, "I love my native land, let me tell you,
but . . . the people of my country did not care for me; they called
me 'seedy.' I was so very small they banished me from their gardens. I am glad to find in my new home one who makes me welcome." A child actually trying to learn botany or genetics by
reading *Stories of Luther Burbank and His Plant School* would have
had every right to be bewildered. Nonetheless, the book was popular, at least on the shelves of elementary school libraries.

There was still demand for other books encapsulating Burbank's garden lessons. Encouraged by his energetic and business-
like wife, Burbank signed a contract with Collier & Son to bring
out a revised and condensed edition of the 1914 *Luther Burbank,
His Methods and Discoveries and Their Practical Application*, the
Cree-Binner volumes he once had dismissed as a foolish pastiche.
How Plants Are Trained to Work for Man came out in 1921 in eight
volumes, in a smaller format with many fewer illustrations. David
Starr Jordan, who always liked and admired Burbank, contributed
a prefatory note that was his final defense of Burbank's claim to
scientific expertise. "Big men are usually of simple, direct sincerity
of character," Jordan wrote. "These marks are found in Burbank,
sweet, straightforward, unspoiled as a child, devoted to truth, never
turning aside to seek fame or money or other personal reward. If
his place be outside the great temple of science, not many of the
rest of us will be found fit to enter."

And still the visitors arrived. Ignace Paderewski, the Polish

pianist and patriot, came for lunch and began a long correspondence on the subject of tomatoes; British music hall star Harry
Lauder visited, as did radical writer Upton Sinclair, the Duc de
Tallyrand, the communist editor of *The Masses*, football hero Red
Grange, Japanese businessmen and nursery owners, movie stars
and opera singers, and a passing array of children's choirs that
serenaded the man who corresponded with kings and princes but
still had time to answer the letters of little children and even write
a book about their welfare.

In 1924, Swami Paramahansa Yogananda toured the United
States, giving lectures and gaining followers from Boston to San
Francisco, and he called on Burbank in Santa Rosa several times.
Over twenty years later, he would dedicate his very popular *Autobiography of a Yogi* "to Luther Burbank, an American Saint," and
devote an entire chapter ("A Saint Amid the Roses") to their discussions of the spirit that flowed through the universe. According
to the yogi, Burbank told him "the secret of improved plant breeding, apart from scientific knowledge, is love." Yogananda also said
Burbank confided he could heal the sick and communicate with
the dead, a statement that matches other accounts from visitors far
less sympathetic to such mental powers. David Fairchild, the
USDA plant explorer, had declared himself nonplussed when Burbank told him that he, his mother, and his sister all shared powers
of clairvoyance, but mystic seekers like Yogananda were happy to
endorse Burbank's vision of universal harmony.

WHILE CHILDREN WERE WEAVING Shasta daisy chains around
Luther Burbank on his birthday and admirers were filling a very
large container in Burbank's office with unsolicited poetic tributes,

it turned out that being the sage of the garden could lead to unforeseen entanglements. Like so many parts of Burbank's story, and the story of our changing relationship with nature, it began with Darwin.

In 1844, almost a decade after his voyage on the *Beagle* and a full fifteen years before he would finally dare to publish *On the Origin of Species by Means of Natural Selection*, Charles Darwin penned a deeply conflicted letter to his friend and fellow scientist Joseph Hooker. "At last gleams of light have come," he wrote, "and I am almost convinced (quite contrary to the opinion I started with) that species are not (it is like confessing a murder) immutable."

Darwin finally published *On the Origin of Species* in 1859, after years of hesitation, because he feared that Alfred Russel Wallace would get all the credit for unveiling the mysterious process of evolution if he waited any longer. Darwin had held back for a number of reasons, but much of his hesitation came from anxiety about what would happen when he challenged the literal truth of the Creation as described in the Bible. To his great surprise and relief, the outcry was not as hostile as he had feared. Over the next sixty years Darwin was corrected, disputed, neglected, and rediscovered, but the greatest attacks from organized religion came long after his death. In the 1920s, as fundamentalist Christianity became a force in American religion, the attacks that Darwin had always dreaded arrived from the evangelical pulpits of the United States.

In March 1925, the state of Tennessee passed a law making it illegal for public schools to teach Darwin's theory of evolution. In response, the American Civil Liberties Union persuaded a high school teacher from Dayton, Tennessee, named John T. Scopes to test the law, leading to what became widely known as the Scopes "monkey" trial. William Jennings Bryan, famous orator, frequent candidate for president, former secretary of state, admirer of Luther Burbank, and ardent believer in the literal truth of the Bible, offered to lead the prosecution. Clarence Darrow, champion of scientific rationalism, leader of the American Civil Liberties Union, and celebrated trial lawyer, was to lead the defense.

Both Bryan and Darrow asked seventy-six-year-old Luther Burbank to appear as a witness, a telling indication of how people had come to attach very different qualities to him while agreeing he was an acknowledged expert on the mysteries of nature. To Darrow, the fundamentalist insistence on creation as a fixed, unalterable event was also an attack on the improvements that Burbank represented. To Bryan, Burbank embodied the reverence for creation that Darwinian science was trying to undermine.

Burbank didn't go to Tennessee for the trial, but he did send a letter unequivocally supporting the teaching of evolution. "Those who would legislate against the teaching of evolution should also legislate against gravity, electricity and the unreasonable velocity of light," Burbank wrote, "and also should introduce a clause to prevent the use of the telescope, the microscope and the spectroscope or any other instrument of precision which may in the future be invented, constructed or used for the discovery of truth." As for Bryan, who had visited Burbank in Santa Rosa more than once, Burbank drily observed, "Mr. Bryan was an honored personal friend of mine, yet this need not prevent the observation that the skull with which Nature endowed him visibly approached the Neanderthal type. Feelings and the use of gesticulations and words are more according to the nature of this type than investigation and reflection."

The trial was broadcast on radio and transcripts appeared in the daily newspapers. Bryan was both victorious and humiliated; put on the witness stand, he revealed an embarrassing ignorance of Darwin's theory of evolution or any other matters of science. Still, the violation of the Tennessee law was clear, and the judge cut the proceedings short by declaring Scopes guilty and fining him one hundred dollars, a penalty that was later waived. Bryan died five days after the trial, but the prohibition against teaching Darwin remained in force in Tennessee until 1967.

In what must have seemed an unrelated event, Henry Ford was quoted in *Collier's* magazine in January 1926 saying that he believed in reincarnation. Questions about the afterlife are not the sort usually referred to a plant breeder, but Burbank was not the usual sort of breeder, and his friendship with Ford was well known. A reporter from the *Oakland Post-Enquirer* came to Santa Rosa to sound out Burbank on the issue.

A long conversation followed, and it was not a casual affair. As had become habit, Elizabeth Burbank was present at the interview with her husband and, again as usual, both Burbanks read and corrected the story before it was published. In discussing his views of immortality, Burbank expressed doubts about the afterlife, preferring to dwell on the infinitude of the natural world as he experienced it in life. In another interview on January 22, this with the *San Francisco Bulletin*, Burbank said that Christ's followers had "so garbled his words and conduct that many of them no longer apply to present life. . . . He was an infidel of his day because he rebelled against the prevailing religions and government. I am a lover of Christ as a man, and his work and all things that help humanity, but nevertheless just as he was an infidel then, I am an infidel today."

Twenty years earlier, in *The Training of the Human Plant*, Burbank had urged parents to substitute communion with nature for the hellfire and brimstone religion he remembered from his own youth, and he had been hailed as a special friend of childhood. Now, however, he had gone too far. The interviews were sent out by wire service and widely reprinted in the national newspapers, where they met the new activism of religious conservatives. Luther Burbank, the beloved sage of the garden, the man for whom schools and nature study clubs were named, the benevolent teacher who showed how both flowers and children could be trained to rise to their best potential, was denounced in pulpits across the country. For the first time in his life, Burbank began receiving hate mail, abusive telegrams, and threatening telephone calls. After a week of grueling attacks, he accepted an invitation to speak at the First Congregational Church of San Francisco on Sunday, January 31, to explain what he had meant.

It was a huge public event. The weather was terrible, a day of cold, hard rain, but more than twenty-five hundred people crammed into the church on Mason Street to hear the famous gardener deliver a fervent statement of his faith in the importance of earthly deeds. Burbank's sermon was broadcast over the radio, published in the next day's newspapers, circulated by wire services, and read aloud in churches the following week.

"I love everybody!" he began. "I love everything! Some people seem to make mistakes, but everything and everybody has something of value to contribute or they would not be here. I love humanity, which has been a constant delight to me during all my seventy-seven years of life. I love flowers, trees, animals and all the works of Nature as they pass before us in time and space."

He then shared the creed he lived by:

What a joy life is when you have made a close working partnership with Nature, helping her to produce for the benefit of mankind new forms, colors and perfumes in flowers which were never known before; fruits in form, size, color and flavor never before seen on this globe; and grains of enormously increased productiveness, whose fat kernels are filled with more and better nourishment, a veritable storehouse of perfect food—new food for all the world's untold millions for all time to come.

Burbank urged his audience not to search the Bible for rules of blind obedience or to frighten children with visions of hell. The meaning of life was to be found in the flow of experience, not in any expectation of heaven. After citing sources of inspiration that included Euripides, Moses, Shakespeare, Franklin, his mother, and his terrier Bonita, Burbank concluded with an assurance that harked back to his favorite author, Ralph Waldo Emerson: "For the soul which knows itself no more as a unit, but as part of the universal Unity of which the beloved is also a part, which feels within itself the throb of the Universal Life—for that soul there is no death." A salvation better than heaven would come to those who were ready to learn the overarching lesson of nature: that all creation was a single, organic whole.

And then he went back to Santa Rosa, trying to act as though the whole affair was settled. The uproar didn't end that quickly, of course, and the entire controversy became yet another proof of the strangely elevated position this one famous plant breeder held in the popular imagination. In the press, from the pulpit, in letters, and in conversation, people continued to debate Burbank's spiritual beliefs, while the man who provoked all that passion and curiosity ignored them as best he could and went back to work. It was time to prepare his new catalog for 1926. He had some very promising gladioli he was looking forward to introducing, as well as a bright red ornamental amaranthus named "Combustion" he had already featured on the cover of last year's catalog.

As the weeks passed, Burbank seemed to be in good spirits. On March 7, Arbor Day in California, he issued his annual birthday message, sounding as serene and chipper as ever: "What a beautiful world we live in!" he joyfully proclaimed. "My seventy-seventh birthday finds me busier than ever in Nature's school, where I have always been a student; it finds me happier than ever because I have strength and the will to work. To all the world but especially to the children who will think of me today—the friends I love best—I send this message: As you hold loving thoughts towards every person and animal and even towards plants, stars, oceans, rivers and hills, and as you are helpful and of service to the world, so you will find yourself growing more happy each day and with happiness comes health and everything you want."

On March 24, 1926, less than three weeks later, Burbank suffered a heart attack. On April 10 he fell into a coma, and at thirteen minutes after midnight on Sunday, April 11, 1926, he died, his wife and his sister at his bedside.

Burbank's death was as much a public event as his life. A reporter from the *Santa Rosa Press-Democrat* had been standing watch for days. He forwarded the news immediately to the waiting editors of the Associated Press wire service, which sent out the first bulletin of the death of "the dean of plant breeders and leader in modern creative plant development." The report made it into the late edition of the *New York Times* on the April 11, with two additional news articles and an unsigned editorial on the April 12.

The *Chicago Tribune* published the AP obituary on the front page on April 11 and followed up with its own reporting the next day, calling Burbank "the world's leading horticulturalist."

The *Los Angeles Times*, which had always followed Burbank's career in great detail, put his obituary on the front page on April 12 and again the next day. In Akron, Ohio, Harvey Firestone told reporters that Burbank's death would "cast a pall" over his summer camping trip with Henry Ford and Thomas Edison, who had once again invited the plant inventor to join them. Miss Katherine M. Lawrence, who had been preparing a historical sketch of the Baptist Church of Still River, Massachusetts, suddenly made national news with her records of Burbank's personal avowal of faith before the congregation in 1866, when he was seventeen. Burbank may have attracted painful attacks in the last months of his life by insisting that he did not believe in heaven or hell, but the important, newsworthy point, as the headlines said, was "Burbank was a Baptist."

Those closest to him knew better. His final wish had been to avoid any religious ceremony. He wanted to return in death to the natural world that was his one constant faith, and that was how his funeral was planned. A public service was held at 4 P.M. on Wednesday, April 14, in a Santa Rosa park that Burbank had often enjoyed visiting. Schools were dismissed for the day in Sonoma County, and three thousand children were expected to sing. Newsreel photographers filmed the ceremony.

That evening, a much smaller group was present when Burbank was buried in the garden near his greenhouse. Boy Scouts formed an honor guard as the coffin was carried across the street from the 1906 home to the garden of his first Santa Rosa house, where he was interred under a Cedar of Lebanon tree he had planted himself.

Elizabeth Burbank and Emma Beeson were the principal mourn-
ers. The Universalist Unitarian minister from San Francisco who
had married Luther and Elizabeth a decade earlier now said a few
words. Judge Ben B. Lindsay, a child welfare advocate who had
given the funeral oration earlier in the day, joined the small circle
at the graveside, along with David Starr Jordan and a long-ago
classmate from Lancaster Academy who now lived in Berkeley.

Burbank's body had returned to nature, becoming part of the
endless cycle of energy and vibration he had so often described.
After the burial came the harder decision of what to do with his
horticultural legacy. Both his reputation and his garden creations
were more available than ever to the many people interested in
asserting their own authority over the natural world, and they
would not wait long to make their claims.

Agriculture. This stained-glass tribute to Luther Burbank, over sixteen feet high, is part of the Human Endeavor series of windows completed in the 1970s, expressing the creative and sustaining action of God's grace for the betterment of humanity. Grace Cathedral, San Francisco.

· 15 ·

TRANSPLANTING THE LEGACY

Before his death Luther Burbank said that he wanted Stanford University to carry on his studies of plant life. It is of unique importance that these experiments, some of them representing years of labor, be carried on. The whole safety of the human race depends upon plant life. —RAY LYMAN WILBUR, president, Stanford University, 1927

Before his death in April of 1926, Luther Burbank spoke to his wife about the problem of finding someone to carry on his work. He said, in effect: "there is really only one I think of that could make the most of it." He named the Stark Brothers Organization.

— DICKSON TERRY, *The Stark Story*, 1966

When Burbank died in 1926, David [Burpee] bought his company and acquired the rights to the seeds as well as to his cousin's experimental work—including the breeding records, or "stud book"— and added Burbank's splendid flowers and vegetables to the Burpee line. —W. ATLEE BURPEE COMPANY HISTORY, 2007

Luther Burbank's will left his entire estate to his wife, Elizabeth, who now owned two houses and their grounds in Santa Rosa, Gold Ridge Farm in Sebastopol, over a hundred and sixty thousand dollars in cash and securities, the car, the dog, the scrapbooks, and, most important, the plants. Rooted in the grounds in Sebastopol and Santa Rosa were thousands of specimens still under cultivation. Each was a horticultural experiment in progress, its history and qualities noted in Burbank's typically fragmentary way on charts and in notebooks, but its real significance known only to the man who had just died.

Some hoped to establish a research center that would continue his work. Elizabeth Burbank entered into negotiations with Stanford University about creating a Luther Burbank Institute to take over Gold Ridge Farms and the plants, separately or together with the greenhouse and gardens in Santa Rosa. By September 26, 1926, Ray Lyman Wilbur, who had become president of Stanford in 1916, had signed a formal option to buy the Sebastopol property for fifty thousand dollars.

The plan was to endow a Luther Burbank Foundation to cover the annual operating costs of approximately twenty-five thousand dollars. Twenty years earlier, David Starr Jordan had approached a trustee about funding a center for agricultural research at Stanford, citing Burbank's 1905 lectures as evidence of Stanford's readiness to assume a serious scientific position in the field. Now his successor was raising funds for what the university announcement called "the sole means by which the research, experimentation, improvement and creation in the plant world initiate[d] and perfected by the late Luther Burbank may be carried forward."

The endowment didn't materialize, and neither did the Luther Burbank Institute. But if a satellite campus for plant research in Sonoma County had little appeal to the Stanford donors, that was only one option for continuing Burbank's work. Viewed as a well-established and highly saleable collection of novel plants, with priceless publicity and bragging rights thrown into the deal, the experimental gardens were an attractive acquisition for a commercial nursery. Certainly they were something the owners of Stark Bro's Nurseries were happy to take on.

Whether Elizabeth Burbank approached Stark Bro's Nurseries or it came to her, the arrangement was not the dynastic passing of authority described in the company's corporate history. It was a business deal, pure and simple, and everyone profited. In the summer of 1927, Elizabeth Burbank signed an agreement by which she retained possession of the land in Sebastopol and Santa Rosa but granted Stark Bro's an exclusive license to propagate, publicize, and sell the plants growing there.

It's not clear exactly what they had acquired. A later account described Gold Ridge Farm as holding "120 types of plums, 18 varieties of peaches, 28 varieties of apples, 500 hybrid roses, 30 cherries, 34 pears, and 52 gladioli," which is considerably short of the thousands of new varieties Burbank had claimed to have under development. Over the next two decades, Stark Bro's took many specimens back to Missouri, including the last tree that bore the famous stoneless plums, which died in its new location. They also brought their own new plants, particularly roses, to Sebastopol, thus confusing the record of what had been there before Burbank died. In 1931, Stark Bro's sold the rights to the flower seeds and bulbs growing in Santa Rosa to the Burpee Seed Company, along with the right to use the Burbank name. In the following years, Burpee Seed Catalogs offered "new Luther Burbank introductions," and the Burpee Company, too, claimed to be Burbank's true and rightful inheritor. Long after his death, there was still extra value in anything plant-related attached to Luther Burbank's name.

While Stark Bro's was exploring ways to increase the value of Burbank's plants, a very different effort to claim his material legacy was taking shape in Dearborn, Michigan, the home of Henry Ford. When Ford went to Santa Rosa in 1915, he was just beginning his vast collection of iconic American objects from the fast-vanishing world of his own childhood. A few years later Ford would famously declare, "History is more or less bunk." As he spent the rest of his life trying to explain, he meant the history written in textbooks, a narrative he had never mastered or perhaps even read. To Ford, the past that mattered resided in tangible objects, and he was a man with the resources to make sure they were preserved.

Soon after his visit to Santa Rosa, Ford began plans to display his growing collection of artifacts on a two-hundred-acre site in Dearborn nestled between his home and the Ford Motor Works. Thucydides was unimportant, but cookstoves and scythes and the house where Stephen Foster may or may not have written about the Swanee River were precious. They needed to be saved, and so did just about anything associated with Luther Burbank.

In January 1928, after a respectful interval that allowed Burbank's estate to be settled, Henry Ford's secretary wrote to Elizabeth Burbank asking if there were any papers or tools associated with her late husband that she might donate to the new museum of what Ford called "the history of our people as written into things their hands have made and used." Convinced that objects touched by great people carried that greatness forward, Ford was determined to have relics associated with Burbank, the genius of the garden, planted in Dearborn.

Two months later, Ford's secretary wrote again, inquiring about buildings that might be moved to the museum, and by the end of the year Elizabeth Burbank had sent him not only Burbank's garden tools but also his desk, a shelf of books that had been in his office, a large collection of other people's business cards he had amassed over the years, and several photographs and chromolithographs that had hung on Burbank's office walls. She also offered a small stucco building, little more than a single room, that Burbank had built in 1910 at the intersection of Santa Rosa Avenue and Tupper Street, between his old and new residences. He called it the Information Bureau and used it as a souvenir stand, so "the average visitor who comes here in the future will be allowed to exchange a few dimes for curios, seeds and bulbs." The list of wares had been expanded to include books by and about Luther Burbank, garden manuals, a vast array of postcards put out by commercial photographers, china printed with images of Burbank's home, picture frames, medallions, and other trinkets, until it was taken over as storage space for the Luther Burbank Society. Now the Information Bureau was on its way to Michigan.

On October 21, 1929, fourteen years after Ford's and Edison's memorable visit to Santa Rosa and more than three years after Burbank's death, Thomas Edison joined President Herbert Hoover, scientist and Nobel laureate Marie Curie, inventors Orville Wright and George Eastman, oil magnate turned philanthropist John D. Rockefeller, comedian Will Rogers, and over two hundred other guests for the groundbreaking of Ford's new two-part effort to honor what he saw as the best of America's historical heritage. The Edison Institute, as Ford's museum was first called, would house the many artifacts in Ford's collection of the ordinary implements of everyday life, while Greenfield Village, named for the town where Ford had been born, would hold his collection of historic buildings.

Only a few days later, Wall Street would experience the catastrophic decline in stock prices that marked the start of the Great

Depression. In Dearborn, Michigan, however, the groundbreaking ceremony and banquet revealed no premonitions of economic decline. Held on the fiftieth anniversary of the lighting of Edison's first successful incandescent bulb, the event celebrated what seemed to be a steady line of progress from the hardships of the past to the ingenious improvements of the present day. Ford had transported Edison's first laboratory from New Jersey and reassembled it in Greenfield Village; for added authenticity, he also brought in New Jersey soil. A reenactment of Edison illuminating his lightbulb was the centerpiece of the day, but there was another ceremony that was equally important. Ford wanted Edison's signature on a large cement block that was to be the dedication stone of the new museum, and he wanted Luther Burbank's shovel embedded there, too, as a symbolic proxy of Burbank's presence in this shrine to America's inventive spirit.

The dedication ceremony was filmed. Imagine an elevated wooden railroad platform erected in an open field far from any station or tracks. Wooden stairs on either side give access to the platform, which is otherwise surrounded by a wooden railing. A smiling group of men and women, elegant in their fall coats and hats, gather along the railing and wave to the camera. Then a black sedan arrives bearing Thomas Edison, eighty-two years old and growing frail, but still enthusiastic. Brandishing Burbank's shovel, Edison mounts the stairs and approaches a large, square wooden trough filled with wet cement that occupies the center of the platform. He takes a step forward and thrusts the tip of the shovel deep into the cement, where it stands upright and ready for the return of the spirit of its mythic owner. Then, unsure what to do next, Edison marches across the trough and down the stairs on the other side, leaving a trail of footprints across the wet cement.

Henry Ford, laughing, slips under the railing, takes Edison's elbow and guides him back. After they remount the stairs, Ford hands Edison a long pointed dowel with which the inventor signs his name in the cement in large letters.

Burbank was a central figure in Ford's projected gallery of American heroes, and the shovel, a rustic Excalibur, was only one of the tributes gathered at the new museum and historic village. Objects Burbank had touched seemed to Ford to be charged with some talismanic power, and the ones Elizabeth Burbank had sent were not nearly enough. In 1936, Ford bought the large, two-story wing of the family farmhouse in Lancaster where Burbank had been born. Ford's agents spent months in Massachusetts, carefully taking photographs, drawing diagrams, and numbering the pieces of the frame building as they took it apart for transit to Michigan. They reassembled it on a grassy bank in Greenfield Village, close to the Burbank Information Bureau on a street called Burbank Lane. Stark Bro's Nurseries was hired to design landscaping that used authentic Burbank creations. After Burbank's terrier, Bonita, died and was buried on the grounds at Sebastopol, Ford asked to exhume the remains to add to his collection. Elizabeth Burbank refused, but she did relinquish her husband's childhood cradle, which sat for years in the relocated Burbank homestead in Dearborn when the building was furnished to illustrate New England life in the nineteenth century.

The Burbank house and office took their place in Ford's ideal village of high achievers, along with the Edison laboratory, the house where the Wright brothers were raised, the birthplace of nineteenth-century textbook editor William McGuffey, the one-room schoolhouse where Harvey Firestone learned his letters, a house from the original Plymouth settlement, an immaculately clean reproduction of the slave cabin where George Washington Carver was born, and many other evocative reminders of the heroes and inventors Ford admired. But Burbank was not one of many. He was one of a very select few, and Ford was determined to place him at the forefront of his new museum. The cement dedication stone, with Edison's signature and Burbank's shovel, was installed on a pedestal at the main entrance to the museum, where it remains today.

BY THE END OF BURBANK'S LIFE, the business of writing about him was nearly as big as the business of creating and marketing his plants, and this, too, continued after his death. The first book to appear was by his sister Emma, who published *Harvest of the Years: The Early Life and Letters of Luther Burbank* in May 1926. In a sense, Emma had been working on the book for decades, since she not only maintained her brother's scrapbooks but also saved his letters and made notes of Olive's stories of her childhood in Sterling, Massachusetts, as well as their shared memories of Burbank family days. Soon after, Frederick W. Clampett published *Luther Burbank: "Our Beloved Infidel," His Religion of Humanity*, which Burbank had authorized a few weeks before his death as another way of responding to the outcry over his "infidel" statements. Clampett, a member of the rationalist, antireligious Freethinkers' Society, had sent Burbank a questionnaire that Burbank, after consulting with David Starr Jordan, had replied to at considerable length. His responses, reprinted in *Our Beloved Infidel*, were like a voice from the world of spirits that Burbank himself had so specifically dismissed.

On May 22, 1927, a year after Burbank's death, the Freethinkers' Society of New York added another tribute, planting a Norway maple in Burbank's honor in Central Park near the statue of that other great explorer of cosmic connections, Alexander von Humboldt. Thomas Edison, one of many celebrities with ties to Burbank who had been invited to the ceremony, sent his regrets but declared the tree planting "a most fitting manner of perpetuating the memory of one whose every thought and heart-throb had their inspiration in the glorious beauties of nature." At the tree-planting ceremony, Professor Garrett P. Serviss, an astronomer and writer of science fiction, attacked the *Encyclopaedia Britannica* for according Burbank only twenty-five lines, the same space given to Charlie Chaplin. Poet Edgar Lee Masters spoke, as did Madame Olga Petrova, a silent-movie actress who had started life as Muriel Harding. A heckler disrupted the proceedings and the police had to intervene, distracting the participants from the wise and quiet harmony with the universe that Burbank himself so often described.

There was more to come. Some time in 1921, Burbank had started working on his autobiography with a writer named Burt C. Bean, who had been part of the Luther Burbank Press enterprise in 1916. Bean, who delighted in pursuing all the small details of Burbank's life, had conducted many interviews with Burbank friends and family in New England and compiled an enormous trove of notes. Shortly before the address at the First Congregational Church, Bean had sent Burbank a "Tentative List of Biographical Publications Projected and Now in Hand Based on the Life of Luther Burbank." The list ran to ten volumes, each to be several hundred pages long, because there was no event of Burbank's life, however obscure, that Bean felt the public didn't yearn to know. In May of 1926, a month after her husband's death, Elizabeth Burbank arranged to buy Bean's voluminous notes and drafts for the hefty price of ten thousand dollars. She also reached an agreement with Emma to shorten the title of her book to *The Early Life and Letters of Luther Burbank*. Elizabeth wanted a new and different *Harvest of the Years* written by an author who knew Burbank and had just published a feature about him: Wilbur Hall.

Hall was an experienced journalist but an odd choice to be Luther Burbank's biographer. Since 1914, he had written over fifty short stories and articles published in popular magazines, including a *Saturday Evening Post* series "The Salesman's Kindergarten," which was all about the vital importance of having a purchasing agent if you expected to run an up-to-date business. Needless to say, a purchasing agent was one of the many kinds of managers Burbank had always declined to hire. In addition, Hall was an outspoken atheist who considered Burbank's belief in an all-embracing spiritual force a childish fantasy; he was also a heavy drinker who doubtless would have dismissed Burbank's lifelong aversion to alcohol as another sign of immaturity.

The gossips of Santa Rosa immediately got to work, noting that Hall had arrived on the scene some time before Burbank's death, that he was now in residence in the office space that had been built on the second story of the barn, and, most pointedly, that Burbank's thirty-six-year-old widow was named in Hall's divorce. On the other hand, even the briefest examination of Bean's files suggests Elizabeth Burbank may have simply wanted someone a bit less long-winded to get the job done. *The Harvest of the Years*, published in 1927, is written as though Burbank and Hall had had long conversations, although the better part of it was almost certainly based on Bean's transcripts. In any case, Hall's particular contribution to the Burbank legacy was to preserve for the ages Burbank's image as the elderly and eccentric spirit of the garden. "He was a queer admixture of a little, old-fashioned, careful Massachusetts bachelor," Hall wrote in his preface, "a gnome, a genius, a prankish boy, a spendthrift, and a temperamental artist." Once again, and not for the last time, Burbank's reputation was a commodity over which he had no control.

Ownership of Burbank's significance as a scientist was as much in dispute as control of his experimental plants. Biologists and geneticists in the United States, many of whom now knew little about Burbank beyond the accepted opinion that he was not a scientist, dismissed him as a publicity-seeking amateur. In the new Soviet Union, however, Burbank was still respected as an authority on hybridization and inheritance. As had happened during the Scopes trial, Burbank once again had the dubious honor of being claimed by opposing sides in a debate, this time among Soviet scientists assessing Mendelian inheritance.

Nikolai I. Vavilov, the country's leading plant geneticist and founder of the Leningrad (now St. Petersburg) seed bank, one of the world's great repositories of genetic material, had visited Burbank in Santa Rosa in 1921. Five years later, Vavilov wrote an admiring obituary that described Burbank's extraordinary contributions to hybridization, with particular praise for his work with hybrid plums. When T. D. Lysenko rose to power under Stalin and began imposing an agricultural policy based on an ideological version of the inheritance of acquired characteristics, Vavilov was accused of "bourgeois pseudoscience" and sent to prison, where he died. Lysenko, meanwhile, hailed Burbank for his insistence that environment was as powerful a force as genetics.

While all these different parties were taking possession of Burbank's plants, his tools, his letters, his biographical writings, and his scientific work, others were appropriating the less tangible parts of the Burbank legacy. As had been true since at least the 1890s, Burbank's reputation as a master manipulator of the natural world was treated as a commodity that could itself be altered and controlled, not just for the uses of commerce but also as a source of art.

Frida Kahlo, *Portrait of Luther Burbank*, 1931.

THE CREATOR'S ART

The chief work of the botanist of yesterday was the study and classification of dried, shriveled plant mummies whose souls had fled.
They thought their classified species were more fixed and unchange-
able than anything in heaven or earth that we can now imagine. We
have learned that they are as plastic in our hands as clay in the hands
of the potter or color on the artist's canvas and can readily be molded
into more beautiful forms and colors than any painter or sculptor
can ever hope to bring forth.

—LUTHER BURBANK, address to the Pacific States
Floral Congress, 1901

The desire to turn an orange poppy red or cross an apricot with
a plum comes from a creative impulse that is as much art as
it is science. The determination to start with an ideal and then
labor without cease until that ideal is realized—Luther Burbank's
favorite description of his method—could serve as a definition of
all artistic endeavors. Understandably, then, many creative people
in other fields felt a powerful kinship to Luther Burbank. During
much of his life, amateur poets and painters portrayed their hero
in doggerel verse and sketches, but in the years just before and after
his death, he gathered the attention of far more serious artists.

Edith Wharton and T. S. Eliot were aware of Burbank as a
plant wizard and as a figure in the eugenics movement, and both

mentioned him in their writing. Poet Marianne Moore, who was fascinated by the forces of immigration and hybridization (in plants, in people, and in language), paid far closer attention to Burbank's career. Moore had a lifelong interest in natural history and spent much of 1919 reading Darwin's *Variation of Animals and Plants Under Domestication*, the book that had first inspired Burbank to begin his work in speeding up the evolution of plants. While reading Darwin, Moore also started copying quotations from Burbank's newspaper interviews into her writing notebook. As editor of *Dial* magazine in 1925, she presented a purposely controversial reordering of the heroes of science that used Burbank's popular reputation to topple the hierarchies of conventional history. Luther Burbank, she maintained, was a better model for the modern scientific hero than Isaac Newton, "Since, having been made to understand how five hundred kinds of fruit may be produced on one tree, how white blackberries, stoneless plums, spineless cactus, and sweet lemons may be successfully 'designed,' one cannot but understand somewhat of the water, of the air, and of the sun which contributed to produce these curiosities."

After Burbank's death, his dual reputation as both an interpreter of the natural world and a collaborator in the very human search for profits made him the subject of three distinctly political portrayals by three very different artists: John Dos Passos, Diego Rivera, and Frida Kahlo. *The 42nd Parallel*, the first novel of John Dos Passos's *U.S.A.* trilogy, published in 1930, is a panoramic description of modern American life as a frenzied scene of rapid change and growing economic and social inequality. The book is a modernist collage, with Dos Passos's narrative punctuated by newspaper clippings and biographies of prominent people, including Luther Burbank.

In three long, impressionistic free-verse stanzas, Dos Passos recounts the popular legends of Burbank's life in a way that shows he had read at least one of the biographies published after the plant breeder's death. Here are Burbank's childhood memory of flowers warmed by a thermal spring, blooming amid the snows of a Massachusetts winter; his discovery of the potato seed ball; and his move to Santa Rosa, where "he was a sunny old man where roses bloomed all year everblooming everbearing hybrids." Dos Passos also incorporates the popular legend that Burbank was hounded to death for his beliefs. "He was one of the grand old men until the churches and the congregations got wind that he was an infidel and believed in Darwin," Dos Passos wrote. "Luther Burbank had never a thought of evil, selecting improved hybrids for America those sunny years in Santa Rosa. But he brushed down a wasp's nest that time . . . and they stung him and he died puzzled."

Burbank fares better than many of the business figures in *U.S.A.* since, unlike them, he is not condemned as an exploiter of labor, but Dos Passos understood very well that Burbank was an entrepreneur as well as a sage. "He was an infidel," Dos Passos wrote, "he believed in Darwin and Natural Selection and the influence of the mighty dead and a good firm shipper's fruit suitable for canning." The result is a portrait at once smiling and sinister, as Dos Passos describes Burbank's "apocalyptic dream of green grass in winter and seedless berries and stoneless plums and thornless roses brambles cactus." In this cavalcade of heedless change, Dos Passos uses Burbank's life to suggest the way the natural world has been subsumed by the world of commerce, all in the name of a disorienting but unstoppable progress. It is left to the reader to decide if this "apocalyptic dream" of an eternally verdant garden, stripped of its thorns and stones, is a reminder of paradise or a prediction of the end of the world.

The Mexican artists Frida Kahlo and Diego Rivera shared John Dos Passos's deep skepticism of the virtues of capitalism. Recently married and even more recently arrived in San Francisco, the two painters visited Santa Rosa sometime in the fall of 1930 or early winter of 1931. Both came away with plans for portraits of Luther Burbank.

Rivera, an avowed Marxist, was beginning a three-year stay in the United States working under the patronage of America's leading financial powers. His most famous works of this period would be *Detroit Industry*, a twenty-seven-panel cycle of frescoes sponsored by the Detroit Arts Commission under the leadership of Edsel Ford, and the notorious mural at New York's Rockefeller Center that Nelson Rockefeller commissioned, paid for, and then destroyed when Rivera refused to remove a portrait of Lenin from the center of his design.

Rivera's first project in the United States, however, was *The Allegory of California*, a mural painted on the main staircase wall of the luncheon club for members of San Francisco's Pacific Stock Exchange (now the City Club). After arriving in San Francisco on November 10, 1930, Rivera and Kahlo set out on a series of trips around the state, gathering images of the landscape, the people, and the life the mural was to portray.

Though it was almost five years after his death, Luther Burbank was still regarded as the embodiment of California's hard-won position as the garden of the nation. When Kahlo and Rivera arrived in Santa Rosa, Elizabeth Burbank had already sold the rights to Burbank's plants to Stark Bro's Nurseries and was in the process of sending his garden tools to Henry Ford. She had moved into the old frame house Burbank bought with his first profits as a commercial breeder in the 1880s, next to the greenhouse and the large Cedar of Lebanon under which he was buried. Rivera, Kahlo, Elizabeth Burbank, Betty Jane, and other guests posed together for snapshots outside the greenhouse. It is very likely that Elizabeth Burbank also gave her visitors several photographs of her late husband, including one that had appeared on the cover of the *Mentor* magazine and seems to be Rivera's model for his depiction of Burbank in the City Club mural.

According to Rivera, his object was to represent what he saw as the three bases of California's wealth: gold, petroleum, and fruit. *The Allegory of California* shows an enormous female figure wearing a necklace of wheat, her huge outstretched left hand piled with apples, pears, plums, oranges, and berries while her right hand lifts the surface of the ground to reveal miners using power drills to wrest ore from beneath the earth. Images of industry swirl around this goddess of California plenty: oil derricks, ships, refineries, miners, prospectors, aviators, and engineers. Occupying the middle ground on the right side, opposite the stump of a giant redwood on the left, is the sole human representative of the state's agricultural bounty, Luther Burbank. He kneels under the goddess's fruit-filled hand and examines a large blooming plant, as though the future crops whose growth he nurtures will balance the ancient tree that has been destroyed.

Frida Kahlo's 1931 *Portrait of Luther Burbank* is far more mysterious than her husband's depiction of California as a natural and industrial empire. The painting is unique in her works in that it is not a portrait of herself, her family, a politician, a figure from Mexican history, or anyone she personally knew. It marked a turning point in Kahlo's art, away from more direct representation into surrealism, and it is a haunting inversion of her recurrent theme of the presence of death in life, shown here as life springing from death.

The background of the painting is a bright but cloudy blue sky and the parched brown hills of dry-season California. At the center, Luther Burbank, dressed in a dark suit and starched white shirt, rises magically, as in a myth of metamorphosis, from the trunk of a tree that engulfs him up to the knee. He holds a large philodendron, its oversized leaves obscuring much of his torso, its stem and bare roots dangling at his side. In the otherwise barren background are two other trees, both laden with fruit. One has been severely pruned, its top clipped and its few almost leafless branches sagging with large yellow globes. The other tree, more distant, is covered with leaves, blossoms, and fruits of different colors.

At the bottom of the canvas, the earth is dug away to reveal the roots of the tree from which Burbank emerges. In a shocking contrast to the brilliant sky, fruit, sunlight, and greenery of the top of the painting, a skeletal corpse lies in a dark, muddy hollow, its left arm torn off near the shoulder, its bones already penetrated by the roots of the tree.

Kahlo's painting is both highly symbolic and strikingly literal. The hauntingly empty vistas, the fruit trees that seem to exist outside of any ordinary system of agriculture, and the central figure of Burbank rising from a hollow stump all mark a new spirit of surrealism in Kahlo's work, while the strangely desiccated landscape can be seen as an early example of her many depictions of the United States as a country where nature has been altered and robbed of its lush fertility. *Portrait of Luther Burbank* also can be viewed as a statement of Kahlo's own sense of being a kind of hybrid. Taking Burbank's most famous talent for crossing different species to create something newer and stronger than either parent, Kahlo may have seen Burbank as a way to reconcile her own multiple dualities: a Mexican in the United States, a person of Indian and European heritage, a bisexual woman, and the wife of a famous artist who was an ambitious painter in her own right.

Whatever its other sources and meanings, however, *Portrait of Luther Burbank* also faithfully combines two images Kahlo first encountered during her visit to Santa Rosa. Like Rivera, Kahlo was almost certainly working from a photograph, this one of Burbank standing in his greenhouse and holding a large philodendron in a pose identical to that of the painting. The second image Kahlo took from Santa Rosa existed only in her imagination, but it was based on the knowledge that Burbank was buried under the Cedar of Lebanon tree very near where she and Rivera had stood with Elizabeth Burbank—another much younger wife of a famous man. Nourished by the skeleton, the tree in Kahlo's painting gives birth to the man, Luther Burbank, who embodies the entire cycle of nature. At the bottom of the canvas, painted in large brown letters, are the words "Luther Burbank," identifying the corpse, the resurgent man who rises from his own death, and the bare landscape that is Kahlo's version of California's—and Burbank's—not-quite-natural land. Themes of celebrity, immortality, and the ambiguous interrelationship of the natural and the man-made environment all come together in a painting that manages to be a complex social commentary that draws its meaning from the life of a single man.

As MORE TIME PASSED after Burbank's death, his reputation settled into a simpler, saintlier narrative. He was a great inventor, a national hero, and an uplifting example for children. Popular histories from the 1920s through the 1960s routinely included Burbank on the list of what one author called "the new pioneers" and another deemed "famous men of science." The DuPont *Cavalcade of America* dramatized Burbank's story twice on the radio—in 1937 as "Luther Burbank, the Plant Wizard," and in 1947 as "The Man with Green Fingers," the second starring Lionel Barrymore. In *Webster's Dictionary* he became a verb: to "Burbank" was "to cross or graft (a plant). Hence, figuratively, to improve (anything, as a process or institution) by selecting good features and rejecting bad, or by adding good features." Children were taught to regard Burbank as a great inventor and encouraged to read books with titles like *Luther Burbank: Boy Wizard* (1948), *Luther Burbank: Nature's Helper* (1959), and *Luther Burbank: Partner of Nature* (1963).

By the 1940s, Burbank's popular reputation had been stretched very far indeed. In 1940, the United States Post Office issued fifty-eight million stamps honoring Luther Burbank in its series on Great American Scientists, although hardly any professional plant biologists of the time considered Burbank a significant figure in their field. In 1942, the U.S. Navy commissioned the S.S. *Luther Burbank* as a cargo ship carrying supplies to the Pacific theater during World War II, giving new life to Burbank's fame as a champion of products that could withstand long-distance shipping. Anheuser-Busch used the lifelong teetotaler to advertise Budweiser beer in a 1948 campaign called "Great Contributions to Good Taste": "He gave nature 100,000 new ideas," the advertising copy read. "But before Burbank, Anheuser-Busch in 1876 had made a great contribution to the American table. . . . " The John Hancock Insurance Company also featured Luther Burbank in their advertising as an icon of quality, and the Topps toy company, best known for its baseball cards, issued a Luther Burbank trading card in 1952. Burbank's name and his portrait continued to appear on commemorative silver bars and plaques, teapots, and towels, and his life was retold in several different comic books. In the 1960s, Burbank reached a higher plane when he was immortalized in a stained-glass window in San Francisco's Grace Cathedral, on the summit of the city's most fashionable district, Nob Hill. Along with Albert Einstein, Thurgood Marshall, and John Glenn, he is one of a dozen luminaries portrayed in separate gothic windows on the north side of the cathedral nave.

All of these representations, from trading card to cathedral window, were ways to claim some association with the inventive skill and creative energy Luther Burbank represented. The most significant effort to appropriate Burbank's legacy, however, and the most controversial, came in the form of federal legislation that never mentioned his name. The first self-service supermarket, the Piggly Wiggly store designed by Clarence Saunders, had opened in Memphis, Tennessee, on September 16, 1916. Five weeks later, Saunders filed to patent his concept, the "Self Serving Store." If the aisles and counters from which food was sold deserved legal protection as intellectual property, how long could it be before the same rights were extended to the fruits and vegetables and flowers that nestled in the shopper's cart?

Application for Plant Patent No. 15, "Peach," filed December 23, 1930.
COURTESY LUTHER BURBANK HOME & GARDENS, SANTA ROSA, CALIFORNIA

The Garden as
Intellectual Property

The plant lover can sometimes make a few dollars, if he is also an
active businessman, if he creates a new plant of great value, while the
party who originates a new pin or needle may make untold wealth
from it through a long series of years by patenting it.

—Luther Burbank, *Pittsburgh Dispatch*, 1921

In 1837, the newly reorganized Patent Office received approximately 650 patent applications for the entire year, of which
435 were approved. In 1874, the year Burbank put his first potato
on the market, the number of patent applications had risen to almost 13,000, with 250 patent models arriving in Washington every
week. In 1893, the year of the first *New Creations* catalog, 38,473
patent applications were received by the Patent Office. By 1926,
the year Luther Burbank died, the number was 110,030, a rate of
increase that far exceeded the rate of population growth. Not one
of those applications was for a plant.

Burbank had always wished he could patent his creations. During his lifetime, he was regarded as a great inventor, a master of
the intricacies of evolution, a communicant with the mysteries of
nature, a selfless creator of plants that benefited all humanity, a
sexless god of fertility, and a jolly champion of little children. It

also makes a great deal of sense, however, to see his career as a series of attempts to earn a living from the business of plant breeding in a time when objects of nature, no matter how improved and altered by human ingenuity, could not receive the legal protection patents gave the inventors and improvers of mechanical devices or commercial processes.

Over the years, Burbank's strategies for dealing with the absence of plant patents had been nearly as inventive as his plant creations themselves. He tried retail sales, both at the farmers' market and out of his garden. He accepted commissions to breed new products, payable on delivery. He assumed the risk of development and put out catalogs offering his inventions at high prices to wholesale producers who could then profit from being the first to offer a new creation: what economists call "first mover advantage." He contracted with large plant-selling companies like Jackson & Perkins to market his inventions for him, collecting payments that varied depending on whether they sold wholesale, retail, or from prototypes they propagated in their own gardens. He accepted the support of the Carnegie Institution of Washington, D.C., a generous but somewhat demanding patron. He flirted with academic appointments and made occasional forays onto the lecture circuit, where he could command the modern equivalent of ten thousand dollars for an evening's talk. He turned himself into a marketable commodity, capitalizing on his reputation to sell books. What he could not do was profit from the monopoly on production a patent provides.

The patent laws of the United States, as laid out by Thomas Jefferson in 1793, allowed patents for "any new and useful art, machine, manufacture, or composition of matter, or any new or useful improvement thereof." The stipulations were that the product must be useful, nonobvious, and new. Like the fruits and flowers of Burbank's garden, the interpretation of these original conditions continued to evolve, forcefully prodded by creative interpretations and perceived needs.

There are many justifications for patents, a topic that has long occupied legal and economic theorists, but the one that was most common in the early years of the new nation was the argument that protecting the rights of inventors would encourage innovation. Guaranteed a period when only they could profit from their good ideas, inventors would be willing to bear the significant costs of developing those ideas into new products. Patents also appeal to a deeply held sense of fairness. The view of patents as a way of protecting private property, albeit the abstract, intangible property of ideas, has always coexisted with the view of patents as a means of promoting innovation for the greater goal of progress. In the words of Abraham Lincoln, the only president to hold a patent (for an inflatable device to buoy boats in shallow water), patents "add the fuel of interest to the fire of genius."

For anyone working with the products made from living matter, the barriers to obtaining a patent came from two directions. Long tradition, embodied in many court rulings and even more deeply ingrained in human instinct, held that access to any creation of the natural world—air, water, diamonds, string beans—should not be owned exclusively by a private party. The second barrier was the requirement that an inventor had to submit clear instructions on how to duplicate the process being patented. This requirement, known as "enabling disclosure," exists so that others can benefit after the set period of patent protection has elapsed. The word "patent" also means "open" and "obvious," because the privilege of patent protection carries the demand for disclosure of how your invention is made. In the barely understood processes of hybridization, however, and in the highly variable process of plant selection, enabling disclosure was virtually impossible.

That did not keep plant breeders and plant merchants from trying to protect the literal and figurative fruits of their labors. In the second half of the nineteenth century, as commercial growers banded together in trade associations, the possibility of group action in pursuit of greater legal protection was an important reason for organizing. In 1868, a grape-growers' association in western New York explored the possibility of patent protection for their new varieties of grapes, and by the 1870s a number of horticultural groups were proposing laws protecting plant innovators. In 1881, Congress enacted a new trademark law that allowed breeders to register unique names for what they claimed were distinctive plants. But while trademarks let growers advertise their plants under protected names, it did little to prevent anyone from reproducing the plant itself and selling it under another name. During the period when Burbank was helping transform California from a region of wheat fields and abandoned mining claims into a fertile landscape of orchards, flower gardens, and vegetable fields, the American Seed Trade Association (founded in 1883), the Society of American Florists (founded in 1884), and particularly the American Association of Nurserymen (founded in 1887) all called for legal protection to prevent competitors from reproducing and marketing their new plant varieties.

In 1889, just as Burbank was beginning to gain a reputation as an inventor of new plants, a case brought before the commissioner of patents involving a newly discovered fiber in pine needles ended in the decision (*ex parte Latimer*) that products found in nature were not patentable. That hardly settled the question, however, especially for a "plant evoluter" like Burbank who devoted himself to organisms that were *not* found in nature but developed through his own strenuous intervention. Burbank's introductions were new varieties created on his experimental grounds and they were certainly his inventions, as much as a lightbulb fashioned from naturally occurring raw materials was Edison's invention.

In the 1890s, as Burbank was bringing out his catalogs of *New Creations in Fruits and Flowers*, he began to feel even more strongly that patent protection was his due. In 1898, he joined with H. D. Van Deman, former head of the Department of Agriculture's Division of Pomology and a devoted supporter of commercial fruit interests, in a campaign for plant patents. In a letter that was reprinted in many newspapers and magazines at the time, Burbank declared that plant pirates and imitators were driving him out of the plant business. He threatened to abandon his work if he could not secure legal protection for his inventions. "After all my years of very extensive experience in the special advantages of soil, climate, knowledge of the work and, above all, my character and standing as an originator, patience is at last exhausted," he complained, "and except to complete some of the plant developments now well under way and the pursuit of a few scientific lines, [I] shall quit the work at once and forever." There is no record of any official response to this threat, and Burbank of course continued in business, but the image of him as an ill-used inventor deprived of his rightful profits would linger in public memory.

By the beginning of the twentieth century, Burbank's standing as a plant inventor different from the common crowd of breeders and sellers extended as far as the Patent Office. In 1906, when Burbank's fame as an expert in plant evolution was at its height, a representative of the horticulture industry, Hyland C. Kirk, asked the House Committee on Patents for an amendment of the patent laws to protect the interests of the originators of horticultural products. Kirk's argument was that, in the wake of the rediscovery of Mendel and the publication of de Vries's work on mutation, the technology of plant breeding was now better understood. In light of this new scientific basis, Kirk said, biological innovations could be considered legally equivalent to mechanical or chemical ones. In an addition that may have doomed his case, Kirk also claimed that *the discoverer* of a new variety of plant was as deserving of protection as the inventor of a new motor or a chemical compound.

Kirk's argument found a formidable opponent in Albert H. Walker, an expert on patent law. Walker was the author of *Text-Book of the Patent Laws of the United States of America*, which had been judged by the *Harvard Law Review* in 1904 to be "probably the best modern text-book on the law of patents, and . . . the only treatment of the modern American law of patents." Speaking before the same House Committee on Patents, Walker argued that protection of plants as intellectual property should be limited to those who actually create new plants, as opposed to those who merely discover a previously unknown organism. To illustrate the difference, Walker cited Luther Burbank as an example of a plant breeder who *did* deserve such protection. Walker's tribute shows that he was one of the many people who judged Burbank's work to be very different from the common novelties of mere commercial breeders, but the report never made it out of committee, and Burbank probably did not even know about the debate.

In any case, it's not clear that a patent would have improved Burbank's fortunes as much as he may have imagined. Intellectual property history is littered with unhappy tales of competition, theft, endless court cases, and more than a few inventors dying before they could profit from their great idea. But if the absence of patent protection spared Burbank the legal battles that consumed the energies of many other inventors, including Edison, it also eliminated any prospect of great wealth or long-term financial security from his past triumphs. It's not hard to understand Burbank's frustration at the constant pressure to create something new. His income was entirely dependent on his latest marvel.

In interviews, Burbank would sometimes describe himself as a selfless benefactor of humanity, indifferent to profit and happy that his plants were available to all, but at many other moments he had complained that his life would have been very different if only he had been able to patent his creations. In 1921, just as Burbank was completing the revised text *How Plants Are Trained to Work for Man*, a columnist from the *Pittsburgh Dispatch* sent him a form letter requesting a brief reply to her question of the week, "Should the government grant rights to the originators of new varieties of plants and farm products?"

Burbank's answer far exceeded the specified limit of two hundred words. It began with his recollection of "very extensive correspondence with the United States Patent Office" some thirty years before, which he said had ended with the official opinion that the natural variability of seeds, particularly in different localities, made it impossible to prove the novelty of any particular plant and therefore impossible to patent it.

The decision was wrong, Burbank maintained. "As a matter of justice," he wrote, the originator of new plants deserved the same "untold wealth" as the originators of mechanical devices who could patent their inventions. And, as a matter of policy, it would be a benefit to all if plant inventors could obtain patents. "Our very civilization depends on the improvements which have been made with plants," he pointed out, "but there is very little financial inducement for improving them."

IN 1924, commercial seed catalog giants like Burpee, Park, Landreth, Ferry, Morse, and all their smaller brethren were delighted that Congress had finally done away with the free seed program, which had long been regarded as a boondoggle used to curry favor with constituents. But while that eliminated a major grievance of the seed sellers and a major focus of their political lobbying, the tantalizing vision of legal protection for plant inventions still remained out of reach. Not very far out, however, because Paul Stark of Stark Bro's Nurseries was chairman of the National Committee for Plant Patents, a Washington lobbying group supported by the American Association of Nurserymen.

In November 1929, when it began to seem very likely that the next election would bring a change in the composition of Congress that would delay any action on plant patents possibly for decades, the members of Stark's committee began an aggressive campaign to promote their cause, speaking at public hearings and in private meetings with members of Congress. They also drafted the bill that was finally introduced in May 1930, proposing a radical change in the legal and commercial status of both plants and those who breed them.

Six months after the crash of the stock market, the plight of plant inventors yearning for intellectual property protection was nowhere near the top of the country's list of agricultural problems. As the global financial crisis deepened, farmers were among the first to be hurt. Farmers are always debtors, borrowing against the prospects of a future harvest in order to pay for seeds, fertilizer, and machinery. When commodity prices plunged in 1929 and the credit sources farmers depended on collapsed, they had no way to pay their debts. The start of a lingering drought that would turn much of the Great Plains into the famous "Dust Bowl" was also taking a toll. Amid the growing cries to do something for the farmers, the first legislative response had nothing to do with helping those who were suffering most. It was a plant patent law.

Senator John G. Townsend Jr., Republican of Delaware, and Representative Fred S. Purnell, Republican of Indiana, were the bill's sponsors. Townsend, a wealthy grower who had been known as the "Strawberry King" before entering politics, owned 130,000 acres of orchards in 1930, the second largest holding of its kind in the nation. Purnell had a close relationship with the American Association of Nurserymen. Luther Burbank's name and his legend loomed over the entire congressional debate. He was cited repeatedly as a brilliant inventor who had suffered from not being able to profit from his ideas. Congressmen vied with each other to praise him in ever more elevated terms. Glowing descriptions of Burbank's contributions to humanity were interlaced with reminders of the financial sufferings he had endured because he could not patent his creations. He was remembered as a selfless champion of both nature and the national economy, a hero who had been denied the rewards that his labors so richly deserved. In an echo of Burbank's own threats from the 1890s, members of Congress heard dire warnings about the future of plant breeding if other horticultural inventors did not receive better encouragement in the form of patent protection.

Eighty-three-year-old Thomas Edison sent a telegram in support of the legislative change. Edison, holder of a world record

1,093 separate patents, was certainly in a position to speak to the spur to creativity that intellectual property rights provided. "Nothing that Congress could do to help farming would be of greater value and permanence," Edison declared, "than to give the plant breeder the same status as the mechanical and chemical inventors now have through patent law." As executor of her husband's estate, Elizabeth Burbank also wrote in support of the bill, describing it as "one of Luther Burbank's most cherished hopes."

Not everybody was convinced plant patents were either necessary or desirable. Senator Clarence Dill of Washington questioned the wisdom and the constitutionality of allowing private individuals or companies to monopolize "new plants and new food products produced by nature." Senator Royal Copeland of New York moved to postpone discussion for three days to have more time to examine the bill, only to withdraw his objections after his office was inundated with telegrams from the very well organized horticultural and nursery societies of his home state that supported the new legislation.

In the House of Representatives, Fiorello LaGuardia, the "Little Flower" who would soon be elected to the first of his three terms as mayor of New York City, tried to get his colleagues to look more carefully at possible consequences of plant patents. LaGuardia's constituents, residents of East Harlem's Twentieth District, did not include the grape growers and orchard owners of western New York State or any other plant breeders pressuring their congressman for patent privilege, so he felt free to express his many doubts about the proposed legislation.

LaGuardia's comments were a survey of issues that had made and would continue to make plant patents a divisive issue. Fearing

the effects of patents on competition, he asked how small producers would be able to compete with patented varieties developed by
large growers with greater resources for investment. He worried,
too, about farmers who inadvertently cultivated seeds of what
turned out to be a patented plant, and he asked if they would be
liable for accidental infringements on patent rights. More pointedly, he wondered why Congress wasn't working on more extensive
farm relief instead of focusing on the rather small population of
developers of new plant varieties.

These were all good questions, but they were silenced by the
enduring power of a dead man's reputation. Asked if he would
agree that "there is no man who is a greater benefactor to the
human race than the man who produces a new vegetable or a new
fruit," the representative from what was arguably the least gar-
dened district in America answered without hesitation or qualification. "I will go further and state that I consider Luther Burbank
the outstanding American of his time," LaGuardia declared, leaving a field of other heroes that stretched from Abraham Lincoln
to Charles Lindbergh to fight it out for second place. He added,
however, that Burbank had managed to make a living without
patent protection, and he imagined that other plant breeders could
do the same.

In response, Purnell read a letter Burbank had written despair-
ing over his inability to profit from his plants:

> A man can patent a mouse trap or copyright a nasty song, but if
> he gives to the world a new fruit that will add millions to the value
> of earth's annual harvests he will be fortunate if he is rewarded by
> so much as having his name connected with the result. . . . I would

hesitate to advise a young man, no matter how gifted or devoted, to adopt plant breeding as a life work until America takes some action to protest his unquestioned rights to some benefit from his achievements.

LaGuardia remained unconvinced, but the bill passed both House and Senate with little opposition or further discussion as the Plant Patent Act of 1930. It was the first legislation anywhere in the world that treated growing things as intellectual property. In the early months of the Depression under a probusiness Republican administration, extending new incentives to the breeders and sellers of new plants seemed a small but easy way of assisting the flagging economy. And five years after his death, the powerful public image of Luther Burbank, the benevolent inventor in the garden, was still sufficient to overcome fears of a new natural order in which the living substance of creation could be privately owned and controlled.

Not all creation, however. The congressional debate had included grand pronouncements about how the new legislation would benefit farmers and feed the people of America, but in fact its terms were so restricted that few farmers noticed any change at all, either in what they could buy or what they could sell. The Plant Patent Act of 1930 offered intellectual property protection "for a new and distinct, invented or discovered asexually reproduced plant including cultivated sports, mutants, hybrids, and newly found seedlings, other than a tuber propagated plant or a plant found in an uncultivated state." The exclusion of plants propagated by sexual reproduction meant that corn, wheat, rice, and other grains could not be patented, ostensibly because of the great variation in plants grown from seed, but also because of a deep reluctance to grant exclusive control to private interests over any of the plants that were major sources of food. In an irony that Burbank would have noted, the unexplained exclusion of tubers meant that potatoes were also specifically ineligible for patents, even though they fit the otherwise rather strict requirements of the new legislation. What that left was mostly tree fruits, nuts, roses, and lilies—all plants that were part of the Luther Burbank legacy that now belonged to the inventory of Stark Bro's Nursery.

PAUL STARK'S SUCCESSFUL LOBBYING for plant patent protection was doubtless meant to be the start of much more aggressive efforts to develop the Gold Ridge Farm and market Luther Burbank's plant inventions. Soon after the company reached an agreement with Elizabeth Burbank to take over the plants, Stark Bro's had hired Dr. John Bregger from Clemson University to select specimens he thought had commercial potential. When he got to Santa Rosa, Bregger became enamored of Burbank's plums and thought his hybrid lilacs would sweep the market. Little was done at first, however, beyond a good deal of bragging about how Stark Bro's was the inheritors of Burbank's legacy. A publicity photograph from the period, taken in Missouri, shows seventeen men and an adolescent girl gaping at an open trunk and a scattering of small paper bags tumbled together on the ground. The caption says they are "listing the contents of Burbank's Treasure Chest of seeds of rare hybrids, trees and plants, descriptions and notes which Stark Bro's inherited," although nobody appears to be making such a list.

In the fall of 1930, soon after the Plant Patent Act became law, Elizabeth Burbank, acting as executrix of Luther Burbank's estate, applied for six plant patents that were immediately assigned to Stark Bro's Nurseries and Orchards. Five of those applications were for plums and one was for a large freestone peach; all were granted in 1932, the first year of plant patent approvals, as was a patent for a cherry submitted in December 1931. More Burbank patents followed during the decade, mostly for roses but including a double-flowering peach described as a hybrid between the ornamental varieties from Asia and the edible Muir peach. The last Burbank patent was granted in 1951, twenty-five years after Luther Burbank's death. It was for a dwarf prune plum described as "a seedling resulting from deliberate cross-pollination of two varieties of unidentified parentage, as performed and propagated by the late Luther Burbank at the Burbank Experimental Gardens at Sebastopol, California." In all, Burbank's creations received a total of sixteen posthumous patents—a tiny fraction of the new cultivars under development at his death, let alone perfected in his lifetime, and an indication of the difficulties that remained in the quest to establish exclusive rights to Burbank's work.

Still, the power of the new legal protection remains clear. One of Elizabeth Burbank's patent applications was for "a new and distinct variety of peach" called the July Elberta. By virtue of various changes and improvements in the original tree, the July Elberta patent has been extended far beyond its original seventeen years. Over the ensuing decades, Stark Bro's Nurseries has had its own travails, with several changes of ownership, but in 2008, the company still advertised the Burbank July Elberta peach, proclaiming, "Luther Burbank himself created this wonder-tree. Stark Bro's gave it to the world! . . . We're proud to bring this tree to you . . . and prouder yet that you can get it only from Stark Bro's."

. . .

LIKE PAUL STARK, Thomas Edison had had a personal interest in the Plant Patent Act, beyond his firmly held conviction that every inventor should receive legal and financial credit for his creations. Late in his career, after a lifetime of chemical and electrical experiments, Edison turned his attention to possibilities Burbank had suggested long ago in Santa Rosa. Edison had never forgotten Burbank's idea at the time of the Panama-Pacific Exposition that domestic sources of latex might decrease reliance on distant rubber plantations. In 1927, the year after Burbank's death, Edison took up the mantle of the garden inventor, announcing he would make the quest for domestic rubber the sole object of his research. At his winter home in Fort Myers, Florida, Edison had begun cultivating milkweed and ficus for their sticky sap, using a vacuum pump to extract enough material for his experiments.

It was his final challenge and "the most complicated problem I have ever yet tackled," Edison told the editor of *Popular Science Monthly*. He had spent a lifetime mastering inorganic materials, but now he was entering Burbank's realm of living things. Edison pored over books of botany and sent agents to comb forest and meadow for likely plants whose practical uses could be tested in the laboratory. Even as his sons were moving their father's business into the new field of radio communication, Edison set up a temporary laboratory at the New York Botanical Garden to analyze the rubber content of different plant sources. He built a new laboratory in Florida and a large herbarium in West Orange, New Jersey, to contain the specimens sent in by his various botanical collectors.

Early in 1929, before the stock market crash or the dedication of Henry Ford's museum, Edison announced that he had managed to extract one hundred pounds of rubber from an acre of goldenrod, a prolific weed more often associated with allergies than with strategic materials. Ford, who was eager to develop new material for tires and other automobile parts, gave Edison land to build a processing facility, but there was more to be done. Edison wanted to breed a new kind of goldenrod with a higher latex content, a goal that invigorated his lobbying the following summer when he campaigned in Burbank's name for the Plant Patent Act.

Edison continued his breeding program to the very last weeks of his life, paying more attention to his goldenrod than to his daughter's new baby or his son's departure from the family company. It was only when he stopped visiting the greenhouse that people who worked for him knew the end must be near. When Edison died in October 1931, the goldenrod experiments ended with him.

ONCE THE PRINCIPLE was established that nature could be subject to exclusive ownership, it was only a matter of time before the initial limitations on plant patents were removed. The Plant Patent Act of 1930 was amended in the 1950s to allow patent protection for plants that had been newly recognized as well as newly created, including not only mutants and sports, but also varieties discovered in other countries and brought to the United States for propagation.

In 1970, the Plant Variety Protection Act extended patentlike protection to seeds, through a protection certificate that allowed sale only by permission of the certificate holder and required labels indicating protection on seed containers. For over twenty years, an exemption was granted to farmers, who could save the seed of patented varieties for their own use and sell them to other farmers. Breeders were allowed to use patented seeds as the basis for further experiments that might lead to new patentable varieties (the kind of jump-start many breeders had taken by buying Burbank's new creations). In 1994, however, the Plant Variety Protection Act was amended to restrict farmers and breeders from selling any seeds from protected varieties and from breeding new varieties from protected seeds. The 1994 amendment also extended patent protection to potatoes and other tubers, a change that was probably less a tribute to Luther Burbank than an anticipation of the Monsanto Corporation's 1995 introduction of the Bt "Newleaf" Russet Burbank potato, which had been genetically engineered to produce an insecticide that repelled the Colorado potato beetle.

AND SO WE RETURN to where we began, only to discover how much our perspective has changed. In 1906, the *Florists' Exchange* had described the blight-resistant Burbank potato as "the salvation of parts of Ireland from famine." A century later, the potato that was hailed for many years as the answer to potato growers' problems now literally contains the problem itself, as debates over risks and benefits of genetically modified organisms polarize an increasingly global community of breeders, growers, and consumers. To many opponents of bioengineering, the Bt Russet Burbank potato has become the centerpiece of legal and political campaigns to ban genetically modified plants, and it is reviled as a leading example of large multinational corporations' attempting to monopolize international agriculture at the expense of environment, health, local culture, and regional economies. To advocates of that same genetic engineering, the Bt Russet Burbank represents a triumph in the ongoing effort to provide more food for an expanding global population.

Like the man whose name it bears, the Burbank potato now comes wrapped in a reputation that has little to do with the virtues it first demonstrated on a small farm in Massachusetts. Its evolution as both plant and symbol epitomizes the vast balancing act of reverence and greed that has always marked the human relationship to every other element of the natural world. The road from the nineteenth-century farm to the twenty-first-century global market twists and turns, of course, but a good part of it still passes straight through Luther Burbank's garden.

"Sunberry, the Improved Wonderberry," John Lewis Childs catalog, 1910.

Epilogue: Searching for Luther Burbank

A lot of it boils down to what's natural and what's not. . . . There's nothing wrong with improving plants. Luther Burbank—he did that. But he didn't violate nature doing it. —Alice Waters, 2001

rom the Plant Patent Act of 1930 to the contemporary battles over bioengineered crops, the history of modern agriculture and horticulture is a record of increasing claims of property rights over what once was the common heritage of nature. But that was hardly the idea behind the enormous enthusiasm for new plant varieties in the years when Luther Burbank was the most visible practitioner of the plant inventor's art.

A century ago, innovation in the garden was not synonymous with ownership, and new plant introductions were not regarded as a threat to biodiversity. Even as the environmental movement was coming into being and broad swatches of wilderness were being set aside by Congress as national parks, there had been little question that improving cultivated plants was a worthy goal and that anything that increased yield or improved marketability was an asset. Burbank and all his many plant-breeding brethren were dedicated to *expanding* the grower's options, supplementing known varieties of just about every kind of plant with new ones that looked better, lasted longer, grew more lushly, tasted sweeter, could be shipped farther, and could be afforded by every consumer.

By contemporary standards, Burbank's famous grafts and hybrids, once so miraculous, seem almost quaint. It's hard to be amazed by a winter-bearing rhubarb or a dahlia that has been bred to lose its unpleasant smell when molecular biologists have learned how to move genetic material between animals and plants, breed crops to resist specific herbicides, or guarantee the sterility of that profligate of pollen, corn.

Burbank could not have imagined how much plant breeding would change in the years after his death, or the changes that would come to his beloved Sonoma County. In Burbank's era and for years after, Santa Rosa was all about plums, Petaluma was eggs, and Sebastopol was filled with rows of apple trees with pink and white blossoms that drifted from the trees and coated the ground, announcing the arrival of spring. Now the few farms in the area are holdouts, small patches of green amid more profitable residential and commercial developments. Orchards and fields remain, but their edges are fringed with signs advertising real estate, ayurvedic yoga, wine country balloon tours, self-storage lockers, and lawyers eager to help you get the disability payments you surely deserve.

The heart of agriculture has moved east to the mammoth industrial farms of California's Central Valley, while some might argue that its soul is to the south and west of Santa Rosa, in the organic farms of Marin County. Down in Berkeley, forty-six miles from the Burbank cottage, Alice Waters of Chez Panisse restaurant fame is fostering schoolyard gardens to introduce city children to the experience, once so normal, of seeing food grow before it is eaten. From New York's Union Square to the San Francisco Ferry Building, farmers' markets are now a familiar sight in urban venues around the country. In Chicago's stately Lincoln Park, built in the nineteenth century to civilize unimproved nature, signs for the twice-weekly greenmarket now exhort the passersby: "Know your food. Know your farmer." In the abandoned centers of many cities, barren blocks are being rescued, patch by patch, to start neighborhood gardens where people can, once again, grow their own food.

Today, the Wizard of Santa Rosa rarely gets more than a passing mention in discussions of cloning, gene-splicing, bioengineering, and what is often called the future of food. The art of making new organisms has progressed far beyond anything Burbank ever attempted. His techniques were a combination of selection, cross-pollination, and grafting. His scientific vocabulary was considerably smaller than that found in any modern textbook of high school biology. The patents that were not available during his lifetime have become a force of economic consolidation that makes many long for a return to the "heirloom" crops that were once so eagerly replaced.

And yet Burbank's work and his inventions are all around us. His daisies and gladioli have so changed our image of these flowers that we might not even recognize the varieties that preceded his improvements. The pluot, a hybrid fruit derived in part from Burbank's plumcot, is patented and trademark protected but often sold interchangeably with plumcots in the grocery aisles. The small, dark berry that created so much controversy when it was marketed as the Wonderberry in 1908 is being grown again as the Sunberry, the name Burbank preferred. Moving far beyond jams and jellies, the restaurant chefs who frequent today's urban greenmarkets use it as a garnish for summer cocktails and even for a chutney to accompany fois gras.

Outside a market stall, a child plays air guitar with a fresh head of elephant garlic, the cloves as big as his hands, the stalk a crisp green shaft that rises four feet into the air and ends in a white turban of a flower bud that Burbank spent years cross-pollinating. Wickson plums, their yellow skins showing a pink blush when they are ready to eat, are too fragile for long-distance shipping, but they still ripen in home gardens and the orchards of smaller farms. The Russet Burbank potato (usually without the Bt gene) continues to dominate the global potato patch. And the Burbank tomato, introduced in 1915 as a new cultivar that was earlier, smoother, larger, and more productive than its rivals, is now offered as an heirloom variety, even though it hasn't quite reached the century mark that some say is a defining requirement for heirloom status.

Luther Burbank's legend and his legacy also live on in many of the places where he lived and worked, and in the written records of his career. In Massachusetts, the Lancaster Public Library still stands on the Lancaster town green, renamed the Thayer Memorial Library and much expanded since Luther Burbank walked there to read Darwin. The Bulfinch church built of Burbank bricks is still there, too, not far from the two-story brick building that once held the Lancaster Academy and is now a private home. The Burbank farmland is now part of a military base, Fort Devens. The brick home that stood there has been destroyed, but the large wooden wing of the farmhouse where Luther Burbank was born remains intact as part of the Greenfield Village outdoor museum, where it now serves as a gift shop.

The white frame house in Lunenburg where Burbank, his

mother, and his sister lived when he was cultivating his first commercial garden remains largely unchanged, surrounded by descendants of the maple trees that made a brilliant display that distant October when Luther Burbank left Massachusetts for California. In the undeveloped fields that still line some of the roads between Lancaster and Lunenburg, immigrants from Laos, Cambodia, Vietnam, and Brazil arrive after work to grow vegetables in areas where the owners wish to keep their land in cultivation.

The first house Luther Burbank owned in Santa Rosa was renovated and occupied by his widow, Elizabeth, until her death in 1977. The house, the barn, the greenhouse, and the grounds are now all part of the Luther Burbank Home & Gardens museum in Santa Rosa. The garden beds display beautiful roses and daisies and cacti that are close to those Burbank created, though often not exactly the real thing, because no one is quite sure at this point what the originals were like. The barn where Burbank stayed to get away from his first wife and where Wilbur Hall lived while writing *Harvest of the Years* now holds a gift shop, a visitor center, and a changing exhibition of material from the archives, which are expertly tended by well-informed and dedicated volunteers. Inside the small frame house, visitors can see some of the original books, chromolithographs, carved walnut furniture, and even an early hand-powered sewing machine like the ones Burbank sold door-to-door as a young man in Massachusetts. They are all powerful evocations of the modest life that was a significant part of Luther Burbank's personal charm.

In 1974, almost fifty years after her husband's death and after her agreement with Stark Bro's Nurseries had ended, Elizabeth Burbank sold the land that held Gold Ridge Farm to the Sebastopol Area Housing Corporation, a government agency, to be used for the low-cost senior housing that now occupies the site. She stipulated that three acres, including plantings and the caretaker's cottage, be left undisturbed. This area is now owned by the city of Sebastopol and maintained by the Western Sonoma Historical Society and the Burbank Farm Committee, two organizations formed to care for the Burbank legacy.

What remains of the original experimental grounds is a thin slice of sloping land wedged between the Memorial Lawn cemetery to the west and the Burbank Heights Senior Living Apartments to the east, a juxtaposition that forces a certain contemplation of mortality. The grounds are very much alive, however, and full of Burbank creations, including some of his less successful experiments. Here a visitor can see the white blackberries marked as "not as tasty as the black kind," the recently rediscovered row of hybrid nightshade, and the not-quite-spineless cactus that never became the success as cattle feed that Burbank had hoped it would be. The winter-hardy Chinese oranges he thought might extend the citrus industry to northern climates outlived him, unimproved, with fruit that is said to have the taste and tenderness of golf balls.

The triumphs are there, too. Pink and yellow Burbank roses climb the pillars of the cottage porch, while all around are wonderful beds planted with Shasta daisies, many of them varieties created by later breeders who used Burbank's breakthrough as the start of further work. A venerable Royal walnut tree, one of Burbank's original plantings, continues to shower down tons of nuts every year. An apple tree bears sixty different kinds of grafts, fewer than in Burbank's day but still a very impressive sight, especially in spring when the branches are covered with multicolored blossoms. Roses and lilacs bloom in season, along with plums and plumcots and the apple trees that bear their varied fruit, a testament to Burbank's inventiveness and to the careful vigilance of the knowledgeable volunteers who keep the wilderness at bay.

On the wall of the cottage at Gold Ridge Farm is a copy of a garden chart that Burbank had prepared some time in the 1920s, showing every experimental plant in its position on the experimental grounds. Four feet high and six feet wide, made of paper mounted on canvas stretched between wooden poles, the chart was written in code, inscribed in tiny letters, and rolled up like a sea chart. We can see the careful use of land, the thousands of varieties under study, the enormous inventory of Burbank's work. We cannot tell what anything means. It's a treasure map that waits to be deciphered.

LUTHER BURBANK'S CAREER was very well recorded, and documents associated with his work are now housed in a number of different places that remain important settings for his story. The Library of Congress has 12,500 items in its Luther Burbank Collection, close to the Capitol and not very far from the Patent Office that had so much to do with the plant breeding industry before, during, and after Burbank's life. The holdings include personal and professional correspondence, family papers, catalogs, advertising broadsheets, price lists, subscription lists, garden charts, notes on curious seeds and roots (received, sent, sold abroad), membership cards, birthday cards, Christmas cards, postcards, calling cards, admiring poems, fan mail, hate mail, classroom exercises in group adulation, transcripts of interviews conducted by actual or would-be biographers, typescripts and outlines of unpublished biographies, and nine of the seventeen oversize, overstuffed scrapbooks full of newspapers clippings about Luther Burbank assembled primarily by his sister Emma. Here, too, are the scripts and programs for pageants enacted in honor of Luther Burbank's birthday, the many posthumous tributes, the even more voluminous proposals for posthumous tributes, the centennial celebrations of Burbank's birth in 1849 and of his move to California in 1875, and a list of other archives with significant collections.

These start where much of his work was done, at the Luther Burbank Home & Gardens in Santa Rosa, California, and Gold Ridge Farm in Sebastopol, California, which retain a number of Burbank papers and personal effects. The Bancroft Library at the University of California in Berkeley holds many of the papers of Edward Wickson and other associates of Burbank during his long career, as well as an invaluable collection of "Burbankiana" put together by Walter Howard, head of the Department of Pomology at the University of California at Davis in the 1930s and 1940s. Howard, who met Burbank only once, in 1915, spent almost twenty years compiling *Luther Burbank's Plant Contributions*, which documented Burbank's introduction of over eight hundred original varieties of fruits, flowers, vegetable, nuts, and grains—an impressive number for any breeder, much less one who was accused of not understanding what he was doing. The Howard collection includes a unique run of Burbank catalogs, interviews with his contemporaries, and unpublished writings about Burbank done by other people. Among these is the unpublished manuscript about Luther Burbank written by Donald F. Jones, the plant biologist at the Connecticut Agricultural Experiment Station who perfected the "double cross" method of breeding hybrid corn and became yet another plant scientist who had a long and almost grudging fascination with Burbank's work.

Edward Wickson's letters to and from Oscar E. Binner when he worked on the twelve-volume *Luther Burbank, His Methods and Discoveries and Their Practical Applications* are now in the Special Collections at the University of California at Davis, the "University Farm" Wickson worked so hard to establish; they can be read in a room hung with glorious Maxfield Parrish paintings commissioned by the Ferry Seed Company for their advertisements. In Palo Alto, where Burbank lectured on evolution in the early years of the twentieth century, the Stanford University Library holds many letters from and about Burbank that passed through the hands of two of his most active supporters, David Starr Jordan, the first university president, and Judge Samuel Leib, Burbank's close friend and one of the early university trustees.

The American Philosophical Society in Philadelphia houses the papers of George H. Shull, who was sent by the Carnegie Institution of Washington, D.C., to make a scientific report of Burbank's work; the Carnegie Institution has its own records of the deliberations that led to their funding of Burbank's research. The Benson Ford Research Center at The Henry Ford in Dearborn, Michigan, holds another collection of papers by and about Luther Burbank, along with writings about him by other people, ephemeral papers and tributes to Burbank that were given to Henry Ford after Burbank's death, and extensive records of the Ford collection of Burbank items, many of which (starting with the shovel) can be seen in the Henry Ford museum or the adjoining Greenfield Village.

To anyone trying to capture Luther Burbank's special place in the world of growing, selling, understanding, and celebrating plants, this abundance of written material is a mixed blessing. It can be overwhelming, of course. It can be misleading, too, because it makes it seem as though the story of the garden somehow happens indoors and can be enclosed within boxes and files containing endless reams of papers. Instead, we should begin where Burbank began and where every gardener, farmer, and plant lover starts, which is outside.

People who love to grow things have a very expansive embrace. They want flowers and fruits, trees and bulbs, acres of vegetables, an herb garden by the kitchen door, an orchard not much farther away, and a sunny window behind which they can nurture potted plants to get them through the winter. One of Burbank's charms was that he shared this all-embracing passion. He wanted to feed the world, and he also wanted to shade it with fast-growing trees and deck it with flowers in colors never seen before. From window box to farm and orchard, the garden remains what it has always been, a place of inexhaustible invention.

Le géranium de M. Burbank comparé au
géranium ordinaire, *Le Globe*, May 1906.

ACKNOWLEDGMENTS

This book began in a garden in Italy with a debate about the origins of plants, took me to California where my subject quickly expanded to include the business of plant breeding and the marketing of crops, and led from there to Chicago where I grappled with unanticipated issues of property rights, patent protection, and the marketing of fame itself. As I traveled this unfamiliar territory, I had a great deal of help. The progress I've made in understanding gardens, plants, Luther Burbank, and most of the other areas I've tried to explore in this book has depended on the expertise, patience, insight, and generosity of many people. The mistakes are entirely my own.

To start with Burbank's own gardens, I am enormously grateful for the help of the volunteers who staff both the Luther Burbank Home & Gardens, in Santa Rosa, and Gold Ridge Farm, in Sebastopol. Rebecca Baker, volunteer archivist and historian at the Luther Burbank Home & Gardens, provided invaluable insight and repeated access to the wealth of material in the Santa Rosa collection, as did assistant archivist Lori Ross. Patty Levenberg, president of the Western Sonoma County Historical Society, was a wonderful guide to Gold Ridge Farm and host in Sebastopol, and Bob Hornback helped me understand the past and current intricacies of the plantings there. On the other side of the continent, Marcia Jakubowicz, special collections clerk of the Thayer Memorial Library in Lancaster, Massachusetts, shared both historical and contemporary understanding of the history of Burbank's family and the setting of his earliest experiences.

I am also very grateful to the many librarians who helped me navigate the different archives where Burbank's papers now reside: David Kessler at the Bancroft Library at the University of California, Berkeley; Pat White and her colleagues in Special Collections at the Green Library at Stanford University; John Skarstad and colleagues in Special Collections at the University of California, Davis; librarian Katherine Powis and volunteer archivist Joan Nichols at the Library of the Horticultural Society of New York; Sherry Vance of the Bailey Hortorium at Cornell University; Leora Siegel, Stacy Stoldt, and Edward Valauskas of the Lenhardt Library at the Chicago Botanic Garden; Jennifer Hart of the John Crerar Library at the University of Chicago; Clay and Sally Logan and Martha Sue Smith of the Louisiana Area Historical Museum; Valerie-Ann Lutz of the American Philosophical Society; Kathy Steiner and her knowledgeable and infinitely patient colleagues at the Benson Ford Research Center at The Henry Ford in Dearborn, Michigan; and the many expert librarians and staff who made it a pleasure to work in the Manuscript Division at the Library of Congress.

The Northwestern University Department of History graciously gave me a home from which to write this book. At the Northwestern University library, Harriet Lightman helped me find my way through the web of online resources and Charmaine Henriques revealed the secrets of government publications. Thanks go to Jennifer Chen, my resourceful research assistant and ace retriever of ancient newspapers and magazines, and to M. Leigh Harrison, LiAnn Yim, and Anthony Abata, who stepped in to provide much-needed research help at different times. Phillip Nolte of the University of Idaho graciously answered many random questions about potatoes, and Charles Valauskas generously corrected some of my errors on patent law. The staff at Lincoln Park Conservatory in Chicago shared their horticultural knowledge and were a constant reminder that the most important thing is to love plants; I am particularly indebted to Brian Houck for his informed observations and keen editorial eye. Photographs of archival material at the Library of Congress are the expert work of David B. Smith.

To my editor, Janie Fleming, and my agent, Rob McQuilkin, I give great thanks for all their help and encouragement, with special gratitude for their insistence on keeping my spirits and my standards high.

Many friends put up with me as I traveled to collections and made them listen to perhaps more than they wanted to know about the wonders of plant breeding. Special thanks goes to Michael Janeway and Barbara Maltby, Mark Aaronson and Marjorie Gelb, Randy Byrne and Susan Cohen-Byrne, and Margot and Greg Squires.

Carl, Jeremy, and Lucia Smith—great readers, astute critics, endlessly generous supporters—know how much I rely on them, which is beyond expression in mere words. Last but not at all least, I thank my mother, Sylvia Schur, grocer's daughter and food editor extraordinaire, who first taught me about fruits and flowers, and my father, Saul Schur, who loved books.

NOTES

xiii **"Not one man in a thousand"**: Charles Darwin, *On the Origin of Species by Means of Natural Selection*. (London: John Murray, 1859), p. 32.

PROLOGUE

3 **"the simple dignity and modesty"**: All quotations from "Complimentary Banquet in Honor of Luther Burbank" (San Francisco: California State Board of Trade, *Bulletin* No. 14, 1905).

CHAPTER 1: NATURE IN AN AGE OF INVENTION

13 **"The greatest service"**: Thomas Jefferson, "A Memorandum (Services to My Country)," in *Writings/Thomas Jefferson*, ed. Merrill D. Peterson. *The Library of America*. (New York: Literary Classics of the United States, 1984), p. 703.

13 **Ellsworth envisioned his office**: For a fuller description, see Henry L. Ellsworth, "Letter from the Commissioner of Patents," 25th Congress, 3d. Session, January 28, 1839.

17 **"Luther has his days"**: Herbert Burbank, October 27, 1856, Box 1, Luther Burbank Papers, Manuscript Division, Library of Congress, Washington, DC.

18 **"accepted so literally"**: Emma Burbank Beeson, *Early Life and Letters of Luther Burbank* (San Francisco: Harr Wagner Publishing Company, 1927), pp. 68–69.

20 **"He was very ingenious"**: Letter, Jane [Burbank] Bell, February 28, 1903. Box 1, Luther Burbank Papers, Manuscript Division, Library of Congress, Washington, DC.

24 **"grand Waschusett"**: Emma Burbank Beeson, *Early Life and Letters of Luther Burbank* (San Francisco: Harr Wagner Publishing Company, 1927), p. 71.

25 **"a Cosmist"**: Luther Burbank to David Starr Jordan, December 10, 1925. David Starr Jordan Papers, SC 058, Stanford University Archives, Stanford, CA.

27 **"It opened a new world to me"**: Luther Burbank and Wilbur Hall, *The Har-*

vest of the Years (Boston: Houghton Mifflin Company, 1927), p. 22.

29 "It is an error": Charles Darwin, *The Variation of Animals and Plants Under Domestication* (New York: Orange Judd, 1869), vol. 1, p. 2.

29 "When we ask ourselves what is the cause": Ibid., vol. 1, p. 493.

30 "every thing is made perfectly plain": First advertising page in Darwin, *Variation of Animals and Plants*, vol. 1, opp. p. 494.

30 On his twenty-second birthday: Burbank Personal Inventory, Box 22, Luther Burbank Collection, Manuscript Division, Library of Congress, Washington, DC.

CHAPTER 2: THE LUCKY SPUD

35 "And he gave it for his opinion": Jonathan Swift, *Gulliver's Travels*, part 2, chapter 7.

44 "D[ear] S[ir]": James J. H. Gregory to Luther Burbank, October 5, 1874. Luther Burbank Home & Gardens, Santa Rosa, CA.

45 "Dear Sir, In reply to your letter": Washburn to Luther Burbank, December 3, 1874. Luther Burbank Home & Gardens, Santa Rosa, CA.

46 "a very worthy lady": Letter by James J. H. Gregory to *The Magazine of Horticulture*, December 1857, quoted in http://www.saveseeds.org/biography/gregory/hubbard_origin_article.htm.

CHAPTER 3: THE SECOND GOLD RUSH

51 "Within the limits of our State": Charles H. Shinn, *Pacific Rural Handbook* (San Francisco: Dewey & Co., Publishers of the *Pacific Rural Press*, 1879), p. 34.

52 "a young man who will not drink": Letters from Luther Burbank to his mother and sister, published in Emma Burbank Beeson, *Early Life and Letters of Luther Burbank* (San Francisco: Harr Wagner Publishing Company, 1927), pp. 89–112.

57 "she will never": Herbert Burbank letter of October 27, 1856, to unidentified recipient, Box 1, Luther Burbank Papers, Manuscript Division, Library of Congress, Washington, DC.

60 "One sentence in the very introductory": Luther Burbank and Wilbur Hall. *The Harvest of the Years* (Boston: Houghton Mifflin Company, 1927), p. 33.

62 "the sexuality of plants": Henry L. Ellsworth, "Letter from the Commissioner of Patents," 25th Congress, 3d. session, January 28, 1839.

68 "The Burbank Seedling Potatoes": Quotations from unidentified scrapbook clippings, Luther Burbank Home & Gardens, Santa Rosa, CA.

69 "I will remember you": James J. H. Gregory to Luther Burbank, December 31, 1877. Luther Burbank Home & Gardens, Santa Rosa, CA.

71 "New Potato": Walter Howard Collection, the Bancroft Library, University of California, Berkeley.

72 "I have given you great fame": James J. H. Gregory to Luther Burbank, August 19, 1880. Luther Burbank Home & Gardens, Santa Rosa, CA.

CHAPTER 4: FASTER, BETTER, SWEETER

75 "The market for dried and canned fruit": Robert A. Thompson, *Resources of the Santa Rosa Valley and the Town of Santa Rosa, Sonoma County, California*, 1884, quoted in Gaye LeBaron, Dee Blackman,

Joann Mitchell, Harvey Hansen, *Santa Rosa: A Nineteenth Century Town* (Santa Rosa: Historia, Ltd., 1985), p. 68.

85 **"budded over apricots"**: Nursery Plan book, 1881. Luther Burbank Home & Gardens, Santa Rosa, CA.

CHAPTER 5: A PERSONAL INTERLUDE

99 **"Have never enjoyed"**: All quotations from Burbank's letters in 1888 are from Emma Burbank Beeson, *Early Life and Letters of Luther Burbank* (San Francisco: Harr Wagner Publishing Company, 1927), pp. 121–44. The pocket diary and other souvenirs from Burbank's 1888 trip from California to Massachusetts and Washington, DC, are in Box 2, Luther Burbank Collection, Manuscript Division, Library of Congress, Washington, DC.

100 **"Mr. Gregory expects to have a monument raised"**: Emma Burbank Beeson, *Early Life and Letters of Luther Burbank* p. 125.

103 **"Luther and all his family"**: Walter L. Howard, "Papers relating to Walter Howard's biography of Luther Burbank." BANC MSS C-R 6, the Bancroft Library, University of California, Berkeley.

105 **"normal male sexual drives"**: Ken Kraft and Pat Kraft, *Luther Burbank, the Wizard and the Man* (New York: Meredith Press, 1967), p. 62.

CHAPTER 6: MARKETING THE NEW CREATION

118 **"Mr. Burbank has devoted a life's work"**: Testimonials are from Burbank scrapbook, vol. 1. Luther Burbank Home & Gardens, Santa Rosa, CA. Many are also included in *New Creations in Fruits and Flowers*, 1893.

129 **"$500 FOR ONE TREE"**: Hale

Nursery advertisement. Collection of Luther Burbank Home & Gardens, Santa Rosa, CA.

CHAPTER 7: THE PHILOSOPHER IN THE ORCHARD, THE SCIENTIST IN THE PEA PATCH

133 **"The statements made"**: Scrapbook, Luther Burbank Collection, Manuscript Division, Library of Congress, Washington, DC.

137 **"Mr. B. believes that thought vibrations"**: Samuel Green, "Notes made by the late Professor Samuel B. Green when he visited Luther Burbank in 1899." Walter Howard Collection, BANC MSS C-R 6, the Bancroft Library, University of California, Berkeley.

142 **"So keep my bob"**: Luther Burbank, September 26, 1900. Box 1, Luther Burbank Papers, Manuscript Division, Library of Congress, Washington, DC.

147 **"Then the photographer must be taken to Gold Ridge"**: May Benedict Maye to Emma Burbank Beeson, from Emma Burbank Beeson, *Early Life and Letters of Luther Burbank* (San Francisco: Harr Wagner Publishing Company, 1927), p. 148.

149 All quotations from "Some of the Fundamental Principles of Plant Breeding" and from the second International Conference on Plant Breeding and Hybridization are from the Horticultural Society of New York, "Proceedings: International Conference on Plant Breeding and Hybridization, 1902," *Memoirs*, vol. 1, (New York: 1904).

CHAPTER 8: CALIFORNIA BOOSTERS AND THE IVORY TOWER

164 **"He cast aside the elaborate armament"**: Edward Wickson, "Luther Burbank, the Man, his Methods and his

Achievements," *Sunset,* December 1901, p. 62.

166 "A friendship sprang up": Letter, October 11, 1901, Samuel Leib to E. J. Wickson. Wickson Papers, Special Collections/General Library, University of California, Davis.

167 "listen patiently, quietly and reverently": Proceedings of the American Pomological Society, 1895, p. 59, quoted in Edward Wickson, "Luther Burbank, Man, Methods and Achievements," *Sunset*, February 1902.

169 "all motion, all life, all force": Box 14, Luther Burbank Papers, Manuscript Division, Library of Congress, Washington, DC.

170 "Yes, and I suppose": Ibid.

172 "in that, when one was with him": David Fairchild, *The World Was My Garden: Travels of a Plant Explorer* (New York: Charles Scribner's Sons, 1938), p. 264.

CHAPTER 9: THE CARNEGIE
INSTITUTION SEAL OF
APPROVAL

175 "It is Mr. Burbank's natural desire": Liberty Hyde Bailey, "A Maker of New Fruits and Flowers," *The World's Work*, 1901, pp. 1209–14.

175 "to encourage in the broadest and most liberal manner": "Our Mission," Carnegie Institution of Washington, DC, www.ciw.edu/about.

180 "worried about men of science" "extraordinary and exceptional faculty": Nathan Reingold, "National Science Policy in a Private Foundation: The Carnegie Institution of Washington," *The Organization of Knowledge in America, 1860–1920*, eds. Alexander Oleson and John Voss (Baltimore: Johns Hopkins University Press, 1979).

185 "the most celebrated grower":

Letter, Julius Schuster, director for Baron Nathaniel v. Rothschild, November 23, 1904. Box 9, Luther Burbank Papers, Manuscript Division, Library of Congress, Washington, DC.

185 "I am happy as a clam": Letter, Luther Burbank to Hugo de Vries, n.d., circa 1906. Box 4, Luther Burbank Papers, Manuscript Division, Library of Congress, Washington, DC.

CHAPTER 10: THE TRAINING OF
THE HUMAN PLANT

189 "If we had paid no more attention": Luther Burbank, quoted in Elbert Hubbard, *Elbert Hubbard's Scrapbook* (East Aurora, NY: The Roycrofters, 1923), p. 227.

192 "The nation, or the commonwealth": Luther Burbank, *The Training of the Human Plant* (New York: Century Company, 1907), p. 44.

193 "Go to the mother": Ibid., p. 56.

193 "What we should do": Ibid., p. 55.

193 "Every child": Ibid., p. 91.

CHAPTER 11: LEARNING FROM
LUTHER BURBANK

197 "How can and will Burbank live as Pliny lives": Oscar Binner to Mrs. Comstock, February 25, 1910. Luther Burbank Home & Gardens, Santa Rosa, CA.

198 "The clock jumped off the shelf": Luther Burbank to the children of the Forestville School, April 30, 1906. Item 00.4.7142, Benson Ford Research Center, The Henry Ford, Dearborn, MI.

201 "The general methods used by Mr. Burbank": "G. H. Shull's Initial Report on Luther Burbank to the Carnegie Institution of Washington," reprinted in Bentley

Glass, "The Strange Encounter of Luther Burbank and George Harrison Shull," *Proceedings of the American Philosophical Society*, vol. 124, no. 2 (April 29, 1980).

205 "Mr. Burbank informed me that the Cree books": Quoted in Bentley Glass, "The Strange Encounter of Luther Burbank and George Harrison Shull."

208 "determined to discontinue subsidies": Letter, Robert Woodward to Luther Burbank, December 1909. Box 3, Luther Burbank Papers, Manuscript Division, Library of Congress, Washington, DC.

209 "I have greatly rejoiced": Letter, Luther Burbank to Samuel F. Leib, January 20, 1910. Samuel F. Leib Papers, Department of Special Collections, Stanford University Libraries, Stanford, CA.

211 "as necessary as a plow": Luther Burbank Society *Prospectus*, 1912. Luther Burbank Home & Gardens, Santa Rosa, CA.

217 "a large personal equity": Letter, George Harrison Shull to Nelle Branch, January 20, 1941. Walter Howard Collection, BANC MSS C-R 6, the Bancroft Library, University of California, Berkeley.

CHAPTER 12: THE CORN PALACE AND THE EMPIRE OF THE PRICKLY PEAR

220 "over a million seedling plants": Letter, Burbank to Carnegie Institution, *Year book No. 6*, Carnegie Institution of Washington, 1907, pp. 176–77.

223 "[makes] it necessary to go back": George Harrison Shull, "Importance of the Mutation Theory in Practical Breeding," *American Breeders' Association Proceedings*, vol. 3 (1907), pp. 60–67.

224 Tater Tots: See "Soaring Corn Prices Hit U.S. Cattle Farmers," afp.google.com, September 24, 2007.

229 "to have nutritive powers": This

and other testimonials to the potential of cacti as cattle feed are reprinted in *The New Agricultural-Horticultural Opuntias: Plant Creations for Arid Regions* (Santa Rosa: 1907).

230 "Of course my first object": "Wizard's Wisdom," *Los Angeles Times*, September 6, 1907, p. I1.

235 "a man of the finest, cleanest character": Letter, George Harrison Shull to Walter Howard, November 25, 1939. Walter Howard Collection, BANC MSS C-R 6, the Bancroft Library, University of California, Berkeley.

CHAPTER 13: THE MEETING OF THE MASTERS

243 "I saw you meet Edison": Letter from Bob Lyle, quoted in Luther Burbank and Wilbur Hall, *The Harvest of the Years* (Boston: Houghton Mifflin Company, 1927), p. 223.

245 "Who will be the one": Henry Smith Williams, Robert John, and John Whitson, *Luther Burbank, His Methods and Discoveries and Their Practical Applications*, vol. 1 (Santa Rosa: Luther Burbank Press, 1914), p. 271.

246 "Edison and Ford and the Wright brothers": Luther Burbank and Wilbur Hall, *Harvest of the Years*, p. 110.

246 "some of my friends in the rubber business": Ibid., p. 36.

249 "My heart is with you": Telegram, Burbank to Henry Ford, November 1915. Box 4, Luther Burbank Papers, Manuscript Division, Library of Congress, Washington, DC.

250 "my friend sister wife": June 10, 1919, on the occasion of Luther Burbank's gift of ten thousand dollars to Elizabeth Burbank. Microfilm Reel 1, Luther Burbank Papers, Manuscript Division, Library of Congress, Washington, DC.

250 "I have had some success": Let-

ter, Burbank to Elizabeth's father. Luther Burbank Home & Gardens, Santa Rosa, CA.

CHAPTER 14: THE GARDEN OF BEAUTIFUL THOUGHTS

253 "Is it not inspiring": William Ellsworth Smythe, *City Homes on Country Lanes: Philosophy and Practice of the Home-in-a-Garden* (New York: Macmillan, 1921), p. 102.

259 "To apprehend": Ibid., p. 104.

263 "At last gleams of light have come": Letter, Charles Darwin to Joseph Hooker, January 11, 1844. See http://www.darwinproject.ac.uk/darwinletters/calendar/entry-729.html.

264 "Those who would legislate": Luther Burbank, *Why I Am an Infidel* (Girard, KS: Haldeman-Julius Company, Little Blue Book no. 1020 [n.p., n.d.]).

264 "Mr. Bryan was an honored": Ibid.

266 "I love everybody": The complete text of Burbank's sermon was printed in the *Los Angeles Times* on February 1, 1926, among other newspapers, and is also reprinted in Frederick W. Clampett, *Luther Burbank: "Our Beloved Infidel," His Religion of Humanity* (New York: Macmillan, 1926).

CHAPTER 15: TRANSPLANTING THE LEGACY

273 "Before his death Luther Burbank said that he wanted Stanford University": Box 1, Luther Burbank Collection, Manuscript Division, Library of Congress, Washington, DC.

273 "Before his death in April of 1926": Dickson Terry, *The Stark Story: Stark Nurseries 150th Anniversary* (St. Louis: Missouri Historical Society, 1966), p. 33.

273 "When Burbank died in 1926":

See http://www.fundinguniverse.com/Company-histories/W-Atlee-Burpee-amp;-Co-Company-History.html.

275 "120 types of plums": Dickson Terry, *The Stark Story*, p. 34.

277 "the average visitor who comes here in the future": Letter, Luther Burbank to Samuel F. Leib, January 20, 1910, Samuel F. Leib Papers, Department of Special Collections, Stanford University Libraries, Stanford, CA.

281 "Tentative List of Biographical Publications": Box 15, Luther Burbank Papers, Manuscript Division, Library of Congress, Washington, DC.

283 "He was a queer admixture of a little, old-fashioned": Luther Burbank and Wilbur Hall, *The Harvest of the Years* (Boston: Houghton Mifflin Company, 1927), p. xxiv.

CHAPTER 16: THE CREATOR'S ART

287 "The chief work of the botanist of yesterday": Luther Burbank, "How to Produce New Flowers," *Proceedings, Pacific States Floral Congress* (San Francisco: Academy of Sciences, 1901).

288 "Since, having been made to understand": Marianne Moore, *Complete Prose of Marianne Moore* (New York: Penguin Books, 1986), p. 154.

289 "he was a sunny old man": John Dos Passos, *The 42nd Parallel* (New York: Harper's, 1930).

293 Like Rivera, Kahlo was almost certainly working from a photograph: Credit for discovering the photographic source for Kahlo's portrait goes to Rebecca Baker, volunteer archivist at the Luther Burbank Home & Gardens in Santa Rosa. The photograph can be seen in the Corbis archive (http://pro.corbis.com), U240045INP ©Bettmann/CORBIS.

CHAPTER 17: THE GARDEN AS
INTELLECTUAL PROPERTY

297 "The plant lover can sometimes
make a few dollars": "The Wanderer,"
Pittsburgh Dispatch, 1921. Benson Ford Research Center, The Henry Ford, Acc. B, Box
4, Luther Burbank Birthplace.

299 "add the fuel of interest to the fire
of genius": Abraham Lincoln, "Lecture on
Discoveries and Inventions," *Collected Works
of Abraham Lincoln*, vol. 2 (New Brunswick,
NJ: Rutgers University Press, 1953).

301 "After all my years of very extensive experience": Luther Burbank scrapbooks, Luther Burbank Home & Gardens,
Santa Rosa, CA.

302 "probably the best modern text-
book": *Harvard Law Review*, vol. 17, no.
8, June 1904, pp. 593–94.

303 "As a matter of justice": Luther
Burbank, 1921. Benson Ford Research Cen-
ter, The Henry Ford, Acc. B, Box 4, Luther
Burbank Birthplace.

306 "Nothing that Congress could
do": All quotations from congressional
debate on the Plant Patent Act of 1930 are
in the *Congressional Record*, 71st Congress,
2nd session (April 1930), and U.S. Congress, House Committee on Patents, Plant
Patents, April 9–10, 1930.

307 "A man can patent": Ibid.

310 "a seedling resulting from deliberate cross-pollination": Quotations from
all Burbank's posthumous patent applications are from Luther Burbank Home &
Gardens, Santa Rosa, CA.

313 "the salvation of parts of Ireland
from famine": E. O. Orpet, *Florist's Exchange*, November 24, 1906. The full statement was, "For many years the Burbank
potato was the salvation of parts of Ireland
from famine, it being the best disease-
resister known."

EPILOGUE: SEARCHING FOR
LUTHER BURBANK

317 "A lot of it boils down": Greg
Krister, "Mean Cuisine," *Washington
Monthly*, July/August 2001.

SELECTED BIBLIOGRAPHY

Acquaah, George. *Principles of Plant Genetics and Breeding*. Oxford, UK, and Malden, MA: Blackwell Publishing, 2007.

Alston, Julian M., and Philip G. Pardey. *Making Science Pay: The Economics of Agricultural R&D Policy*. Washington, DC: American Enterprise Institute Press, 1996.

Ausubel, Kenny. *Seeds of Change: The Living Treasure*. San Francisco: HarperSanFrancisco, 1994.

Bacon, Paul. *Luther Burbank: Creating New and Better Plants*. Chicago: Encyclopaedia Britannica Press, 1961.

Bailey, Liberty H. *Garden Making: Suggestions for the Utilizing of Home Grounds*. New York: Macmillan, 1898.

———. "A Maker of New Fruits and Flowers." *The World's Work* (September 1901).

———. *The Survival of the Unlike: A Collection of Evolution Essays Suggested by the Study of Domestic Plants*. New York: Macmillan, 1899.

Bailey, Liberty H., and A.W. Gilbert. *Plant Breeding*. New York: Macmillan, 1915.

Baldwin, Neil. *Edison: Inventing the Century*. Chicago: University of Chicago Press, 2001.

Baumol, William J. *The Free Market Innovation Machine: Analyzing the Growth Miracle of Capitalism*. Princeton, NJ: Princeton University Press, 2002.

Beaty, John Y. *Luther Burbank, Plant Magician*. New York: J. Messner, Inc., 1943.

Beeson, Emma Burbank. *Early Life and Letters of Luther Burbank*. San Francisco: Harr Wagner Publishing Company, 1927.

Bergson, Henri. *Creative Evolution*. New York: Modern Library, 1944.

Bledstein, Burt. *The Culture of Professionalism: The Middle Class and the Development of Higher Education in America*. New York: W. W. Norton & Co., 1976.

Bonnen, James T. "Historical Sources of U.S. Agricultural Productivity." *American Journal of Agricultural Economics*, vol. 65 (1983).

Boswell, Victor R. "Potatoes." *After a Hundred Years: Yearbook of Agriculture*. Washington, DC: Government Printing Office, 1962.

Bowers, Ray. *Mr. Carnegie's Plant Biologists: The Ancestry of Carnegie Institution's DPB*. Washington, DC: Carnegie Institution of Washington, 1992.

Boyes, B. C. "The Impact of Mendel." *BioScience*, vol. 16, no. 2 (February 1966).

Bragdon, Lillian J. *Luther Burbank, Nature's Helper.* New York: Abingdon Press, 1959.

Brandes, Stanley. "The Perilous Potato and the Terrifying Tomato." *Consequences of Cultivar Diffusion*, ed. Leonard Plotnicov and Richard Scaglion. Pittsburgh: University of Pittsburgh Press, 1999.

Burbank, Luther. "Another Mode of Species Forming." *Popular Science Monthly* (November 1909).

———. "Some of the Fundamental Principles of Plant Breeding." New York: 1902.

———. *How Plants Are Trained to Work for Man.* New York: P. F. Collier & Son, 1921.

———. "How to Produce New Flowers." *Proceedings, Pacific States Floral Congress.* San Francisco: Academy of Sciences, 1901.

———. *The New Agricultural-Horticultural Opuntias.* Santa Rosa: Burbank's Experiment Grounds, June 1, 1907.

———. *New Creations in Fruits and Flowers.* Santa Rosa: Burbank's Experiment Grounds, 1893–1926.

———. *The Training of the Human Plant.* New York: Century Company, 1907.

———. *Why I Am an Infidel.* Girard, KS: Haldeman-Julius Company, Little Blue Book No. 1020 [n.p., n.d.].

Burbank, Luther, and Wilbur Hall. *The Harvest of the Years.* Boston: Houghton Mifflin Company, 1927.

Burnham, George P. *The History of the Hen Fever.* Boston: James French and Company, 1856.

"Burpee for Burbank." *Time* (September 21, 1931).

Burt, Olive Woolley. *Luther Burbank, Boy Wizard.* Indianapolis: Bobbs-Merrill, 1948, 1962.

Buttel, Frederick H., and Jill Belsky. "Biotechnology, Plant Breeding, and Intellectual Property: Social and Ethical Dimensions." *Owning Scientific and Technical Information: Value and Ethical Issues.* New Brunswick, NJ: Rutgers University Press, 1989.

Carson, Charles. *The Life of Luther Burbank.* Santa Rosa: Press of the Press Democrat Publishing Company, 1949.

Cerney, Jan. *Mitchell's Corn Palace.* Charleston, SC: Arcadia Publishing, 2004.

Clampett, Frederick W. *Luther Burbank: "Our Beloved Infidel," His Religion of Humanity.* New York: Macmillan, 1926.

Cole, Arthur H. "Agricultural Crazes: A Neglected Chapter in American Economic History." *American Economic Review*, vol. 16, no. 4 (December 1926).

"Complimentary Banquet in Honor of Luther Burbank." San Francisco: California State Board of Trade, *Bulletin*, no. 14 (1905).

Cooke, Kathy J. "Expertise, Book Farming, and Government Agriculture: The Origins of Agricultural Seed Certification in the United States." *Agricultural History*, vol. 76, no. 3 (2002).

Cowen, Tyler. *What Price Fame?* Cambridge, MA: Harvard University Press, 2000.

Crow, James F. "Plant Breeding Giants: Burbank, the Artist; Vavilov, the Scientist." *Genetics*, vol. 158 (August 2001): 1391–95.

Darwin, Charles. *Effects of Cross and Self Fertilisation in the Vegetable Kingdom.* New York: D. Appleton & Co., 1877.

———. *The Variation of Animals and Plants Under Domestication.* New York: Orange Judd and Co., 1868.

De Vries, Hugo. *Plant Breeding: Comments on the Experiments of Nilsson and Burbank.* Chicago: Open Court Publishing Co., 1907.

———. "A Visit to Luther Burbank." *Popular Science Monthly* (August 1905).

DeFelice, Michael S. "The Black Night-shades, Solanum nigrum L. et al.–Poison, Poultice, and Pie." *Weed Technology*, vol. 17 (2003): 421–27.

———. "Prickley Pear Cactus, Opuntia spp.—A Spine-Tingling Tale." *Weed Technology*, vol. 18 (2004): 869–77.

Dobyns, Kenneth. *History of the United States Patent Office*. Sergeant Kirklands Museum and Historical Society, Fredericksburg, VA, 1994.

Dos Passos, John. *The 42nd Parallel*. New York: Harper's, 1930.

Dreyer, Peter. *A Gardener Touched with Genius: The Life of Luther Burbank*. New York: Coward, McCann & Geoghegan, 1975; new and expanded edition, Santa Rosa: Luther Burbank Home & Gardens, 1993.

Faber, Doris. *Luther Burbank: Partner of Nature*. Champaign, IL: Garrard Publishing Co., 1963.

Fairchild, David. *The World Was My Garden: Travels of a Plant Explorer*. New York: Charles Scribner's Sons, 1938.

Fallen, Catherine. *A Botanic Garden for the Nation: The United States Botanic Garden*. Senate Document 109-19. Washington, DC: Government Printing Office, 2006.

Ford, Henry, in collaboration with Samuel Crowther. *Edison as I Know Him*. New York: Cosmopolitan Book Corporation, 1930.

Fussell, Betty. *The Story of Corn*. New York: Alfred A. Knopf, 1992.

Geise, Lucretia Hoover. "Rare Crossing: Frida Kahlo and Luther Burbank." *American Art*, vol. 15, no. 1 (2001).

Glass, Bentley. "The Strange Encounter of Luther Burbank and George Harrison Shull." *Proceedings of the American Philosophical Society*, vol. 124, no. 2 (April 29, 1980).

Gould, Stephen Jay. "Does the Stoneless Plum Instruct the Thinking Reed?" *Dino-saur in a Haystack: Reflections on Natural History*. New York: Harmony Books, 1995.

Grubb, E. H., and W. S. Guilford. *The Potato: A Compilation of Information from Every Available Source*. Garden City, NY: Doubleday, Page & Company, 1912.

Harding, T. Swann. "Henry Ellsworth, Commissioner of Patents." *Journal of Farm Economics*, vol. 22, no. 3 (August 1940).

Harwood, W. S. *New Creations in Plant Life*. New York: Macmillan, 1907.

Hayes, Everis Anson. "Luther Burbank and His Work." Speech in the House of Representatives, February 29, 1912. Washington, DC: Government Printing Office, 1912.

Hedrich, U. P. *A History of Horticulture in American to 1860*. New York: Oxford University Press, 1950.

Henkin, David M. *The Postal Age*. Chicago: University of Chicago Press, 2006.

Herrera, Hayden. *Frida: A Biography of Frida Kahlo*. New York: Harper & Row, 1983.

History of Sonoma County, San Francisco: Alley, Bowen & Company, 1879 (reprinted Petaluma, CA: C. B. Veronda, 1973).

Hobhouse, Henry. *Seeds of Change: Five Plants That Transformed Mankind*. London: Sidgwick, 1985.

Horticultural Society of New York. "Proceedings: International Conference on Plant Breeding and Hybridization, 1902." *Memoirs*, vol. 1. New York: Horticultural Society of New York, 1904.

Howard, Walter. "Luther Burbank, a Victim of Hero Worship," *Chronica Botanica*, vol. 9, no. 5/6 (1945/1946).

———. "Luther Burbank's Plant Contributions." *Bulletin 691*. Berkeley: University of California College of Agriculture, Agricultural Experiment Station, March 1945.

"Hybrid Conference Report." *Journal of*

the Royal Horticultural Society, vol. 24, 1900.

Irvine, Leigh, ed. *A History of the New California, Its Resources and People*. New York: Lewis Publishing Company, 1905.

Israel, Paul. *Edison: A Life of Invention*. New York: John Wiley & Sons, 1998.

Jordan, David Starr. *The Days of a Man*. Yonkers-on-Hudson, NY: World Book Company, 1922.

Jordan, David Starr, and Vernon Lyman Kellogg. *Scientific Aspects of Luther Burbank's Work*. San Francisco: Philopolis Press, 1909.

Kadlec, David. "Marianne Moore, Immigration, and Eugenics." *Modernism/Modernity* vol. 1, no. 2 (April 1994).

Keeny, Elizabeth B. *The Botanizers: Amateur Scientists in Nineteenth-Century America*. Chapel Hill: University of North Carolina Press, 1992.

Kevles, Daniel J. *In the Name of Eugenics: Genetics and the Uses of Human Heredity*. New York: Alfred A. Knopf, 1985.

———. "Patenting Life: A Historical Overview of Law, Interest, and Ethics." Legal Theory Workshop, Yale Law School, December 20, 2001.

———. "Patents, Protections, and Privileges: The Establishment of Intellectual Property in Animals and Plants." *Isis* (June 2007).

Kevles, Daniel J., and Glenn E. Bugos. "Plants as Intellectual Property: American Practice, Law, and Policy in World Context," *Osiris*, 2nd series, vol. 7 (1991).

Kimmelman, Barbara A. "The American Breeders' Association: Genetics and Eugenics in an Agricultural Context, 1903–13." *Social Studies of Science*, vol. 13, no. 2 (May 1983).

Kimmelman, Barbara A., and Diane B. Paul. "Mendel in America: Theory and Practice, 1900–1919." *The American Devel-*

opment of Biology. New Brunswick: Rutgers University Press, 1991.

Kirkendall, Richard S. "Up to Now: A History of American Agriculture from Jefferson to Revolution to Crisis." *Agriculture and Human Values*, vol. 4, no. 1, Netherlands: Springer, December 1987.

Kloppenburg, Jack Ralph, Jr. *First the Seed: The Political Economy of Plant Biotechnology, 1942–2000*. New York: Cambridge University Press, 1988.

Kohlstedt, Sally Gregory. "Nature, Not Books: Scientists and the Origins of the Nature-Study Movement in the 1890s." *Isis*, vol. 96 (2005): 324–52.

Kraft, Ken, and Pat Kraft. *Luther Burbank: The Wizard and the Man*. New York: Meredith Press, 1967.

Lanman, Susan Warren. "'For Profit and Pleasure': Peter Henderson and the Commercialization of Horticulture in Nineteenth-Century America." *Industrializing Organisms: Introducing Evolutionary History*. New York: Routledge, 2004.

"The Last Glacial Epoch in America: Lecture by Professor Gunning." *New York Times*, February 19, 1871.

Laszlo, Pierre. *Citrus: A History*. Chicago: University of Chicago Press, 2007.

Law, Frederick Houk. *Modern Great Americans*. New York: Century Company, 1926.

LeBaron, Gaye, Dee Blackman, Joann Mitchell, Harvey Hansen. *Santa Rosa: A Nineteenth-Century Town*. Santa Rosa: Historia, Ltd., 1985.

LeBaron, Gaye, and Joann Mitchell. *Santa Rosa: A Twentieth-Century Town*. Santa Rosa: Historia, Ltd., 1993.

Leichtman, Robert R. *Burbank Returns (from Heaven to Earth)*. Columbus, OH: Ariel Press, 1983.

Lim, Phillip W. *The Privatization of Species: An Economic History of Biotechnology and Intellectual Property Rights*. Stanford PhD thesis, 1993.

Lynch, Ada Kyle. *Luther Burbank, Plant Lover and Citizen, with Musical Numbers*. San Francisco: Herr Wagner Publishing Co., 1924.

Lyon-Jenness, Cheryl. "Petunias by Post: The Post Office and America's Nineteenth-Century Horticultural Boom." Winton M. Blount Symposium on Postal History, Smithsonian National Postal Museum, November 4, 2006.

Machlup, Fritz, and Edith Penrose. "The Patent Controversy in the Nineteenth Century." *Journal of Economic History*, vol. 10, no. 1 (May 1950).

McKelvey, Blake. "When Science Was on Trial in Rochester: 1850–1890." *Rochester History*, vol. 8, no. 4 (1946).

Moskowitz, Marina. "Broadcasting Seeds on the American Landscape." *Cultures of Commerce*. New York: Palgrave Macmillan, 2006.

———. "Seed Money: The Economies of Horticulture in Nineteenth-Century America." http://www.consume.bbk.ac.uk/researchfindings/CofC_Findings_Moskowitz 02.pdf.

Nasaw, David. *Andrew Carnegie*. New York: Penguin Press, 2006.

Nelson, Lavina. *Luther Burbank and the Human Flower and Some Child Verse*. Indianapolis: Printing Arts Co., c. 1923.

Nevins, Allan, and Frank Ernest Hill. *Ford: Expansion and Challenge, 1915–1933*. New York: Charles Scribner's Sons, 1957.

Nolte, Phillip. "Plant Disease, Politics and an Irish Catastrophe." *American Vegetable Grower Magazine*, April 1997.

Palladino, Paolo. "Wizards and Devotees: On the Mendelian Theory of Inheritance and the Professionalization of Agricultural Science in Great Britain and the United States, 1880–1930." *History of Science*, vol. 32 (1994) .

Pandora, Katherine. "Knowledge Held in Common: Tales of Luther Burbank and Science in the American Vernacular." *Isis*, vol. 92 (2001): 484–516.

Pollan, Michael. *The Botany of Desire: A Plant's-Eye View of the World*. New York: Random House, 2001.

———. *The Omnivore's Dilemma*. New York: Penguin Press, 2006.

Quackenbush, Robert. *Here a Plant, There a Plant, Everywhere a Plant, Plant*. Santa Rosa, CA: Luther Burbank Home & Gardens, 1982.

Reingold, Nathan. "National Science Policy in a Private Foundation: The Carnegie Institution of Washington." *The Organization of Knowledge in America, 1860–1920*s. Baltimore: Johns Hopkins University Press, 1979.

Sachs, Aaron. *The Humboldt Current: Nineteenth-Century Exploration and the Roots of American Environmentalism*. New York: Viking Press, 2006.

Sackman, Douglas Cazaux. *Orange Empire: California and the Fruits of Eden*. Berkeley: University of California Press, 2005.

Salaman, Redcliffe N. *The History and Social Influence of the Potato*. Cambridge and New York: Cambridge University Press, 1985.

Schafer, Joseph. *The Social History of American Agriculture*. New York: Macmillan, 1936.

Scheuring, Ann F. *Abundant Harvest: The History of the University of California, Davis*. University of California Davis History Project, 2001.

Sedgley, George Burbank. *Genealogy of the Burbank Family and the Families of Bray, Wellcome, Sedgley (Sedgeley), and Welch*. Farmington, ME: Knowlton & McLeary, 1928.

Shinn, Charles H. *Pacific Rural Handbook, Containing a Series of Brief and Practical Essays and Notes on the Culture of Trees, Vegetables and Flowers, Adapted to the Pacific Coast. Also, Hints on Home and Farm Improvements.* San Francisco: Dewey & Co., Publishers of the *Pacific Rural Press*, 1879.

Shull, George Harrison. "Importance of the Mutation Theory in Practical Breeding." *American Breeders' Association Proceedings*, vol. 3 (1907).

Simonds, William A. *Henry Ford, His Life, His Work, His Genius.* New York: Bobbs-Merrill Company, 1943.

Slusser, Effie Young, Emma Burbank Beeson, and Mary Bell Williams. *Stories of Luther Burbank and His Plant School.* New York: Charles Scribner's Sons, 1920.

Smith, J. Russell. "The Agriculture of the Future." *Harper's Monthly*, vol. 126 (1913): 752.

Smythe, William Ellsworth. *City Homes on Country Lanes: Philosophy and Practice of the Home-in-a-Garden.* New York: Macmillan, 1921.

Stallmann, Judith I., and A. Allan Schmid. "Property Rights in Plants: Implications for Biotechnology Research and Extension." *American Journal of Agricultural Economics*, vol. 69, no. 2 (May 1987).

Stansfield, William D. "Luther Burbank: Honorary Member of the American Breeders' Association." *Journal of Heredity*, vol. 97, no. 2 (2006).

Starr, Kevin. *Americans and the California Dream, 1850–1915.* New York: Oxford University Press, 1973.

———. *Inventing the Dream: California Through the Progressive Era.* New York: Oxford University Press, 1985.

———. Sunset Magazine: *A Century of Western Living, 1898–1990: Historical Portraits and a Chronological Bibliography of Selected Topics.* Stanford: Stanford University Libraries, 1998.

Stefferud, Alfred, ed. *Seeds: The Yearbook of Agriculture.* Washington DC: Government Printing Office, 1961.

Stern, Alexandra Minna. *Eugenic Nation: Faults and Frontiers of Better Breeding in Modern America.* Berkeley: University of California Press, 2005.

Stewart, Amy. *Flower Confidential.* Chapel Hill, NC: Algonquin Books, 2007.

Stoll, Steven. *The Fruits of Natural Advantage: Making the Industrial Countryside in California.* Berkeley: University of California Press, 1998.

Terry, Dickson. *The Stark Story: Stark Nurseries 150th Anniversary.* St. Louis: Missouri Historical Society, 1966.

Thompson, Robert A. *Central Sonoma: A Brief Description of the Township of Santa Rosa, Sonoma County, California, Its Climate and Resources.* San Francisco: W. M. Hinton & Co., 1884.

———. *Historical Atlas Map of Sonoma County.* Oakland: Thomas H. Thompson & Co., 1877.

Tompkins, Peter, and Christopher Bird. *The Secret Life of Plants.* New York: Harper & Row, 1973.

Tymeson, Mildred McClary. *Two Towers: The Story of Worcester Tech, 1865–1965.* Worcester, MA: Worcester Polytechnic Institute, 1965.

Tyrrell, Ian. *True Garden of the Gods: California-Australian Environmental Reform, 1860–1930.* Berkeley: University of California Press, 1999.

Walker, Richard. *The Conquest of Bread: 150 Years of Agribusiness in California.* New York: The New Press, 2004.

Walls, Laura Dassow. "'Hero of Knowledge, Be Our Tribute Thine': Alexander von Humboldt in Victorian America." *Northeastern Naturalist*, 2001.

Ward, Artemas. *The Grocer's Encyclopedia.* New York: n.p., 1911.

Wechter, Dixon. *The Hero in America: A*

Chronicle of Hero-Worship. New York: Charles Scribner's Sons, 1941.

West-Eberhard, Mary Jane. *Developmental Plasticity and Evolution.* New York: Oxford University Press, 2003.

Western Sonoma Historical Society. *Images of America: Sebastopol.* San Francisco: Arcadia Publishing, 2003.

Wickson, Edward J. *Luther Burbank: Man, Methods and Achievements.* San Francisco: Southern Pacific Company, 1902.

Wilder, Burt G. "Agassiz at Penikese." *American Naturalist,* vol. 32, no. 375 (March 1898).

Williams, Henry Smith. *Luther Burbank, His Life and Works.* New York: Heart's International Library Co., 1915.

Williams, Henry Smith, Robert John, and John Whitson. *Luther Burbank, his methods and discoveries and their practical application: prepared from his original field notes covering more than 100,000 experiments made during forty years devoted to plant improvement, with the assistance of the Luther Burbank Society and its entire membership, under the editorial direction of John Whitson and Robert John and Henry Smith Williams, M.D., LL.D.* New York, London: Luther Burbank Press, 1914.

Yogananda, Paramahansa. *Autobiography of a Yogi.* New York: Philosophical Library, 1946.

Zirkle, Conway. "Plant Hybridization and Plant Breeding in Eighteenth-Century American Agriculture." *Agricultural History,* vol. 43, no.1 (1969).

INDEX

Page numbers in *italics* refer to illustrations.